"With this book, Hofer has done us a huge favor. . . . He gives insight into Lewis's honest wrestling with several of the most important questions that can be asked—and then, as a word artist, conveys his apologetic answers in a way that appeals to Christians and atheists even today. This is what Hofer was able to capture and share with us in this inspiring and instructive book."

—Henk Stoker,
North-West University

"Hofer investigates key challenges to contemporary Christianity presented by alternative worldviews like naturalism, pantheism, and various versions of non-supernatural Christian belief. . . . He indicates how Lewis's approach can fruitfully be employed in a present-day practice of Christian apologetics."

—C. J. Wethmar,
University of Pretoria, emeritus

"Hofer has written a fascinating book that gives real insight into the development of Evangelical Christianity in North America. It is well researched and documented and adds to our knowledge of a topic that is often dismissed with superficial clichés. Anyone teaching on the topic of contemporary religion ought to consider it as a possible textbook. Ministers and laypeople should read it to keep abreast of the way Evangelicalism is constantly adapting to an ever-changing society."

—Irving Hexham,
University of Calgary

"Hofer's work is carefully documented and written with clarity and succinctness. It is an important contribution to the manner in which the concept of worldview effects the discipline of Christian apologetics. In that regard, it can be a valuable resource for the curricula of Christian colleges and seminaries."

—Ronald Galloway,
Greenwich School of Theology

"Hofer allows us to accompany C. S. Lewis on his intellectual and spiritual journey from one worldview to another. This work analyzes key elements of that worldview and identifies several challenges leveled against it. . . . Hofer does an excellent job of presenting comparative analyses of worldviews as they relate to key Christian claims. The reader will appreciate Hofer's very informative and analytical presentation of a great Christian thinker."

—Beat Mertz,
Swiss Association of Pharmaceutical Physicians (SwAPP)

Weltanschauung *and* Apologia

WELTANSCHAUUNG *and* APOLOGIA

A Study in C. S. Lewis

ELIAS HOFER

Foreword by **Paul Chamberlain**

WIPF & STOCK · Eugene, Oregon

WELTANSCHAUUNG AND *APOLOGIA*
A Study in C. S. Lewis

Copyright © 2022 Elias Hofer. All rights reserved. Except for brief quotations in critical publications or reviews, no part of this book may be reproduced in any manner without prior written permission from the publisher. Write: Permissions, Wipf and Stock Publishers, 199 W. 8th Ave., Suite 3, Eugene, OR 97401.

Wipf & Stock
An Imprint of Wipf and Stock Publishers
199 W. 8th Ave., Suite 3
Eugene, OR 97401

www.wipfandstock.com

PAPERBACK ISBN: 978-1-6667-3952-7
HARDCOVER ISBN: 978-1-6667-3953-4
EBOOK ISBN: 978-1-6667-3954-1

FEBRUARY 10, 2026 2:39 PM

Contents

Foreword by Paul Chamberlain | vii

Acknowledgments | xi

Chapter One
OVERVIEW | 1

Chapter Two
CONTEMPORARY CHALLENGES TO CHRISTIANITY | 5

Chapter Three
THE PHILOSOPHICAL AND SPIRITUAL
  JOURNEY OF C. S. LEWIS | 16

Chapter Four
DIMENSIONS OF LEWIS'S WORLDVIEW:
  IMPACT ON HIS APOLOGETICS | 56

Chapter Five
LEWIS'S FUSION OF FICTION AND APOLOGETICS:
  WEAVING REASON WITH IMAGINATION | 163

Chapter Six
C. S. LEWIS'S RELEVANCE FOR PRESENT-DAY
  CHRISTIAN APOLOGETICS | 195

Chapter Seven
CONCLUSION | 217

Bibliography | 229

Index | 241

Foreword

I REMEMBER VIVIDLY my first meeting with Dr. Elias Hofer. It took place a few years ago, when he visited me in my office to inquire about a graduate-level academic program of which I was director. Seldom have I been as thoroughly questioned by a prospective student about the strengths, weaknesses, history, course offerings, and other features of our program as I was that day. When the meeting was over, we said goodbye, and I wondered if I would ever see him again. As he made clear, we were just one of three programs he was considering. I'm happy to say that, a few months later, he entered the program, and today, I count him a lifelong friend.

As a student in our program, Elias's interest in the works of C. S. Lewis moved him to research and write several essays on this astute Christian thinker. These early works, however, turned out to be just the beginning of an extended journey of research into Lewis's life and works and also into the broader concept of worldview.

The notion of worldview is as fascinating as it is critical to the way we all formulate our views on most everything. One's worldview determines how one perceives reality itself. It can be thought of as a set of glasses through which one views one's surroundings and interprets one's experiences. Furthermore, it accounts for the perspectives we all bring to every event in life. Perhaps, most importantly, it explains why different people may see different things when looking at the same set of data or evidence. The same experiences or evidence may lead one person to reject a particular conclusion or even an entire worldview, while moving another to embrace what the other rejected. At times, it's head-shaking, but this portrays the enormous influence of one's worldview.

James Sire, an American academic and publisher who spent a good part of his life considering and writing about the concept of worldview, shows just how influential one's worldview is by describing it as "a fundamental orientation of the heart, that can be expressed as a story or in a set of presuppositions (assumptions which may be true, partially true, or entirely false) which we hold (consciously or subconsciously, consistently or inconsistently) about the basic constitution of reality, and that provides the foundation on which we live and move, and have our being."[1]

Christianity is a worldview. As such, it makes significant claims concerning important areas of inquiry, including the origins of life, the universe, and humans; the existence of a Creator; the reality of good and evil; the need for a Saviour; and the identity and resurrection of Jesus of Nazareth. While Christians accept these claims, many people with alternative worldviews see them differently, and some have mounted objections to them.

Having been an atheist before he was ever a Christian, C. S. Lewis had the relatively unusual experience of thoughtfully viewing and analysing the world through two diametrically opposing worldviews, one after the other. This fact was not lost on him, and once he made the intellectual and spiritual journey to Christian faith, he spent considerable time and effort analysing why he had turned from one worldview to the other, and articulating responses to many of the objections levelled against Christianity from atheism and other worldviews.

Lewis is remembered not only as a highly rated literary scholar but also as a Christian apologist par excellence, perhaps the most significant one of the twentieth century. He not only defended the faith but also developed a methodology for doing so. What may be overlooked is the rather long and winding journey involved in his coming to faith in the first place, and eventually becoming a highly regarded representative of Christian faith.

In this thesis, Elias Hofer allows us to accompany C. S. Lewis on his intellectual and spiritual journey from one worldview, atheism, to another, Christianity. Along the way, this project analyses key elements of Lewis's Christian worldview and then identifies several challenges levelled against it from alternative worldviews. Hofer then examines Lewis's apologetic methodology highlighting how it was shaped by his worldview as all methodologies are. From there, he turns to an analysis of Lewis's specific responses to a number of these objections. As such, this

1. Sire, *Universe Next Door*, 20.

project is also a comparative analysis of worldviews, particularly as they relate to key Christian claims.

Hofer, however, is concerned not only with the past but also with current interactions between alternative worldviews. In this vein, he suggests ways in which certain elements of Lewis's apologetic methodology may still be useful in addressing twenty-first century challenges to the Christian worldview, which come from the representatives of alternative worldviews.

We are all better off for having access to this latest work on one of the world's great Christian thinkers. Put on your thinking cap and prepare for a highly informative read.

Paul Chamberlain, PhD
Professor, Ethics & Leadership
Trinity Western University

NOTE TO READERS: The first two chapters cover the usual structural components associated with dissertations and provide an overview of the characteristics of a given worldview. Some readers may want to start with reading the introduction to C. S. Lewis in chapter 3 and read the first two chapters later.

Acknowledgments

First and foremost, I am indebted to my two supervisors, Dr. Conrad J. Wethmar and Dr. Ronald Gordon Galloway, for their support and guidance throughout the process of researching and writing this dissertation. I am especially grateful for the direction they provided early on in structuring the research proposal; the guidance that they provided during this critical stage of the project was invaluable.

Secondly, I want to express my appreciation to North-West University and the Greenwich School of Theology for their interest in the subject matter and for making this venture possible. I am especially grateful to Peg Evans and Tienie Buys for helping me to stay on track with the procedural details, and to Zine Sapula, Christien Terblanche, and Elsa Esterhuizen for their assistance in formatting the document.

In addition, I am grateful to my master's thesis supervisor, Dr. Paul Chamberlain, for his encouragement to continue my studies in worldviews and to analyse their relationship to Christian apologetics.

I also wish to acknowledge the resources that were made available through the University of Victoria Library. The selection of C. S. Lewis-related works that were gifted to the university by former professor of English Dr. Lionel Adey provided valuable insights to Lewis's body of work.

As well, I am indebted to Dr. James Sire for his advice, wise counsel, and, especially, his patience during our numerous telephone conversations. I'm also appreciative of Dr. David Naugle's and Dr. Paul McCuistion's assistance in outlining the initial contour of the research to be undertaken.

I am particularly indebted to Dr. Irving Hexham for his advice and counsel, and for his timely introduction to North-West University and the Greenwich School of Theology.

And last, but not least, I am grateful to my family for their interest and support of this project, and for their ongoing encouragement to bring it to completion.

Chapter One

OVERVIEW

1.1 TITLE

Weltanschauung *and* Apologia: *A Study in C. S. Lewis*

1.2 ABSTRACT

This thesis introduces worldview as a concept for perceiving reality, provides an overview of contemporary worldviews, and explores the key challenges to Christianity from alternative worldviews. It introduces C. S. Lewis as a Christian apologist, and examines his circuitous intellectual and spiritual journey to Christian faith. It analyses the intellectual and philosophical elements of the Lewisian Christian worldview, and explores the manner in which this worldview affected the methodology for his apologetics. Finally, it examines Lewis's apologetic methods in order to ascertain how key elements from his apologetics may be employed in dealing with present day challenges to the Christian worldview.

1.3 KEY WORDS

Weltanschauung, Apologia, Worldview, Apologetics, Lewis, Plato, Hegel, Kant, Hume, Darwin, Metaphysics, Christianity, Theism, Deism, Naturalism, Materialism, Scientism, Pantheism, Panentheism, Philosophy, Realism, Idealism, Theology, Reason, Rational, Imagination, Belief, Myth, Fideism

1.4 INTRODUCTION

It is often stated that there are a number of mutually exclusive ways to perceive reality. The way in which a person perceives reality is sometimes referred to as one's worldview. According to James Sire, a worldview is a set of presuppositions which we hold, consciously or subconsciously about the basic makeup of the world.[1] Ronald Nash considers worldview to be a conceptual scheme by which we consciously or unconsciously place or fit everything we believe and by which we interpret and judge reality.[2]

David Naugle writes that worldview as a concept originated in the late eighteenth and early nineteenth century. It derives its origin from the German word *Weltanschauung* (world perspective).[3] Wilhelm Dilthey (1833–1911) has been credited as the father of worldview theory. According to Dilthey, worldviews are created through the mind's formation of a cosmic picture or *Weltbild* (world picture), which forms the basis for perceiving reality.[4]

Western society embraces a variety of mutually exclusive worldviews, many of which present significant challenges to Christian faith. Christian apologetics requires an engagement with contemporary societal norms, including its worldviews. A basic understanding of contemporary worldviews is important in order to do apologetics effectively. Accordingly, as David Naugle writes, during the past several decades, there has been an explosion of interest in evangelical circles in the subject of worldviews.[5]

Although various taxonomies have been advocated for creating a framework for analysing worldviews, Dilthey's analysis led him to propose a provisional threefold typology of worldviews that may be characterised as naturalism, pantheism, and theism.[6] A similar organizational structure for studying worldviews has been advocated by Steven Cowan.[7] This enquiry will examine the respective manifestations represented by

---

1. Sire, *Naming the Elephant*, 19.

2. Nash, *Worldviews in Conflict*, 16.

3. See also Hacking, "Introductory Essay" to Thomas Kuhn's *Structure of Scientific Revolutions*; and Bird, "Thomas Kuhn."

4. Naugle, *Worldview*, 87.

5. "Protestant evangelicalism, more than any other Christian tradition, has deployed the idea of worldview most extensively" (Naugle, *Worldview*, 54).

6. Naugle, *Worldview*, 82–98.

7. Cowan, *Five Views on Apologetics*, 24.

this taxonomy and will explore what measures might be employed for responding to the challenges presented.

Derived from the Greek word *apologia*, Christian apologetics seeks to demonstrate the intellectual validity of the Christian faith. Renowned Oxford/Cambridge professor and Christian apologist C. S. Lewis is often credited as having been the most influential Christian apologist of the twentieth century.[8] This study will explore the methods that were employed by Lewis in order to ascertain how his worldview influenced his apologetics, and how his methodology may be applied to the challenges that contemporary worldviews present to Christianity.

An examination of Lewis's spiritual life reveals a circuitous journey from atheism/pantheism to Christian faith; a study of Lewis's spiritual journey and his progression toward a worldview that embraces Christian theism has the potential to make a significant contribution to contemporary Christian apologetics. The study will explore the process by which Lewis came to embrace Christian theism and ascertain how Lewis's apologetic methods might be applied to today's challenges.

1.5 PROBLEM STATEMENT

In their various manifestations, the influences of alternative worldviews are presenting significant challenges to the truth claims of contemporary Christianity. Understanding the basic fundamentals of alternative worldviews and having the ability to respond to the challenges that they pose is vitally important in the work of current apologetics. As one of the premier Christian apologists of the past century and as someone who dealt with many of the challenges encountered today, C. S. Lewis has much to offer to today's apologetics.

Although relatively little has been written about Lewis's worldview, there is much to be gained from a close examination of his highly nuanced perception of reality, or his "account of the world."[9] It is the premise of this thesis that much of Lewis's apologetic work is a defense of the Lewisian worldview. There is therefore much to be gleaned from an in-depth study of the process by which Lewis acquired his perception of reality and the manner in which he defended it.

---

8. Ward, "Good Serves the Better," 59.

9. Wesley Kort refers to worldview as an "account of the world" (Kort, *C. S. Lewis*, 24).

1.6 AIMS AND OBJECTIVES

This study will endeavour to provide an overview of the key challenges that alternative worldviews pose for contemporary Christianity. It will examine the manner in which Lewis's worldview manifested itself in his methodology and will ascertain how Lewisian methods may be applied to today's apologetics.

1.7 CENTRAL THEOLOGICAL ARGUMENT

The central argument of this thesis holds that the core claims of the Christian faith are true and that the truth claims of alternative worldviews, inasmuch as they contradict these Christian claims, necessitate a response. It holds that individuals who are engaged in contemporary Christian apologetics should have an awareness of the core tenets of competing worldviews when responding to the challenges that they pose, and that Lewis offers important insights for countering the challenges.

1.8 METHODOLOGY

The study will begin by categorizing the main alternatives to the Christian worldview, provide a description of their respective characteristics, offer an analysis of their intellectual validity, and identify the main challenges that they present to the Christian faith. This will be followed by an in-depth study of Lewis's apologetic methodology, beginning with an overview of his life's work and followed by an examination of his spiritual journey to Christian faith and the framing of his intellectual world.

Next, this study will examine the complexity of Lewis's worldview, explore the key elements of his faith, and analyse the impact that his faith-endowed worldview had on his apologetics.

This information will be gleaned not only from the many volumes of Lewis's works but also from the body of work written about him.

The study will culminate with an examination of how Lewis's apologetic methods might apply to dealing with Christianity's current challenges.

Chapter Two

CONTEMPORARY CHALLENGES *to* CHRISTIANITY

2.1 CHALLENGES FROM SECULARISM/NATURALISM

Duke University's Wesley Kort claims that Lewis saw modern secularism as the greatest challenge to Christianity and directed his apologetics to this challenge. He writes that "modernity has retained most of the characteristics that Lewis deplored and attacked" and that Lewis's "cultural critique and his alternative way of giving an account of the world continue to apply."[1] McGill University's Charles Taylor agrees. He claims Western society has become considerably more secular since Lewis's time.[2] In his book *A Secular Age*, he writes that "within a relatively short period of time Western society has changed from a condition in which belief was the default option—to a condition in which for more and more people unbelieving construals seem at first blush to be the only plausible ones."[3]

To counter the trend toward secular modernity in contemporary society, Kort recommends the construction of a Lewis-like project. He writes that because we are living in a different time and culture, the project that he envisions would not simply "appropriate Lewis" but would engage in a critique of the objections to today's culture and apply Lewisian ways of "giving an account of the world."[4] Kort argues that those who

---

1. Kort, *C. S. Lewis*, 162.
2. See also Callum Brown, *Religion and the Demographic Revolution*.
3. Taylor, *Secular Age*, 12.
4. Kort, *C. S. Lewis*, 160, 162.

are "concerned about the moral and spiritual well-being of our culture have a responsibility not only to hold a critical, negative attitude to contemporary culture but to propose projects for its cure."[5] And he strongly advises against retreating "from the challenge into the security and relative simplicity of our separate faith communities."[6] Kort thinks that the place to start for this Lewis-like task is to "foster a culture that emphasises a shared sense of right relations between people and their environment, between people and their neighbors, and between people and future prospects for a common life." After sufficient progress has been made in restoring a sense of humanity into contemporary culture, he writes that "Christians can then turn to the larger task of giving a more specifically Christian account of the world and recommending it to their nonreligious neighbors as coherent and revealing."[7]

Although this thesis is not structured in accordance with Kort's suggested framework, nevertheless, it endeavours to explore means by which a Lewis-like methodology might critique our contemporary secular culture and find ways for promoting a Christian worldview or, in Kort's terminology, a Christian account of the world.

Secularism consists of many forms, not all of which are incompatible with Christianity. A reasonable, well-balanced interpretation of the American notion of the separation of church and state need not present any restrictions for the development of a vibrant Christianity. As well, most people in the West believe that a trend toward secularism in countries such as Turkey or Iran would be a positive step, because it would be considered to be conducive to fostering a more tolerant and less restrictive society. Although there are various manifestations of secularism extant in contemporary society, a prevalent version known as methodological naturalism,[8] presents perhaps the greatest challenge to the Christian faith, because it contradicts basic tenets of Christian orthodoxy.

---

5. Kort, *C. S. Lewis*, 162.
6. Kort, *C. S. Lewis*, 163.
7. Kort, *C. S. Lewis*, 170.
8. Methodological naturalism is an epistemological view about practical methods for acquiring knowledge. It is the general notion that explanations of observable effects are considered to be practical and useful only when they hypothesize natural causes, and requires that hypotheses be explained and tested only by reference to natural causes and events (Moreland, *Creation Hypothesis*, 41–51).

Former dean of the faculty of chemistry and material sciences at Helsinki University Matti Leisola and Jonathan Witt at Seattle's Discovery Institute claim: "Christians invented modern science, but a later generation discarded science's fertile theological

When methodological naturalism coexists with Christianity, it can have a corrosive effect on the faith, robbing it of its vitality and reducing it to some form of humanism. Whereas a core tenet of Christian belief holds that a supernatural force outside of the natural order created the natural world, methodological naturalism rejects the notion of there being anything outside of the natural order. Removing its supernatural element diminishes the Christian faith and deprives it of one of its most significant elements. Without its inherent supernatural quality, Christianity becomes impoverished, devoid of much of its transformative power. An account of the world that has the effect of undermining the Christian faith by reducing it to a humanist philosophy presents a significant challenge to a Christian worldview.

Secular humanism is another manifestation of secularism that is often cited as a challenge to Christian theism. It is an anti-theistic naturalistic movement that opposes many of Christianity's truth claims; it also rejects the notion of any absolute moral standard as well as any conception of the supernatural.[9] As this study will show, Lewis offers important insights for countering the various challenges from secularism/naturalism.

2.2 CHALLENGES FROM PANTHEISM/PANENTHEISM

There are significant similarities, as well as strong differences, between pantheism and panentheism. In pantheism, God is everything: all is God, and God is all. God pervades all things and is found in all things. Panentheism is the belief that God is in the world in much the same way as a mind or a soul is in a body, whereas pantheism is the belief that God is the world and the world is God.[10] Both belief systems are in conflict with Christian theism, in that theism holds that God is an eternal Being outside of the natural order that he created.

Pantheism is a worldview found in some forms of Hinduism, Buddhism, and many New Age religions. It is also the worldview of Christian Science and Scientology.[11] According to Alisdair MacIntyre, "Pantheism

---

soil and insisted that science trade only in theories that fit materialism and atheism" (Leisola and Witt, *Heretic*, 228).

9. Geisler, *Big Book*, 250.

10. Geisler, *Christian Apologetics*, 201.

11. Geisler, *Big Book*, 425.

is a doctrine that usually occurs in a religious and philosophical context in which there are already tolerable conceptions of God and of the universe and the question has arisen how these two conceptions are related."[12]

A thorough description of pantheistic beliefs is beyond the scope of this study. However, for the purpose of distinguishing the key challenges that a pantheistic worldview presents to Christianity, it is important to identify some of its key characteristics. According to Norman Geisler, the following are basic beliefs in a pantheistic worldview:[13]

The Nature of God. For most pantheists, God and reality are ultimately impersonal. In God, there is the absolute simplicity of one. There are no parts. Multiplicity may flow from the one, but in and of itself, the one is simple and not multiple.

The Nature of the Universe. Those pantheists who grant any kind of reality to the universe agree that it was created *ex Deo* (out of God), not *ex nihilo* (out of nothing), as theism maintains. There is only one Being or Existence in the universe; everything else is an emanation or manifestation of that Being. Absolute pantheists hold that the universe is not even a manifestation. We are all simply part of an illusion. Creation simply does not exist. Only God exists; nothing else does.

God in Relation to the Universe. In contrast to the theists, who view God as beyond and separate from the universe, pantheists believe that God and the universe are one. The theist grants some reality to the universe, while the pantheist does not. Those who deny the existence of the universe, of course, see no relation between God and the universe. But all pantheists agree that whatever reality exists, it is God. Pantheism essentially involves two assertions: all that exists constitutes a unity, and this all-inclusive unity is divine.

Miracles. An implication of pantheism is that miracles are impossible. For if all is God and God is all, nothing exists apart from God that could be interrupted or broken into, which is what the nature of a miracle requires.

Human Beings. The primary teaching of absolute pantheism is that humans must overcome their ignorance and realize that they are God. The body is believed to hold the human down, keeping him or her from uniting with God. So, each person must purge his or her body so that

---

12. MacIntyre, "Pantheism."
13. Geisler, *Big Book*, 425–26.

the soul can be released to attain oneness with the Absolute One. For all pantheists, the chief goal of humanity is to unite with God.

Ethics. Pantheists usually strive to lead moral lives and encourage others to do so. However, these exhortations usually apply to a lower level of spiritual attainment. Once a person has achieved union with God, he or she has no further concern with moral laws. Since God is beyond good and evil, the person must transcend them to reach God. Morality is stressed as only a temporary concern. Pantheists believe that there is no absolute basis for right or wrong.

History and Human Destiny. Geisler writes that pantheists seldom talk about history. He claims that they believe that, like the wheel of *samsara*,[14] history forever repeats itself. There are no unique events or final events of history. There is no millennium, utopia, or eschaton. Most pantheists, especially Eastern varieties, believe in reincarnation. It is believed that after the soul leaves the body, it enters into another mortal body to work off its karma.[15] Eventually, the goal is to leave the body and, in the case of many pantheists, merge with God. In many Buddhist traditions, this is called nirvana,[16] and it means the loss of individuality.

14. University of Calgary's Irving Hexham claims that in the "Hindu tradition samsara is usually pictured as the ever turning wheel of time to which all living things are bound by karma, [and] in turn, karma is the belief that all things are embraced by a universal law of cause and effect that stretches through time, binding living things to the law of samsara." He writes that "just as humans change clothing, so too does the soul move from body to body in the cycle of transmigration. Inhabiting numerous bodies that live and die, the soul moves on through time until eventually it is liberated from the vicious cycle of birth and death to which it is bound" (Hexham, *Understanding World Religions*, 133).

15. Karma (Sanskrit action) is the central moral doctrine in Hinduism, Buddhism and Jainism. "It is a natural, impersonal law of cause and effect, unconnected with divine punishment from sins. In Hinduism and Jainism karma is the sum of a person's actions which are passed on from one life to the next and determine the nature of rebirth. Buddhism rejects this continuity of the 'soul' through Reincarnation. The intention behind an action determines the faith of an individual. Release from rebirth into Nirvana depends on knowledge of the Real, which in turn enables neutral action" (Humphries et al., *Oxford World Book Encyclopedia*, 369).

16. Arindam Chakrabarti, former University of Delhi professor, writes that nirvana is "in Buddhist philosophy the blowing out of the flame of self. Hence the end of all suffering—by living without craving or dying never to be reborn. Commonly understood as pure extinction, it is described by some Buddhist scriptures as a positive state of perpetual peace" (Chakrabarti, "Nirvana").

University of Vienna professor Ingrid Fischer-Schreiber claims that nirvana is derived from the Sanskrit word translated as extinction, and that it is known as a "state of liberation or illumination, characterised by the merging of the individual, transitory

University of Manchester Buddhist scholar Lance Selwyn Cousins writes that although the "aim of the spiritual life was already described as nirvana before the rise of Buddhism in the fifth century, BC, it is in the Buddhist context that it is most well-known."[17] Professor Irving Hexham writes that, in Buddhism, nirvana means freedom from the bonds of karma and release from samsara, the perpetual cycle of rebirths, and a cessation of our present mode of existence. Buddhist teaching maintains that "while we cannot explain what it is, we can know what enables people to attain it."[18]

Noted former religious studies professor Ninian Smart writes that the spiritual goal in many Hindu traditions is known as *moksha*, which is usually conceived as liberation from the incessant round of reincarnations.[19] *The Encyclopedia of Eastern Philosophy and Religion* defines moksha as "the final liberation and release from all worldly bonds, from karma and from the cycle of life and death through union with God or knowledge of the ultimate reality."[20] Geisler writes that ultimate salvation in this kind of panentheistic system is from one's individuality, whereas Christians believe that salvation, although it may apply to individuals rather than to a group, is obtained through a common faith.[21]

In panentheism, God is not identical with the world, as in pantheism; nor is God distinct from and independent of the world, as in theism. God is seen as being identical with the world in his body but is seen

---

I in *brahman*." Nirvana "frees one from suffering, death and rebirth, and all other worldly bonds," she claims. She writes that "it is the highest, transcendent consciousness, referred to in the *Bhagavad-Gita* as *brahman-nirvana*, in the Upanishads as *turiya*, in yoga as *niribja-samadhi*, in Vedanta as *nirvikalpa-samadhi*," and is the goal of spiritual practise in all branches of Buddhism. She notes that in many Buddhist texts, in describing nirvana, the simile of an extinguishing flame is used. The fire is described as not passing away but merely becoming invisible by passing into space, which illustrates that, even though nirvana is derived from the Sanskrit term meaning extinction, in Buddhism, nirvana does not indicate annihilation but rather "entry into another mode of existence." Fischer-Schreiber claims that in Mahayana Buddhism the notion of nirvana underwent a change that may be attributed to emphasis on the unified nature of the world, in which "nirvana is conceived as oneness with the absolute, the unity of samsara and transcendence . . . and as freedom from attachment to illusions, affects and desires" (Fischer-Schreiber, "Nirvana").

17. Cousins, "Nirvana," 633.
18. Hexham, *Understanding World Religions*, 208.
19. Smart, *Long Search*, 304.
20. Friedrichs, "Moksha," 229.
21. Geisler, *Christian Apologetics*, 214.

as being more than the world. He is understood to be transcending the world as a mind transcends or is more than a body. According to Geisler, panentheism may be summarised as follows:

God is conceived as a dipolarity, both a "potential pole that is beyond the world, and an actual pole that is the physical world." Therefore, God is perceived as consisting of both potentiality and actuality. In contrast to theism, the world is not seen as having been created *ex nihilo*, out of nothing, but is formed out of something eternally there, as manifested through God's potentiality. God and world are as interrelated as mind and body; the world depends on God for its existence, and God depends on the world for his manifestation and embodiment. God is seen as "continually growing in perfections due to the increase in value in the world (his body) resulting from human effort." The universe, understood as God's body, is "undergoing perpetual perfection and enlargement of value."[22].

Although various Christian thinkers have embraced a form of process theology that may be characterised as open theism or free will theism,[23] process theology may have some similarities to the pantheistic notion whereby God is perceived as a dipolar entity in a constant process of change.[24] This concept stands in sharp contrast with the traditional Christian concept of God as an omnipotent, omniscient Being.

Whereas a common challenge from secularism involves the denial of the existence of anything outside of the natural order, both pantheism

---

22. Geisler, *Christian Apologetics*, 214.

23. Alfred North Whitehead and Charles Hartshorne are two philosophers frequently credited with developing the concept of process theology. Key components of process theology include the notion that, although certain features about God remain constant, God is constantly growing; God is related to every other actual being and is affected by what happens to it; every actual being has some form of self-determination, and God's power is reconceived as the power to persuade each actual being to be as God wishes it to be. By picturing God as supremely relating to and responding to every actuality, some elements of process theology share the panentheistic notion, whereby the universe is characterised as being God's body (Keller, "Process Theology"; Sherburne, "Whitehead"; Viney, "Charles Hartshorne"). Fuller Seminary's professor emeritus Colin Brown writes: "In so far as process philosophers say that God is active in all nature and history they are saying no more than orthodox Christian Theism. But in so far as they say that the universe is an aspect or manifestation of God they are rejecting Christianity. If there is one thing that the Bible, secular science and common sense are agreed upon it is that nature is not God either in its sum total or its particular parts" (Colin Brown, *Philosophy and Christian Faith*, 241).

24. Roberts, "Processing Theology."

and panentheism challenge the Christian concept of transcendence. Having abandoned atheism in favour of some form of pantheism during his pre-conversion years,[25] Lewis offers insights for dealing with these challenges. Insights from Lewis will be explored in subsequent chapters.

2.3 CHALLENGES FROM DEISM

Norman Geisler writes that although deism is "not presently a major worldview," its significance is long lasting. He characterises deism as having been hostile to Christianity and engaged in a destructive criticism of some of its core beliefs, including miracles and supernatural revelation. While it was critical of many of the practises of Christianity, it adopted some of Christianity's underpinnings and, as a philosophical movement, borrowed its theistic concept of God. Deism's concept of God has not been depicted within orthodox Christianity, however, but has been understood in terms of a mechanistic or "watchmaker" model. Geisler describes deism as having gained influence during the seventeenth century, flourished in the eighteenth, but declined as a movement in the nineteenth century. In spite of its decline, however, deism has had a lasting impact on contemporary society. According to Geisler, earlier proponents of deism were instrumental in creating the present climate of anti-supernaturalism, especially in regards to miracles, and fostering the current trend toward naturalism.[26] In his book *Good without God*, Greg Epstein writes that the Enlightenment provided a pathway to deism by introducing a new way of perceiving God. Epstein claims that deism introduced a concept of God that was different from the Christian notion of God manifested in the biblical narrative; although deism subscribed to a notion of God as creator of the universe, its conception was that of a God who "did not appear to interact with the world other than by assigning nature's laws."[27]

In his 2007 opus, *A Secular Age*, Charles Taylor reflects much of what Geisler has written about the historic rise and present-day influence of deism. In his analysis of Western society's drift toward secularism, he credits a form of deism as having been a stepping-stone or "intermediate stage" to the present state of unbelief and secularism in the West. He

---

25. Lewis, *Surprised by Joy*, 235.
26. Geisler, *Christian Apologetics*, 139.
27. Epstein, *Good without God*, 50.

claims that the general orthodox notion of God as having designed the world went through an anthropocentric shift in the seventeenth and eighteenth centuries, resulting in what he calls providential deism. This led to a notion of what he calls "the primacy of impersonal order," in which God is believed to relate to humans primarily through having created a certain order of things for humans to inhabit.[28]

In Taylor's view, this led to a profound change in the understanding of God and his relation to the world. It resulted in a drift away from orthodox Christian conceptions of God as interacting with humans and intervening in human history, and led to a conception of God as an architect of a universe operating by unchanging laws to which humans have to conform or suffer the consequences. Rather than being conceived as a Supreme Being with powers analogous to what we call agency and personality, God was seen as relating to us only as the architect of the law-governed structure he had created. This resulted in the perception of humans as having an existence within an indifferent universe, with God either indifferent or nonexistent. From Taylor's perspective, deism should be seen as a kind of "half-way house on the road to contemporary atheism."[29]

Although Geisler and Taylor regard deism as having lost much of its appeal as a current movement, they contend that it has been highly instrumental in reshaping contemporary society. Deism has resulted in a drift away from orthodox Christianity toward alternate forms of belief or toward some form of unbelief. According to Taylor, much of this shift would have been evident during Lewis's day, and in that regard, there is much to be gleaned from a study of Lewis's writings and from Lewisian methodology.

2.4 CHALLENGES FROM PRAGMATICISM/ UTILITARIANISM/NEW AGEISM

Utilitarianism is a philosophy that was founded by Jeremy Bentham (1748–1832) and was largely popularized by his student and secretary John Stuart Mill (1806–1873). Bentham and Mill devised the principle of utilitarianism as a universal mode for ethics and proposed the notion that the optimum ethical standard for a society was one whereby

28. Taylor, *Secular Age*, 221.
29. Taylor, *Secular Age*, 270.

individuals consider themselves obligated to act in a manner that they believe is likely to bring the greatest amount of good to the largest number of people.[30] Mill denied the existence of any absolute ethical norms; he believed that optimum ethical societal standards were to be achieved only when a society implemented the best standards that it knew until it discovered better ones.[31]

Although utilitarianism was developed as an ethical model, its influence extended well beyond its ethical origins. Bentham and Mill's utilitarian principles were expanded to include a wide range of topics, ranging from property rights to the status of women in society.[32] Charles Taylor claims that a form of utilitarianism, materialist utilitarianism, is one of Western modernity's most suppressing movements. Even though it was formed as a movement that seeks to establish a form of life that is "unqualifiedly good," utilitarianism has become insensitive and intolerant of alternate notions, including religious ones, writes Taylor.[33]

Perhaps as an outgrowth of postmodernism, a utilitarian notion has also made inroads into various religious philosophies. This trend is characterised as a focus on practical utility when determining a person's decision about adopting a religious practise or subscribing to a particular religious philosophy. Whereas Lewis converted to Christianity because of his belief in its inherent truth, individuals who subscribe to a utilitarian religious philosophy typically do so because of the practical utility experienced by the practitioner. The choice is based on "what works" for the individual, rather than on what's true; it contains elements of consumerism and could be described as a form of pragmaticism or privatism.

A utilitarian-like notion is sometimes manifested in some elements of Christianity, in that a belief in Jesus is deemed to benefit the practitioner in a practical manner. Its utilitarian attraction cannot be the prime motive for embracing the Christian faith, however, without attracting severe criticism from believers who embrace a more traditional/orthodox form of Christianity. The critique that is often directed to a form of Christianity known as the "health and wealth gospel" can be seen as a traditional Christian response to the presence of overt utilitarian overtones within the faith community.

---

30. See Mill, *Utilitarianism*, and Troyer, *Classical Utilitarians*.
31. Geisler, *Christian Apologetics*, 165.
32. See Brock, "Utilitarianism," and F. Wilson, "John Stuart Mill."
33. Taylor, *Secular Age*, 617.

Although a utilitarian context is manifested in a range of religious philosophies, it is especially prevalent within New Age pantheistic notions. Even though traditional utilitarianism is rooted in the philosophy of Jeremy Bentham and John Stuart Mill, it has adopted elements of postmodernism, in which the preference for practitioners is to choose *what is true for them*, and allows individuals to engage in a religious practise because of its practical utility. As someone who converted to Christianity because of the authenticity of its truth claims, Lewis's writings offer important insights into dealing with the challenges from contemporary forms of utilitarianism.

Chapter Three

THE PHILOSOPHICAL *and* SPIRITUAL JOURNEY *of* C. S. LEWIS

3.1 INTRODUCTION

Although C. S. Lewis was a scholar in medieval literature and had been trained in philosophy and classics, he is best known for his contribution to Christian apologetics. Lewis is often credited as being the most influential religious author and Christian apologist of the twentieth century. (MacSwain, 2010:3). His contribution to Christian apologetics is multifaceted and includes exposition of major tenets of the Christian faith, as well as a rigorous defense of the Christian worldview. Lewis's apologetic method cannot be easily categorized within any school of apologetics (McGrath, INTEllectual World:43). It encompasses a wide range of applications. This diversity is attributable to multiple factors: Lewis's training and intellectual capacity enabled him to conceptualize a significant number of relevant factors simultaneously, his worldview was highly complex, and he came to embrace the Christian worldview via a long and tortuous spiritual journey. His spiritual pathway included the abandonment of his childhood faith to a form of naturalism,[1] after which he was temporar-

---

1. Naturalism may be summarised as a "system of thought holding that all phenomena can be explained in terms of natural causes and laws" (*American Heritage Dictionary*, 1172).

ily drawn to pantheism,[2] from which he was attracted to theism, which ultimately led him to embrace orthodox Christianity. Although most of his adult life was spent in the academy, teaching at two of his country's most prestigious universities, Oxford and Cambridge, he is best known for his popular writings in the field of Christian apologetics.

3.2 LEWIS'S PUBLIC SCHOOL YEARS

Lewis was born into a middle class family in Belfast, Northern Ireland, in 1898, the younger of two brothers. The Lewis family attended a Belfast congregation of the Church of Ireland. His father, Albert, was a successful lawyer, and his mother, Florence, was a graduate of Queens College, Belfast, who endeavoured to bring him up in the faith as practised by that denomination.[3] When he was nine years old, Lewis's mother died of abdominal cancer. The resultant grief following his wife's death so unsettled Lewis's father that it rendered him virtually incapable of caring for his sons, and he sent them away to boarding school in England, where Lewis attended various schools throughout his teenage years.[4]

This proved to be an exceedingly difficult period for Lewis, as is described in *Surprised by Joy*[5] and in some of his other writings. Eventually, Lewis was granted a reprieve from the drudgery of the public school system that he detested; his father decided to send him to be tutored by William Kirkpatrick at Great Bookham in Surrey. Kirkpatrick had been Lewis's brother Warren's tutor, and Lewis's father thought that tutoring would be a good alternative to the public schools that Lewis despised. Kirkpatrick served as his tutor from September 1914 to March 1917. The move to Great Bookham proved to be a welcome reprieve from the public schools that he had attended. Lewis thrived under Kirkpatrick's tutelage.

---

2. A succinct definition of pantheism characterises it as a "doctrine identifying the Deity with the universe and its phenomena" (*American Heritage Dictionary*, 1271).

3. Lewis, *Surprised by Joy*, 3–7; Griffin, *C. S. Lewis*, 32–33.

4. Lewis's schooling, mostly in England, following the death of his mother, may be summarised as follows (McGrath, *C. S. Lewis*, 26):
Wynyard School, Watford: Sept. 1908–June 1910
Campbell College, Belfast: Sept.–Dec. 1910
Cherbourg School, Malvern: Jan. 1911–June 1913
Malvern College (pseudonym Wyvern College), Malvern Sept. 1913–June 1914
Private tutelage at Great Bookham: Sept. 1914–Mar. 1917

5. Lewis, *Surprised by Joy*, 18–21.

Lewis's spiritual life underwent a series of different phases during his public school years and during his tutelage under Kirkpatrick. Lewis had prayed fervently for his mother's recovery when she was stricken with abdominal cancer, and her subsequent death challenged his Christian beliefs. Lewis writes, however, that it was at one of the public schools that he first "became an effective believer," and he attributes the "instrument" of this belief to the school's practise of having the boys attend church on a regular basis, where they "were taken twice every Sunday."[6] At that time, he was attending Wynyard School—which he had dubbed Belsen, after the World War II concentration camp—in Watford, Hertfordshire, and the church that the students attended was high Anglo-Catholic. Although he was an Ulster Protestant and had a strong reaction against what he called the "peculiar rituals" of the church service, he was impressed when he heard the doctrines of Christianity being "taught by men who obviously believed them," the effect of which was "to bring to life" the things he already believed. Interestingly, Lewis thinks that concerns about the future of his soul, as well as the notions about hell that are expressed in his later writings, have their origin in his church attendance and schooling at Wynyard.[7]

Wynyard School closed in the summer of 1910, and Lewis was sent to Campbell College, a school "founded for the purpose of giving Ulster boys the advantages of a public-school without the trouble of crossing the Irish Sea."[8] Lewis's attendance at Campbell was brief; before the first term ended. he became ill and went home for the balance of the term. For reasons unknown, Lewis's father had become dissatisfied with Campbell, and in January of 1911, he sent his two sons to Malvern, in Worcestershire, England; Warren attended Malvern College (pseudonym, Wyvern College), and C. S. Lewis attended Cherbourg School (dubbed Chartres by Lewis), a preparatory school there. Lewis's studies at Cherbourg School continued from January 1911 until the end of the summer term in 1913. From September 1913 to September 1914, Lewis attended Malvern College, but it was during his time at "Chartres" (Cherbourg) that he "ceased to be a Christian," he writes.[9]

---

6. Lewis, *Surprised by Joy*, 33.
7. Lewis, *Surprised by Joy*, 33.
8. Lewis, *Surprised by Joy*, 49–50.
9. Lewis, *Surprised by Joy*, 58.

In his book *Surprised by Joy*, Lewis describes some of the circumstances that led to the abandonment of his Christian faith. He claims that although "the chronology of this disaster is a little vague . . . I know for certain that it had not begun when I went there and that the process was complete very shortly after I left."[10] In a chapter titled "I Broaden My Mind," Lewis gives his account of the process by which he came to be an unbeliever. Much of the process revolved around conversations that he had with the school's matron, whom he identifies as Miss C. Although she "seemed old" to Lewis, he saw her as someone who was still in a state of spiritual immaturity. "As I should now put it," writes Lewis, "she was floundering in the mazes of Theosophy,[11] Rosicrucianism,[12] Spiritualism[13] . . . the whole Anglo-American Occult[14] tradition."[15] Since the book was first published in 1955, Lewis would have been in his mid- to late fifties when this was written. Lewis was at Cherbourg when he was ages

10. Lewis, *Surprised by Joy*, 58–59.

11. "In its general sense theosophy denotes a variety of embracing pantheism and natural mysticism in which the divine is claimed to be intuitively known" (Colin Brown, *Philosophy and Christian Faith*, 119n2). Theosophy is a religious philosophy or speculation about the nature of the soul, based on mystical insight into the nature of God (*American Heritage Dictionary*). In a narrower sense, theosophy may refer to the philosophy of Emanuel Swedenborg or Rudolf Steiner. Swedenborg's theosophy attempted to explain the connection between soul and body, while Steiner's was a reaction to the standard scientific theory of his day. It purported to be as rigorous as conventional scientific theory but superior to it, because it incorporated spiritual truths about reality (Martinich, "Theosophy"). Harold Netland, professor of philosophy of religion and intercultural studies, writes: "The central message of Theosophy (the term means 'divine wisdom') is that all phenomena arise out of an eternal, unitary principle which is spiritual in essence and which is manifested most conspicuously in individual enlightened souls" (Netland, *Encountering Religious Pluralism*, 109). The adoption of some of Steiner's notions by Lewis's friend Owen Barfield eventually led to major disagreements between Lewis and Barfield during their Oxford years. These disagreements will be dealt with in a subsequent chapter.

12. Rosicrucianism is embraced by members of an organization that is usually secretive and that is devoted to the study of how ancient mystical, philosophical, and religious doctrines may have application to modern life (*American Heritage Dictionary*, 1515).

13. Spiritualism is a belief that spirits of the dead have both the ability and the inclination to communicate with the living, especially through the agency of a medium (*New Lexicon Webster's Dictionary*).

14. Occultism is the study of supernatural practises, including (but not limited to) magic, alchemy, extra-sensory perception, astrology, spiritualism, and divination (*American Heritage Dictionary*, 1215).

15. Lewis, *Surprised by Joy*, 59.

twelve through fourteen. How much he knew about these "mazes" at the time is difficult to ascertain, but it seems likely that he would have gotten a greater understanding of some of Miss C's notions and her search for spirituality later on as an adult. His description of the nature of the impact that she had on his spiritual life at the time is instructive, however. Lewis is highly appreciative of the kindness and comfort he received from Miss C and impresses upon his readers that he does not consider her to be responsible for his loss of faith. Rather than having been responsible, he sees her as having become a catalyst for the transformation of his beliefs, a transformation made possible by a number of factors. Lewis's description of these factors comprises almost an entire chapter in *Surprised by Joy*.[16] What follows is a description of three of these factors.

Although he had become an effective believer while at Wynyard School from 1908 through 1910, a faith that at first seemed plain sailing eventually became burdensome to him. He cites the manner in which he was taught to pray as an example. Students at the school were instructed to pray regularly, with the added injunction to be "really thinking about what you said." Lewis writes that he tried to follow through on these instructions but was frequently troubled about whether he had really been thinking as taught. To compensate for the perceived shortcomings in his prayer life, he attempted to set a standard for himself that he called a "realization." Lewis writes that in order for this realization to "pass muster" required a "certain vividness of the imagination and the affections." By having set this standard of performance in his prayer life, he had resigned himself to a nightly task to "produce by sheer will power a phenomenon which will power could never produce."[17] He claims that the endeavour to "pump up realizations" frequently left him "dizzy with desire for sleep and often in a kind of despair."[18] After having placed such an impossible spiritual burden on himself during his early teenage years, it is not surprising that Miss C's alternate notions of spirituality had a strong attraction for him. He found in her a guide to lead him out of the troubled predicament in which he found himself. A spirituality of "Higher Thought, where there was nothing to be obeyed, and nothing to be believed except what was either comforting or exciting," offered a

---

16. Lewis titled this chapter "I Broaden My Mind." The title's irony is apparent: rectifying this "broadening" effect required extensive remedial work in later years.

17. Lewis, *Surprised by Joy*, 61.

18. Lewis, *Surprised by Joy*, 62.

welcome reprieve from the rigid version that he had imposed on himself. He found his conversations with her to be liberating and enlightening.[19]

Lewis considers the profound sense of pessimism that he harboured in his adolescence to be another factor in the abandonment of his Christian belief. Although, for the most part, he was "not unhappy," he "had very definitely formed the opinion that the universe was, in the main, a rather regrettable institution," he writes. He felt traumatized by the death of his mother and his subsequent enrollment in a series of boarding schools. But Lewis thinks that his sense of pessimism was prevalent even before his mother's death. He thinks that the physical anomaly that he shared with his brother had something to do with it; the Lewis bothers had both been born with a single joint in their thumbs. Their joints closest to the nail were rigid and unbending, which hampered their athletic prowess, as well as their ability to perform certain mundane tasks. Also adding to his pessimism was a prevailing sense that life was full of dreariness and toil, consisting of mandatory school attendance during a person's youth, which was to be followed by a lifetime of work-related duties. Lewis credits his father for having instilled in him at a very early age the notion that the adult working condition was an unremittent struggle for survival. Despite their being laced with rhetorical flourishes, Lewis took his father's regular admonishments at face value. His was a middle-class home life, but his father's dire rhetoric seemed to imply that there was an ever-present threat to the family's future solvency. Lewis apparently took these admonishments more seriously than his father intended. The spiritual world that Miss C represented was a welcome reprieve from the dreariness that seemed to prevail in his own life.[20]

Lewis writes that his fixation on the preternatural was another factor in his loss of faith during his Cherbourg years. He had developed a lust for the occult, a desire for the power seemingly exhibited by magicians. He was attracted to the "vagueness, the merely speculative character of all this Occultism." To him, its "delicious" quality stood in sharp contrast to "the stern truths of the creeds." His preoccupation with the occult created the notion "that there might be real marvels all about us, that the visible world might be only a curtain to conceal huge realms uncharted by . . . very simple theology." His fixation on the occult had the "power of

---

19. Lewis, *Surprised by Joy*, 59–61.
20. Lewis, *Surprised by Joy*, 63–65.

making everything else in the world seem uninteresting."[21] Lewis's vivid imagination helped fill in the details to this imaginary world that Miss C[22] had been instrumental in creating for him. Eventually, his Christian conception of spirituality receded, and a new spiritualism emerged. What emerged during his Cherbourg school years stood in sharp contrast to the Christian faith he had adopted as a child and had intellectually embraced during his time at Wynyard.

In Lewis's description of the process by which he "became an apostate," there is a sense that while his schooling advanced his academic life, it left his Christian faith intellectually impoverished. His youthful version of Christianity was seemingly unable to keep up with his more robust personal intellectual development. He cites his study of the classics as an example: "Here, especially in Virgil, one was presented with a mass of religious ideas; and all teachers and editors took it for granted at the outset that these religious ideas were sheer illusion," he writes. And he comments that "no one ever attempted to show in what sense Christianity fulfilled Paganism or Paganism prefigured Christianity."[23] To him, it seemed that the accepted position was "that religions were normally a mere farrago of nonsense, though our own, by a fortunate exception, was exactly true."[24] He thinks that if his instructors had compared and contrasted other religions or had even made an effort to argue that other religions were "a work of the devil," that he "might conceivably have been brought to believe." But instead, he got the impression "that religion in general, though utterly false, was a natural growth, a kind of endemic nonsense into which humanity tended to blunder." And he could not see on what grounds it could be argued that Christianity was the exception. He got the impression that in "the midst of a thousand such religions stood [Christianity], the thousand and first, labeled True." Eventually, Lewis came to believe that Christianity "obviously was in some general sense the same kind of thing as all the rest." He saw no need to "continue to treat it differently . . . [and] was very anxious not to."[25] The result of

---

21. Lewis, *Surprised by Joy*, 60.

22. In a letter to his father on May 5, 1912, Lewis identifies her as Miss Cowie and says that she has been replaced by "a new matron, Miss Gosling, who seems to be passably inoffensive—but of course is not nearly as decent as Miss Cowie" (Lewis, *Collected Letters*, 1:19).

23. Lewis, *Surprised by Joy*, 62.

24. Lewis, *Surprised by Joy*, 62–63.

25. Lewis, *Surprised by Joy*, 63.

which, "little by little," he became an "apostate," abandoning his faith. Lewis is unsure about the exact chronology of events, but he thinks that his "slow apostasy" took place gradually sometime during the spring term of 1911 and the end of the summer term in 1913, all of which occurred "with no sense of loss but with the greatest relief."[26]

Abandoning his Christian faith brought an accompanying loss of the ethical and moral restraints that he had associated with Christianity. This included indulging himself in sexual fantasies and relaxing the restraints on his sexual appetite. Although dealt with only cursorily, Lewis identifies his tenure at Cherbourg as the period during which he lost his virginity via a "wholly successful assault of sexual temptation," a consequence of the deliberate withdrawal of himself from "Divine protection."[27]

Despite his aversion to the social aspects at Cherbourg, Lewis experienced an intellectual "renaissance" during his time there. He was enthralled by reading Norse mythology, especially *Siegfried and the Twilight of the Gods*, and by listening to Wagnerian music. He was exhilarated by the sense of what he calls "Northernness" that he experienced from his reading the likes of *Myths of the Norsemen*, *Myths and Legends of the Teutonic Race*, and *Mallet's Northern Antiquities*. The self-described renaissance of his imaginative and intellectual life stood in sharp contrast to the perceived drudgery of his social life, however. The growth in his intellectual and imaginative life was accompanied by doubts about his Christian faith. His "steadily growing doubts about Christianity" were accompanied by a growing fascination with Norse mythology. Lewis's sense of "Northernness seemed then a bigger thing" than his Christianity. He attributes this to the fact that his "attitude toward it contained elements which [Christianity] ought to have contained and did not."[28] He considers these elements to having been "something very like adoration, some kind of disinterested self-abandonment to an object which securely claimed this by simply being the object it was." Lewis concedes that, although he was "taught in the Prayer Book to 'give thanks to God for His great Glory,' for being what He necessarily is than for any particular benefit He confers," he thinks that he "had been far from any such experience." Interestingly, he claims: "I came far nearer to feeling this about the Norse gods whom I disbelieved in than I had ever done about the true God while I

---

26. Lewis, *Surprised by Joy*, 66.
27. Lewis, *Surprised by Joy*, 68.
28. Lewis, *Surprised by Joy*, 76.

believed." Looking back on his adolescence from the vantage point of a Christian apologist, Lewis wonders if he might not have been "sent back to the false gods there to acquire some capacity for worship against the day when the true God should recall" him to himself. And he wonders if he "might not have learned this sooner, and more safely . . . without apostasy." He views his eventual conversion as an instance in which "Divine punishments are also mercies, and particular good is worked out of particular evil, and the penal blindness made sanative."[29]

While Lewis was attending Cherbourg School in Malvern, his brother, Warren, was enrolled in Malvern College. Warren enjoyed many of the social aspects of the college, but his academic performance gradually deteriorated. As his academic reports worsened, his father sought a remedy for his older son's education and eventually sent him to William Kirkpatrick in Great Bookham for private tutelage. Kirkpatrick was his father's former headmaster when his father had been a student, but Kirkpatrick and his wife were now tutoring a few students in their private residence. While his older brother was at Great Bookham, Lewis completed his schooling at Cherbourg and subsequently, too, enrolled in Malvern College.

Although he managed to adjust to the routine of college life, unlike his brother Warren, he never enjoyed the social life at the college. He didn't care for most of the activities, disliked the mandatory participation in the clubs to which all students were assigned, and didn't enjoy the mandatory participation in sports activities. In *Surprised by Joy*, Lewis gives an unflattering account of some of his behaviour during his tenure at Malvern College. He describes himself as having become a "prig," who had developed a tendency toward snobbery. He detested many of the customs at the college, including the custom of "fagging," whereby the younger, incoming students were subjected to a form of hazing that included doing monotonous, and sometimes burdensome, errands for the upperclassmen.[30] "Spiritually speaking," he writes, "the deadly thing was that school life was dominated by the social struggle; to get on, to arrive, or, having reached the top, to remain there was the absorbing preoccupation."[31]

29. Lewis, *Surprised by Joy*, 77.
30. Lewis, *Surprised by Joy*, 107.
31. Lewis, *Surprised by Joy*, 108. Paul Piehler claims that the practise of "fagging" was still prevalent in the English school system when he was at King William's College during the 1940s (Piehler, "Encounters with Lewis," 116).

Lewis was there for only one year. He characterises his spiritual life toward the end of that year as a "whirl of contradictions." He writes that he was "at that time living, like so many Atheists, or Antitheists" who "maintained that God did not exist" but were "also very angry with God for not existing" and were "equally angry with God for having created a world." His letters to his father were replete with complaints about various aspects of his college life. He "never ceased, by letter and by word of mouth, to beg to be taken away," he writes.[32] His expressions of dissatisfaction and frustration increased to the point that he finally persuaded his father to look for an alternative for him by which to continue his schooling.

Much to his father's relief, Warren had eventually excelled under Kirkpatrick's tutelage and had subsequently enrolled in officers' training at Sandhurst. Kirkpatrick's influence on Warren's schooling so impressed the elder Lewis that he decided to send his younger son to study under Kirkpatrick's tutelage as well. In September 1914, Lewis moved to Great Bookham to continue his education. He describes his delight about the prospect of leaving the English public school system behind as somewhat akin to "waking up one morning to find that income tax or unrequited love had somehow vanished from the world."[33]

3.3 TUTELAGE AT GREAT BOOKHAM

Lewis writes that during the school break, just before his last term at Malvern College, he received a message that Arthur Greeves, a boy who lived near his own family home on the outskirts of Belfast, was at home convalescing and had asked that one of the Lewis brothers come over for a visit. Lewis reluctantly agreed to visit him. When Lewis got to his house, Greeves was sitting up in bed with the book *Myths of the Norsemen* beside him. Lewis was thrilled to discover that Greeves shared his enthusiasm for "Northernness."[34] The two became close friends and remained in touch until Lewis's death in 1963, exchanging letters regularly.[35]

---

32. Lewis, *Surprised by Joy*, 115.
33. Lewis, *Surprised by Joy*, 129.
34. Lewis, *Surprised by Joy*, 130.
35. For a sample of the Lewis/Greeves letters that includes a discussion of the Anglo-Saxon classic *Beowulf*, see Lewis, *Collected Letters*, 1:244–245. See D. Wright for a prose translation of *Beowulf*.

Lewis's first letter to Greeves as recorded in Walter Hooper's collection of letters is dated June 5, 1914. Although the two friends corresponded frequently, very little is mentioned about Lewis's religious views until Lewis's letter to Greeves written from Great Bookham in October 1916. Lewis had by that time been studying under Kirkpatrick for two years. In his letter to Greeves, he writes that he had renounced his Christian faith and that he considered all religions to be human constructs.[36] His views, although already formed, were reinforced by Kirkpatrick's rational form of atheism and were not disclosed to his father. In what he characterises as "one of the worst acts of my life," in November 1915, he had allowed himself to be pressured into being confirmed in the Church of Ireland at St. Mark's Church, Dundela, and to make his "first Communion, in total disbelief, acting a part." He attributes his confirmation to having been motivated by a desire to appease his father, and considers it to have been an act of "cowardice" and "hypocrisy."[37]

Lewis and Greeves corresponded on a regular basis. In an October 1916 letter, Lewis answers questions that Greeves had asked him about his religious views: "You ask me my religious views," he writes. "I think that I believe in no religion. There is absolutely no proof for any of them, and from a philosophical standpoint Christianity is not even the best," he tells Greeves. In Lewis's opinion, all religions are mythologies, "merely man's own invention—Christ as much as Loke."[38] He theorizes that because primitive man found himself surrounded by all sorts of terrible things he didn't understand, such as thunder, pestilence, or even snakes, that it was perfectly natural to "suppose that these things were animated by evil spirits trying to torture him," which in turn led to "singing songs and making sacrifices." Eventually, the nature-spirits were transformed into "more elaborate ideas, such as the old gods," Lewis claims. "Once man became more refined he pretended that these spirits were good as well as powerful. Thus religion, that is to say, mythology grew up," he writes Greeves. Lewis describes how the Christian faith, especially belief in Jesus, may have developed over time. He postulates how "great men . . . such as Heracles or Odin were regarded as gods after their death" and theorizes that "thus after the death of a Hebrew philosopher Yeshua

36. Lewis, *They Stand Together*, 134–37.

37. Lewis, *Surprised by Joy*, 160. See also Lewis, *They Stand Together*, 63.

38. Lewis, *Collected Letters*, 1:230. In Norse mythology, Loke, sometimes spelled Loki or Lokke, is a god who creates discord among other gods (*American Heritage Dictionary*, 1029).

(whose name we have corrupted into Jesus), he became regarded as a god, a cult sprang up, which was afterward connected with the ancient Hebrew Yahweh-worship, and so Christianity came into being—one mythology among many, but the one we happen to have been brought up in."[39]

Lewis then tells Greeves how his changing views about religion have affected his sense of morality: "I must only add that one's views on religious subjects don't make any difference in morals, of course. A good member of society must of course be honest, chaste, truthful, kindly etc. [because] these are things we owe to our own manhood and dignity and not to any imagined god or gods," he tells Greeves. "Of course, mind you," Lewis continues, "I am not laying down as a certainty that there is nothing outside the material world: considering the discoveries that are always being made, this would be foolish," he insists. Although, "anything MAY exist . . . but until we know that it does, we can't make any assumptions," he declares. In Lewis's opinion, "the universe is an absolute mystery . . . man has made many guesses at it, but the answer is yet to seek. Whenever any light can be got as to such matters, I will be glad to welcome it," he tells his friend and concludes with these words: "In the meantime I am not going back to the bondage of believing in any old (and already decaying) superstition."[40]

Lewis's letters to Greeves appear to reflect the views of David Hume. Hume attributed "speculative dogmas of religion" as having emerged in prehistoric time, "when mankind, being wholly illiterate, formed an idea of religion more suitable to their weak apprehension."[41] McGrath characterises such notions as rhetoric, to be understood as "a long-standing atheist caricature of faith as wish-fulfillment," which is an idea with a long pedigree and given classic expression in the writings of Sigmund Freud (1859–1939).[42]

As his October 1916 letter indicates, Lewis had by this time adopted a wholly naturalistic worldview. While he is not claiming "as a certainty that there is nothing outside the material world . . . until we know that it does, we can't make any assumptions," he writes. Although he will be open to "any new light that can be shed on such matters" he cannot

---

39. Lewis, *Collected Letters*, 1:231.
40. Lewis, *Collected Letters*, 1:231.
41. Hume, *Enquiry Concerning Human Understanding*, 168.
42. McGrath, *C. S. Lewis*, 146–47.

envision himself "going back to the bondage of believing in any old (and already decaying) superstition," he tells Greeves.[43]

Christianity, with its supra-naturalistic notions, was no longer something to which he could subscribe. In his opinion, it was a relic of an unsophisticated age, a consequence of misdiagnosed natural phenomena combined with mythology. Even though he respected the Christian faith's moral underpinnings, he thought that a sound moral regime could well be developed without any unnecessary attachments to what he considered to be illogical religiosity. In his opinion, religious views had no impact on one's morals, and therefore he saw no purpose in returning to what he considered to be an obsolete belief system.

In Kirkpatrick, Lewis had found a kindred spirit for his acquired naturalism. Right from the start, he was attracted to his new teacher, Kirk or Knock, as he had come to be known by his father and older brother. "If ever a man came near to being a purely logical entity," he writes, "that man was Kirk." Lewis thinks that if he had been born a little later, "he would have been a Logical Positivist." The most casual remark was taken as a summons to disputation, he writes. In Lewis's view, Kirk thought that the idea that human beings should exercise their vocal organs for any purpose except that of communicating or discovering truth was preposterous. Although he thinks that "some boys would not have liked it," to him, "it was red beef and strong beer."[44] (Lewis, Surprised by Joy:136).

Lewis was introduced to Kirkpatrick's rigorous logic immediately upon arriving at Great Bookham. He discovered that his training began even before he got to the Kirkpatrick house. His new tutor had met him at the train station, and during their walk to the Kirkpatricks' home, Lewis, in an effort to engage his host in conversation, remarked that the Surrey scenery was "wilder" than he had expected. "What do you mean by wildness and what grounds had you for not expecting it," Kirkpatrick wanted to know.[45] Lewis's responses didn't impress his tutor; he thought his attempted explanations woefully inadequate and tore them to shreds. Lewis writes that by the time their "acquaintance had lasted about three and a half minutes," he had to accept his tutor's admonishment that he "had no right to have any opinion on the subject," because he had never

---

43. Lewis, *Collected Letters*, 1:231.
44. Lewis, *Surprised by Joy*, 136.
45. Lewis, *Surprised by Joy*, 134.

been there before and had never seen any maps or photographs of the area.[46]

Lewis quickly took to Kirkpatrick's teaching methods. These were not limited to dialectics. Within days after his arrival, Kirkpatrick sat down with him and began to "read aloud about twenty lines or so" of Homer's *Iliad* to him in the original Greek. Kirkpatrick then translated about a hundred lines for him, offered him a lexicon, asked him to continue on his own, and left the room. Lewis writes that Kirkpatrick's method of teaching worked so well that gradually he began to think in Greek, a key to learning any new language. Kirkpatrick then had him concentrate on other languages, including Latin, Italian, and German.[47] He thrived under Kirkpatrick's tutelage, started "to put on intellectual muscle," and eventually "became a not contemptible sparring partner."[48] Lewis's list of his "greatest teachers" includes only two names, Smewgy and Kirk. Smewgy, one of his teachers at Cherbourg, had taught him grammar and rhetoric, and Kirk had taught him dialectic. "My debt to him is very great, my reverence to this day undiminished," he writes.[49]

Even though Kirkpatrick was a confirmed atheist, Lewis never heard him disparage someone else's religious views. He writes that, perhaps because of Kirk's having been influenced by his Presbyterian youth, he always "gardened in a different, slightly more respectable suit on Sundays." Lewis saw in him a "rationalist" of the old nineteenth-century type.[50] Although he was able to glean material from him to use in his arguments against the Christian faith, he got this "indirectly from the tone of his mind and independently from reading his books," he claims.[51]

According to Lewis's official biographers, Walter Hooper and Roger Lancelyn Green, although Lewis and Greeves had occasional discussions about religion, it was always Greeves, a Christian, who brought religion up for discussion.[52] This may have been because Lewis was still formulating his views, but it may also have to do with his desire not to

46. Lewis, *Surprised by Joy*, 135.
47. Lewis, *Surprised by Joy*, 140.
48. Lewis, *Surprised by Joy*, 137.
49. Lewis, *Surprised by Joy*, 148.
50. Lewis, *Surprised by Joy*, 139.
51. Lewis, *Surprised by Joy*, 140.
52. Green and Hooper, *C. S. Lewis*, 31.

publicize the agnosticism/atheism that he had acquired. As mentioned previously, in an apparent attempt to hide his apostasy, in late 1916, he had acquiesced to his father's wishes and allowed himself to be confirmed in the Church of Ireland.[53]

In another letter, Lewis addresses the subject of his religious views again. Apparently, Greeves had challenged some of Lewis's notions, and Lewis responds to his objections. In his counter-argument to Greeves, he invites him to read his letter more carefully before rushing to answer it. Lewis had made a reference to Jesus, a reference he says that Greeves had misunderstood as a challenge to the historicity of Jesus. "I distinctly said there was once a Hebrew called Yeshua," he writes. He disagrees, however, with the Christian doctrine of Yeshua having become "the mythological being into whom he was afterwards converted by popular imagination."[54] And he rejects "the legends about his magic performances and resurrection," he tells Greeves. He thinks it certain "that the man Yeshua or Jesus did actually exist." In fact, "Tacitus mentions his execution in the Annals," he reminds Greeves. But he doesn't subscribe to "all the other tomfoolery about virgin birth, magic healings, apparitions and so forth." He places it "on exactly the same footing as any other mythology," he tells Greeves.[55] In Lewis's view, the "legends" about the historical Jesus should be understood within the context of some of the "nonsense" associated with the "adventures which the Middle Ages related" to Alexander the Great or "to such a man as Odin, who was deified after his death."[56]

As his account in *Surprised by Joy* attests, Lewis enjoyed his time at Great Bookham. He had been extricated from the English public school system that he had come to despise and quickly adjusted to the routine of Kirkpatrick's tutelage. His description of British public schools takes up seven of the fifteen chapters of the book, three of them dealing with his one year at Malvern College. The copyright date of the book is shown

---

53. Griffin, *C. S. Lewis*, 36.

54. In formulating his beliefs about imagination, Lewis appears to have been influenced by the likes of David Hume, Samuel Taylor Coleridge, and William Wordsworth. This will be discussed further in subsequent chapters. In Hume's classic work *Enquiry Concerning Human Understanding*, Hume argues that we make inferences from what we experience and perceive by means of our memories and imagination. Hume claims that through our imagination, we not only make inferences about issues in our present world but also extrapolate possibilities and probabilities for both a previous and future world (Hume, *Enquiry Concerning Human Understanding*, 90–93).

55. Lewis, *Collected Letters*, 1:234.

56. Lewis, *Collected Letters*, 1:235.

as 1955. Although the manuscript itself may well have been written before that date, Lewis was likely in his fifties when he wrote the first draft. Clearly, the negative experience of his early schooling affected him still, as is witnessed by his memories in later years.

Having been sent to an English boarding school shortly after his mother died, he says that he reacted to the English countryside "with immediate hatred. . . . [which] took many years to heal."[57] Apparently, he had questions about his objectivity toward those early years even as he was writing the manuscript. "Reading through what I have just written about Wyvern, I find myself exclaiming, 'Lies, lies!'" he writes.[58] Lewis seeks to reconcile this dichotomy by his explanation that his is a "story of two lives." His outer life was characterised by "sordid, hopeless weariness," whereas his inner life contained moments of ecstasy when he "was too happy to speak."[59] His inner life was enriched by the images of his rich imagination, much of it fueled by the books he was reading. His gifted imagination was later put to good use not only in his now famous works of fiction but also in his depiction of the Christian worldview and his defense of it.

Perhaps Lewis's dissatisfaction with the English public school system in which he spent much of his youth was simply due to the fact that it was unsuited for him. The system was heavily influenced by the dominant educational philosophy of athleticism, whereby intellectual achievement was devalued and athletic prowess was encouraged. English parents wanted their young boys to exhibit a sense of manliness, and the schools were structured to foster the desired qualities. Lewis didn't fit the mold. His accelerated physical growth impaired his athletic ability, and his subsequent lack of enthusiasm to participate in school games made him an outsider. His preference for intellectual endeavours over athletic pursuits was in conflict with the schools' culture at the time.[60] Jack Sayer, a close friend of Lewis's who has written an insightful biography of him, writes that a classmate of Lewis, Donald Hardman (later Air Chief Marshal Sir Donald Hardman), had written Sayer a letter in which he describes Lewis's depiction of life at Malvern as somewhat exaggerated. "He was a bit of a rebel; he had a wonderful sense of humour, and was a past-master of

57. Lewis, *Surprised by Joy*, 24.
58. Lewis, *Surprised by Joy*, 118.
59. Lewis, *Surprised by Joy*, 119.
60. McGrath, *Intellectual World*, 34–35.

mimicry. I think he took his work seriously, but nothing else; never took any interest in any games and never played any as far as I can remember unless he had to. . . . It is surprising that he should forget the happy times and remember only the unhappy ones," Hardman wrote to Sayer.[61] Even if Lewis's recollection of his public school years is less than accurate, there is little doubt that his memory of it is largely negative. He was still highly critical of the English schools when he wrote *Surprised by Joy* many years later. "But whatever the rationality of the design [of the school system], I contend that it did not achieve its object. For the last thirty years England has been filled with a bitter, truculent, skeptical debunking, and cynical *intelligentsia*. A great many of them were at public schools," he writes. And he thinks that many of them were "products of the system."[62] For Lewis, Kirkpatrick's tutelage was a welcome reprieve from the rigid scheduling of the public schools that he had attended. He claims that during his time at Great Bookham, he "reached as much happiness as is ever to be reached on earth."[63]

Although Lewis professed a strong belief in materialism in his letters to Greeves, his writings about that period of his life indicate that those views were not held nearly as firmly as he had intimated, because in his words, there was an "intermittent wavering in my materialistic 'faith' (so to call it) which set in toward the end of the Bookham period." The challenge to materialism came from reading the poetry of Yeats, who, in Lewis's opinion, "really thought that there was a world of beings more or less like the 'ever living ones'" about which Yeats had written.[64] Interestingly, Lewis thinks that if Yeats had been a Christian, he would likely have discounted his notions. From reading Yeats, he "learned that there were people, not traditionally orthodox, who nevertheless rejected the whole Materialist philosophy out of hand." This caused him considerable discomfort, because it brought back memories of the "old Occultist lore, and all the excitement which the Matron of Chartres [Miss C] had innocently aroused" in him, as a consequence of which, he writes, "a disturbing doubt fell into my Materialism."[65]

---

61. Donald Hardman, in Sayer, *Jack*, 84–85.
62. Lewis, *Surprised by Joy*, 107.
63. Lewis, *Surprised by Joy*, 147.
64. Lewis, *Surprised by Joy*, 174.
65. Lewis, *Surprised by Joy*, 175.

Throughout his book, appropriately titled *Surprised by Joy*, Lewis writes about experiencing an often-recurring sensation of imaginative longing that he calls Joy. Jack Sayer writes that these experiences of Joy described by Lewis were actually mystical experiences of the presence of God, similar to those described by William Wordsworth. He thinks that Lewis valued these experiences more than anything else he had known and that these experiences set him apart from other boys.[66] Lewis's experience of Joy at times provided relief from the despair that he often felt during his time in the English public school system.[67] Alister McGrath characterises Lewis's notion of Joy as "experiencing deep feelings of desire, to which he had attached the name, 'Joy.'" He writes that the most important of these took place when he read George MacDonald's fantasy novel *Phantastes*.[68] Lewis writes that this imaginative longing for Joy created a "stirring of unease" toward the seemingly residual notions of Miss C's "Occultist lore" described above. Lewis writes that he felt conflicted by the "ravenous, quasi-prurient desire for the Occult" and "the longing for Joy," and he thinks that his "known nature of Joy" acted as his "best protection" against Occultism.[69] How Lewis's notion of Joy affected his Christian worldview and what impact it had on his apologetic methods will be explored in subsequent chapters.

Eventually, Lewis's naturalism gave way to a form of pantheism. Although he eventually discusses his new view with Greeves, the exact date of this transformation is difficult to quantify.[70] Upon completing his studies at Great Bookham, Lewis decided to seek enrollment at Oxford University, and in December 1916, he learned that he had been accepted.

3.4 OXFORD STUDENT AND MILITARY OFFICER

The country had been engaged in World War I (the Great War) since 1914; with his eighteenth birthday approaching, Lewis faced some critical decisions. Although there was an exemption in place for students who were residing in England for the purpose of advancing their education,

---

66. Sayer, *Jack*, 52.

67. His attendance at Belfast's Campbell College was cut short by illness after less than a full term.

68. McGrath, *C. S. Lewis*, 42.

69. Lewis, *Surprised by Joy*, 177.

70. Lewis, *They Stand Together*, 217.

Lewis felt that the exemption was temporary. In April 1917, Lewis applied for the Oxford University Officers' Training Corps. In September of that year, he was commissioned as second lieutenant, and by November, he was engaged in trench warfare with the British army in France.

By midwinter, he came down with a bout of trench fever, and after a three-week hospital stay in Le Treport, France, he returned to his battalion. In early 1918, he was wounded in action, and by May, he was back in England for convalescence. His fighting days over, he returned to Oxford in January 1919.

Lewis's military experience takes up only a few pages in his autobiographical book *Surprised by Joy*. He writes that he was surprised that he didn't dislike the army more and that he found his "military elders and betters incomparably nicer than the Wyvern Bloods" of his college years. He felt that nearly everyone whom he met considered that the "whole thing was an odious necessity, a ghastly interruption of rational life, [which somehow] made all the difference."[71] Ironically, he seems to have better memories of the challenges that he faced in wartime than of his public school experiences. Although "there were nasty people in the army," he writes, "memory fills those months with pleasant, transitory contacts. Every few days one seemed to meet a scholar, an original, a poet, a cheery buffoon, a raconteur, or at least a man of good will."[72]

The exchange of letters between Arthur Greeves and Lewis continued throughout Lewis's time at Great Bookham and during his application and eventual acceptance at Oxford. Their letter-writing continued, although intermittently, during Lewis's deployment in France and eventual repatriation to England. There is much to be gleaned from Lewis's letters about his religious views during those years. From the time that he wrote his October 1916 letters to Greeves and his return to Oxford in 1919, naturalism seems to have lost some of its appeal for him. Judging from the letters, it was Greeves who initiated the discussions about religion.

By the time Lewis returned to England and was recovering from his wartime injuries, his metaphysical views had undergone some significant changes. The exact details and timing of these changes is unclear. What is known, however, is that in a letter to Greeves dated May 25, 1918, Lewis tells his friend that he has changed his views on the nature of reality.

71. Lewis, *Surprised by Joy*, 187.
72. Lewis, *Surprised by Joy*, 189.

He does so by taking issue with Greeves's reference to beauty in nature. Lewis objects to his sentiments and insists that our impression of things is caused by our sensory perception. We can never see things as they are, he claims. Our sense of colour and shape, of a tree, for instance, is merely a matter of sensations in our eyes caused by the vibrations of colourless shapeless atoms. "The beauty therefore is not in matter at all," he writes, "but is something purely spiritual, arising mysteriously out of the relation between me and the tree . . . or perhaps out of some indwelling spirit behind the matter of the tree." In the letter to Greeves, he discloses a growing conviction "that after all Spirit does exist." By experiencing a sense of "thrill" in what we are able to observe, we "come in contact with this spiritual element," he writes.[73]

Based on his letters to Greeves during the war, it becomes apparent that Lewis is no longer confident that naturalism has the requisite explanatory power to explain his perception of reality. "I fancy that there is Something right outside time and place . . . frankly I admit that my views have changed," he writes. This change did not lead him to embrace Christianity or any form of theism, however. Judging from the letter, it seems as though Lewis, while rejecting naturalism, has embraced a form of pantheism. He tells Greeves that he doesn't believe that something outside time and place had created matter "as the Christians say, but is matter's great enemy." In one of his letters to Greeves during this time, he writes that, "Matter=Nature=Satan." He claims that on the other side of that equation "is Beauty, the only spiritual and not-natural thing that I have found."[74]

Some of those views are expressed in a series of poems that he had written. In September 1918, Lewis wrote a letter to his father and one to Arthur Greeves, in which he mentions that the William Heinemann Company had agreed to publish a small book of poems that he had composed. He writes that the book was going to be titled *Spirits in Prison*. Interestingly, in the letter to his father, he refers to the book only as a "cycle of lyrical poems."[75] In the letter to Greeves written only a few days later, however, he states that the book is going to be published as "*Spirits in Prison* by Clive Staples & is mainly strung round the idea that I mentioned before—that nature is wholly diabolical & malevolent and

---

73. Lewis, *Collected Letters*, 1:374.
74. Lewis, *Collected Letters*, 1:374.
75. Lewis, *Collected Letters*, 1:396.

that God, if he exists, is outside of and in opposition to the cosmic arrangements."[76] The notion of the selection of poems being centered around an overall theme is confirmed in a letter to his father in October of that year, confirming his previous letter in which he writes that "the book is not a collection of really independent pieces, but the working out . . . of a general idea."[77] Lewis's recently acquired beliefs appear to be a composite of materialism and spiritualism and seem to have elements of some form of duality and notions of Gnosticism,[78] characterised by a perceived conflict between spirit and matter. According to his correspondence during the fall of 1918, Lewis was abandoning the naturalism worldview in favour of a worldview in which matter was not the only component in the universe; reality consisted of spirit, as well as matter. In his newly acquired worldview, matter was only one of two components and was essentially malevolent, whereas spirit was a force for good, a key characteristic of which was beauty.[79]

In his book *The Literary Legacy of C. S. Lewis*, Chad Walsh (1914–1991) writes that Lewis had a "fluctuating philosophy" when he wrote *Spirits in Bondage*, and that while he "yearns for transcendent beauty and

---

76. Lewis, *Collected Letters*, 1:397.

77. Lewis, *Collected Letters*, 1:396.

78. Gnosticism was a "dualistic religious and philosophical movement in the early centuries of the Christian church, especially important in the second century under the leadership of Valentinus and Basilidies [who] taught that matter was evil, the result of a cosmic disruption in which an evil *archon*, (often associated with the god of the Old Testament, Yahweh) rebelled against the heavenly *pleroma* (the complete spiritual world)" (Pojman, "Gnosticism").

Richard Valantasis writes: "Gnostics believed that an evil demiurge—the term they used to describe the fabricator of the physical universe—created the material world and the bodies that inhabit it. The true spiritual God—another deity altogether—created the spiritual bodies and humans. The demiurge, who opposed the true God, probably out of arrogance and ignorance, entrapped people in their bodies and within the material world to prevent them from attaining the purely spiritual and immaterial world that was created by the true God. This problem of materiality and its deleterious effect on the human pursuit of reality was the foundation of all Gnostic systems" (Valantasis, *Beliefnet Guide*, 16).

Gnostics emphasised knowledge over practise, Andrew Smith writes: "If an ancient Gnostic had been asked . . . what did Gnostics actually do . . . he may well have answered 'It is not what we do, but what we know that is important. This is what sets us apart from others'" (Smith, *Secret History of Gnostics*, 79). "There was no single monolithic Gnostic Church, no single redeemer figure and no single time or place at which Gnosticism hatched. . . . It seems to have emerged spontaneously in a variety of places in the first and second centuries" (Smith, *Secret History of Gnostics*, 106).

79. Lewis, *Collected Letters*, 1:396–97, 400.

joy and fleetingly affirms their possibility," he seemingly "suspects that the ultimate is malevolent."[80] Walsh notes that his "fluctuating philosophy" becomes evident when Lewis, who considered himself an atheist when he wrote the poems in *Spirits*, makes reference to God as though God exists.[81] Below is a sample of his work:[82]

> The sky above is sickening, the clouds of God's hate cover it . . .
> But now one age is ending, and God calls home the stars
> And looses the age of the ages and sends it spinning back
> Amid the death of nations, and points a downward track
> And madness is come over us and great and little wars.

Walter Hooper claims that although they appreciated some of the literary merits of *Spirits in Bondage*, Lewis's father, Albert, and his brother, Warren, were not favourably impressed by the apparent atheism manifested in some of the poems. Hooper writes that when Albert and Warren read the book, "Jack's atheism was evident to both." Although Albert was impressed with the quality of some of the poems, he expressed his disapproval of "the spirit which pervades the book." Warren opined that although he thought that "Jack's Atheism was purely academic . . . it would have been better if it had never been published."[83] Judging from the response to a letter that his father had written to Jack in early 1919, Lewis seemed to feel the need to allay his father's concerns about some of the book's contents. "I don't think that anyone who takes the trouble to read my book thoroughly will seriously call it blasphemous, whatever criticism he may make on artistic grounds," he writes to his father. "You know who the God that I blaspheme is and is not the God who you or I worship, or any other Christian," he claims.[84] Apparently, Albert had sent him a letter in which he expressed his appreciation for the literary merits of the book but indicated that he also had some serious misgivings about certain parts that he considered to be bordering on blasphemy. Judging from the response to his father's letter, Lewis seems to be unprepared to defend the metaphysical views he had embraced.[85]

---

80. Walsh, *Literary Legacy*, 39.
81. Walsh, *Literary Legacy*, 38.
82. Lewis, *Spirits in Bondage*, 23–24.
83. Walter Hooper, in Lewis, *Collected Letters*, 1:443n44.
84. Lewis, *Collected Letters*, 1:443.
85. Walter Hooper, in Lewis, *Collected Letters*, 1:443n44.

Walter Hooper notes that a monthly magazine, *The Bookman*, which published a catalogue of current publications at that time, characterised *Spirits in Bondage* as a book of forty poems from which readers can "reconstruct a cosmogony"—a cosmogony that purports that "somewhere, far too far off for thought or prayer, there is a god who created the world but subsequently lost interest in it; nearer and more active is a lesser god, who is also Satan, and is responsible for, among other things the war; then there is the world of men, who suffer from and are degraded by this second god's irresponsible iniquities."[86]

The worldview as expressed by the *Bookman* article depicts a reality that consists of equal or nearly equal entities that are in conflict with each other, a manifestation of which is being played out in the world, of which the war that had just been fought was a prime example. Judging from the letter that he had written to Greeves a few months earlier, in May of 1918, Lewis perceived nature as an evil creation of Satan, offset by beauty, which is created by what he calls Spirit. Lewis's search for a metaphysical explanation for the harsh reality of the natural world appears to be a driving force during his late teens and throughout his twenties. When tracing his pursuit of an intellectual answer to his perception of reality, it is apparent that this search was highly instrumental in eventually leading to his conversion to theism and ultimately to Christianity. Chad Walsh writes: "From a purely literary point of view, the most fortunate thing that ever happened to Lewis was his embrace of Christianity in his early thirties."[87] Apparently, Walsh thinks that Lewis's Christianity not only provided him with a framework for formulating a coherent worldview but also enhanced the literary quality of his writing.

A review of the contents of Lewis's letters during this time reflects Lewis's search for a metaphysical framework within which to accommodate his emerging worldview. This is evidenced in his letters to Leo Baker, who was one of his colleagues at Oxford. Although, unlike Lewis, Baker was a Christian, the two colleagues found that they had much in common. Baker, like Lewis, had served in the war and shared Lewis's love of poetry. Much of their correspondence revolves around the composition of poetry, but occasionally Lewis comments on his emerging worldview. In one of the letters, Lewis compliments Baker for expressing some doubts about his Christian beliefs. Although he fully expects Baker

---

86. Walter Hooper, in Lewis, *Collected Letters*, 1:457n69.
87. Walsh, *Literary Legacy*, 245.

"to return to the household of faith," he expects "great good" to come to him from his "excursion." He tells his friend that "blind faith is indeed unsuitable" for any thinking person, and advises him to "make use of our widened landscape." In Lewis's opinion, "the comfortable little universe with heaven above and hell beneath, an absolute up and down and a bare six thousand years of recorded history could furnish well enough with a world-view that a man could write in his pocket book," but was insufficient for the "data" that is available in contemporary times.[88]

In another letter to Baker, dated September 25, 1920, a few months earlier, he writes: "You will be interested to hear that in the course of my philosophy—on the existence of matter—I have had to postulate some sort of God as the least objectionable theory." Lewis appears to be wrestling with the nature of matter—whether it was intrinsically evil or simply neutral. As well, once he had rejected the notion that naturalism held the requisite explanatory power to account for his perception of reality, he struggled to find a satisfactory framework for the entity that he postulated to be in existence beyond the natural order.[89]

Interestingly, despite his ambivalence about the supernatural, Lewis seemingly expected Anglican clergymen to embrace the church's core beliefs or resign from the ministry if unable to do so. In a letter to his brother dated May 10, 1921, he strongly objected to an Anglican priest, who, although still in the employ of the church, was espousing heterodox views. "Strange mortals, these knights of the cloth are," he writes, "on the divinity of Christ, of which the point is that he was only a man, you can still apparently go on being a parson [by saying] 'We don't worship Jesus Christ, only the Christ THAT WAS in Jesus'—a beautiful distinction."[90] Even though he was no longer a believer himself, Lewis considered Christ's divinity to be a seminal belief for Christian clergy.

Glimpses of Lewis's worldview in letters to family members and friends is sometimes supplemented by entries in a diary that Lewis kept between 1922 and 1927. Entries in his diary had been strongly encouraged by the family matron, Janie Moore, with whom Lewis had shared a home virtually since being relieved from active military service. Mrs. Moore was the mother of his friend and fellow Irishman, Paddy Moore, and Paddy's sister Maureen. Lewis and Paddy had become close friends

---

88. Lewis, *Collected Letters*, 1:520.
89. Lewis, *Collected Letters*, 1:509.
90. Lewis, *Collected Letters*, 1:548.

during their military training and subsequent war service and had agreed to take care of each other's parents if either one of them didn't survive the war. Shortly after Paddy Moore had been killed in France, Lewis was wounded in battle and transferred to a military hospital in England to recover from his wounds. After his convalescence, Lewis moved in with Mrs. Moore and her daughter and made the Moore household his permanent home.[91]

Although references to his fluctuating views are mentioned only infrequently, they reveal an ongoing quest for a comprehensive framework to encompass his perception of reality. Lewis's views are often reflected in his disagreements with the opinions of some of his friends, rather than as statements of his own beliefs. In an entry in his diary on July 5, 1922, Lewis describes having a laugh with Owen Barfield about their colleague Leo Baker and his seemingly absurd notions about reincarnation and the "mystifying fragments of his previous lives." A few weeks later, on July 29, 1922, he describes a conversation during which he discussed reincarnation with Baker, in which Baker largely attributed his "reincarnation experiences" and "visions" to fancy and "his faculty for seeing the aura" to hallucination.[92]

In an entry in his diary on July 7, 1923, Lewis describes a visit that he had with another Oxford colleague, Cecil Harwood, during which Harwood told him about "his new philosopher, Rudolf Steiner." Lewis describes Steiner as "a sort of panpsychist,[93] with a vein of posing superstition." His entry in his diary indicates that he was "very much disappointed to hear that both Harwood and Barfield were impressed by him." In Lewis's opinion, Barfield and Harwood were attracted to Steiner's notion of immortality. "I argued that the 'spiritual forces' which Steiner found everywhere were either shamelessly mythological people

---

91. A full treatment of the relationship between Lewis and Mrs. Moore is not germane to this paper and has been addressed in several biographies. See especially McGrath, *C. S. Lewis*; Sayer, *Jack*; and Green and Hooper, *C. S. Lewis*.

92. Lewis, *All My Road*, 30, 77.

93. Panpsychism holds that mentality extends from humans to animals, insects, plant cells, and other natural bodies exhibiting persisting unity of organization. It is a notion that the physical world is pervasively psychical, sentient or conscious, and that all matter has consciousness. The view that the universe has universal consciousness is shared by some forms of religious thought such as theosophy, pantheism, new age thought and panentheism (*American Heritage Dictionary*, 1270; D. Clarke, *Panpsychism*; Sprigge, "Panpsychism").

or else no-one-knows-what," he writes. When Lewis denounced Steiner's notions, Harwood accused him of a "materialistic way of thinking."[94]

Lewis's involvement and eventual reservations about some of the notions associated with spiritualism hearkened back to his public school years during which he came under the influence of Miss C. Although at the time he had found some of her concepts liberating, in subsequent years, he had become alarmed about the destructive potential that similar notions seemingly had on the mental health of people with whom he had come in contact. In an April 1923 letter, he cautions Arthur Greeves to keep "clear of spiritualism" and "of everything eccentric."[95] Lewis's cautionary comments to Greeves had been occasioned by the tragedy that had befallen Mrs. Moore's brother, Dr. Askins, who had died a tragic death after succumbing to mental illness, which, in Lewis's opinion, was at least partially induced as a consequence of dabbling in some form of spiritualism. In one of his notations in *The Collected Letters of C. S. Lewis*, Walter Hooper writes that "it would be difficult to exaggerate this [Askins'] experience on Lewis. He does not reveal Dr. Askins name in his autobiography, but it is the 'Doc' he has in mind when he cites a friend's madness as one reason for a retreat, almost a panic-stricken flight from all that sort of romanticism."[96] The Lewis and Barfield disagreements over Steiner's notions continued after Lewis's conversion to Christianity and will be covered in greater detail in a subsequent chapter.

Judging from the entries in his diary during the 1920s, Lewis was exploring a wide range of viewpoints in order to find a coherent philosophical framework. Many of his comments reflect a growing frustration with his search to find a comprehensive method in which to frame what he perceived to be reality. An entry posted as late as January 18, 1927, reflects the philosophical "muddle" in which he found himself. Lewis writes:[97]

> Was thinking about imagination and intellect and the unholy muddle I am in about them at present, undigested scraps of anthroposophy[98] and psychoanalysis jostling with orthodox

94. Lewis, *All My Road*, 254.
95. Lewis, *Collected Letters*, 1:605.
96. Walter Hooper, in Lewis, *Collected Letters*, 1:606n6.
97. Lewis, *All My Roads*, 431–32.

98. Anthroposophy is a system of beliefs and practises based on the teachings of Rudolf Steiner. Steiner advocated the notion that through correct training and personal discipline, one can attain experience of the spiritual world to which humans

idealism over a background of good old Kirkian rationalism.[99] Lord what a mess! And all the time (with me) there's the danger of falling back into childish superstitions, or of running into dogmatic materialism.

Lewis covers a lot of ground in this brief entry in his diary. Letters to friends disclose a growing awareness about the limitations of reason and the role that imagination played in one's perception of reality. His conversations and communication with Owen Barfield reveal sharp disagreements with the influence that Rudolf Steiner's notions were having on his friend. He had received a good grounding in rational thinking from Kirkpatrick, his former tutor, but had since realized its limitations and was attempting to work out the role that imagination played in the process of acquiring knowledge. When he made the diary entry, he had already come to believe that materialism lacked the requisite explanatory power for encompassing reality and, as has been discussed above, had come to believe in the existence of some entity outside of the material world. His reference to orthodox idealism[100] and childish superstitions seems to indicate a growing acceptance of some form of idealism, which is somewhat muted by concerns about relying on what he considered to be unproven, unsophisticated beliefs from childhood that he had since denounced. Although Steiner's theosophy embraced some adaptation of pantheism, and even though Lewis had been attracted to pantheistic notions in the past, his comments reveal a level of discomfort with every philosophy that he had encountered.

Lewis's quest for a philosophy that could encompass his perception of reality continued throughout his years as a student at Oxford and through the early years of his tenure as an Oxford don. Entries in his

---

had originally been attuned. Steiner embraced a spiritualism that emphasized a form of knowledge that transcended sensory experience. He held that humankind had regressed from having been attuned to spiritual processes because of preoccupation with material entities (Stack, "Rudolph Steiner").

99. This is a reference to his former tutor, William Kirkpatrick, and his rigid rationalism.

100. Idealism is the philosophical doctrine that assigns metaphysical priority to the mental over the material. It holds that reality is somehow mind-correlative or mind-coordinated and that real objects constituting the external world are not independent of cognizant minds but exist in some way correlative to mental operations. It denies the claim within realism that material things exist independently of the mind. Idealism in the West dates from the teachings of Plato (Humphries et al., *Oxford World Encyclopedia*, 335; Rescher, "Idealism," 412–413).

diary, as well as references in his letters to friends and family, are indicative of his ongoing quest.[101] By the summer of 1923, Lewis had been awarded three first-class honours in classics, humanities, and English by the Oxford examiners. This eventually led to a modest stipend as a temporary tutor, and in October 1925, he was awarded a fellowship at Oxford's Magdalen College.[102]

3.5 OXFORD DON: CONVERSION TO CHRISTIANITY

Lewis's fellowship at Magdalen College offered him a new lease on life. Although the financial support with which his father had provided him throughout his school years was more than adequate for a single person, it was insufficient to provide for the needs of a family of three (Lewis, Mrs. Moore, and her daughter Maureen). Lewis had found himself financially strapped throughout most of his years as a student. The Magdalen fellowship offered him the financial security that had previously eluded him.

Besides the reference to Steiner's influence on his friends and the cautionary note to Greeves, Lewis's letters during 1923 and 1924 rarely refer to notions about his fluctuating worldview. However, as attested in a letter to his father, dated August 14, 1925, a few weeks after being selected for the Magdalen fellowship, Lewis confirms his increasing disenchantment with materialism. "It will be a comfort to me all my life," he tells his father, "to know that the scientist and the materialist have not the last word: that Darwin[103] and Spencer[104] undermining ancestral beliefs

---

101. See Lewis, *All My Roads* and *Letters of C. S. Lewis*.

102. McGrath, *C. S. Lewis*, 382.

103. This is a reference to Charles Darwin's theory of origins and his classic 1859 work *On the Origin of Species*.

104. Lewis is likely referring to Herbert Spencer (1820–1902). Spencer differed from modern Darwinism in that he thought that biological changes could not be accounted for by mutation and natural selection alone but included elements of Lamarckian evolution, a process whereby not only inherited changes are transmitted to succeeding generations, but acquired characteristics are transmitted to future generations as well. The popular, modern form of Darwinism, which is restricted to natural selection and mutation only, is frequently identified as Neo-Darwinism. For the purpose of convenience, when used in this paper, the word Darwinism refers to the modern version. Spencer expanded evolutionary theory by developing a system of thought that set forth the idea in which the evolutionary process is depicted as a means for explaining the emergence of not only biological systems but also philosophical and

stand themselves on a foundation of sand; of gigantic assumptions and irreconcilable contradictions an inch below the surface."[105]

Lewis's characterisations of Darwinian and Spencerian notions offer significant insight into his quest for a satisfactory worldview within which to frame reality. Whereas his earliest letters to Greeves had indicated a level of satisfaction with the materialist worldview, later correspondence between the two reveals some doubts about its adequacy. Lewis then postulates the existence of a form of spiritual essence in addition to the material order but later cautions about the potential risk of engaging with certain components of spirituality. Although he characterises himself as being in a "muddle" in his 1927 diary entry, as early as 1925, he appears to have decided against materialism's adequacy to encompass reality and had earlier admitted to Leo Baker that although "we know nothing . . . I have had to postulate some sort of God as the least objectionable theory."[106]

Although Lewis and Owen Barfield were the best of friends and engaged in countless hours of conversation, neither Lewis's diary nor the published collections of his letters prior to his conversion reveal any discussions between the two friends about Spencer or Darwin. However, in a book published after Lewis's death, Barfield expresses some of his own reservations about the ability of Darwinian processes to account for the emergence of the bio-system. Barfield, in a chapter titled "The Coming Trauma of Materialism," postulates about the likelihood of a future crisis engulfing Darwinian theory: "One has to imagine a twentieth-century biologist being asked to accept that the whole library of textbooks from which a man learned at school and university, from which he himself has been teaching all his life, and to which he has perhaps added an

---

ethical systems. In the Spencerian system of thought, progress was the supreme law of the universe. It acquired broad appeal, in part because "it offered a comprehensive worldview, uniting under one generalization everything in nature from protozoa to politics. . . . It soon gave Spencer a public influence that transcended Darwin's" (Hofstadter, "Vogue of Spencer," 389). Spencer was the chief exponent of agnosticism in nineteenth-century England and divided all reality into the knowable (the principles of science) and the unknowable (the principles of religion). Spencer's division of reality appears to be a forerunner to Harvard paleontologist Stephen Jay Gould's concept of NOMA (non-overlapping magisterium) whereby science is deemed to be the instrument for acquiring knowledge and religion is to be understood as a means for acquiring meaning (*American Heritage Dictionary*, 1671; Butts, "Spencer, Herbert"; Gould, *Rocks of Ages*, 5–6).

105. Lewis, *Collected Letters*, 1:649.
106. Lewis, *Collected Letters*, 1:509.

original contribution of his own, is in fact largely irrelevant," he writes.[107] In Barfield's opinion, "the crust of congealed Darwinism is . . . ominously thinning from the bottom upwards."[108] Barfield's reference to the thinning of the Darwinian crust is reminiscent of Lewis's earlier statement about assumptions and contradictions "an inch below the surface." Although Lewis makes frequent references to Darwinism in his post-conversion writings, his pre-conversion material makes scant reference to this topic. The limits of materialism were likely frequent topics of discussion during the many conversations that took place between Barfield and Lewis before and after Lewis's conversion.

During his formative years at Oxford, Lewis was wrestling not only with the framework of his worldview but also with critical epistemological issues. His 1927 diary entry shows him being in an intellectual "muddle," attempting to come to grips with the role that imagination plays in acquiring knowledge. Lewis and Barfield frequently exchanged letters and, as mentioned, engaged in many hours of discussions. Because Barfield had written his thesis and, later, several books[109] on imagination's role in acquiring knowledge, imagination's role was undoubtedly a topic of discussion. Lewis and Barfield were well versed in the works of Samuel Taylor Coleridge and his friend William Wordsworth and their references to the power of imagination.[110] Barfield's book *What Coleridge Thought* describes many of Coleridge's views, including his views on the role of imagination and its relation to knowledge. Lewis's view about the relationship that imagination has to knowledge, especially as it relates

107. Barfield, *Rediscovery of Meaning*, 292.
108. Barfield, *Rediscovery of Meaning*, 289.
109. See Barfield, *What Coleridge Thought* and *Poetic Diction*.

110. Kristine Ottaway Wilson writes: "With the publication of the *Lyrical Ballads*, Wordsworth and Coleridge launched the Romantic Movement in poetry. In this genre the power of imagination is stressed and poems are viewed as external expressions of the poet's internal thoughts. Romantic themes range from the ordinary and mundane to the supernatural, apocalyptic, and mysterious. In Romantic poetry, landscapes are endowed with human life, passion, and expressiveness. Wordsworth is known as a 'lover of nature,' for his poetry is filled with this expression of the grandeur and glory of nature. *The Prelude*, Wordsworth's intellectual and spiritual autobiography, was noted by Lewis for his portrayal of awe and fear in the midst of nature. Although Lewis mentioned Wordsworth's art and imagination fondly, he critiques Wordsworth in *The Pilgrim's Regress* for the extreme value he gives to the love of nature—making one believe 'the picture [of Nature] itself was the thing you wanted.' The title for Lewis's autobiography, *Surprised by Joy*, came from a Wordsworth sonnet by that name" (Ottaway, "William Wordsworth").

to the formation of belief, is an important component in his journey to Christian faith and will be explored more fully.

Coleridge's theory of imagination is succinctly summarised by Ahmed Hasnain:[111] according to Coleridge, human imagination consists of three elements: primary imagination, secondary imagination, and fancy. In Coleridge's system, primary imagination has the capacity to receive the perceptions derived from the senses. Coleridge considered primary imagination to be universal, possessed by everyone. Secondary imagination, on the other hand, although mainly the purview of artists and poets, "requires an effort of the will, volition and conscious effort."[112] It requires our active thinking. Secondary imagination was believed to work with the raw material that was received as sensations and perceptions by the primary imagination. In Coleridge's view, imagination and fancy differ in kind, constituting two different activities. Fancy is not a creative power in Coleridge's system. For instance, it puts together only what it perceives into "beautiful shapes," but in his opinion, unlike the imagination, it does not "fuse and unify."[113]

Coleridge appears to expand on David Hume's notions regarding imagination's function. Hume writes, "It is evident that that there is a principle of connexion between the different thoughts or ideas of the mind, and that, in their appearance to the memory or imagination, they introduce each other with a certain degree of method and regularity."[114] In Hume's view, several mental faculties are responsible for producing our various ideas, one of which is imagination, which he believed to be merely a complexity of ideas. Hume held that our sensory perceptions create impressions, which are stored in our memory. These impressions are then transformed into ideas via our memory and our imagination. He distinguishes between those ideas produced by memory and those produced by imagination; memory conjures up ideas based directly on experiences that were perceived by the senses, whereas imagination, by contrast, is a faculty that breaks apart and combines ideas, thus forming new ideas and more complex ones.[115]

---

111. Hasnain, "Coleridge on Imagination."

112. Hasnain, "Coleridge on Imagination."

113. Hasnain, "Coleridge on Imagination." See also Barfield, *What Coleridge Thought*, 27; Coleridge, *Samuel Taylor Coleridge*, 313.

114. Hume, *Enquiry Concerning Human Understanding*, 69.

115. Hume, *Enquiry Concerning Human Understanding*, 63–70.

Judging from the entries in his diary, Lewis was very well acquainted with the writings of Wordsworth, Coleridge, and Hume. Even as a tutor, prior to becoming a fellow at Magdalen College, he gave lectures on Hume.[116] In an entry dated January 19, 1927, he writes about going for a walk while "still puzzled about imagination etc." and found himself thinking that "imagination at its highest is the real in some way."[117] But he couldn't understand how, and decided to work up the whole doctrine of imagination in Coleridge as soon as time permitted. He found Wordsworth's notion of imagination somehow very reassuring. In his opinion, Wordsworth's view of imagination was "the real imagination, no bogies, no Karmas, no gurus, no damned psychism." And he resolved not to wander "astray among second rate ideas" any longer.[118] In Lewis's references to Rudolf Steiner's teachings and to Owen Barfield's embrace of those teachings, it is clear that he considered at least some elements of anthroposophy to be "second rate ideas."[119] In a diary entry dated January

---

116. Lewis, *All My Road*, 350.
117. Lewis, *All My Road*, 432.
118. Lewis, *All My Road*, 432.

119. In his commentary to a book review Lewis had written for one of Barfield's books, Walter Hooper claims that Barfield's conversion to anthroposophy created considerable conflict between Lewis and Barfield: "Anthroposophy is a system of theosophy evolved by Rudolf Steiner (1861–1925), based on the premise that the human soul can, of its own power, contact the spiritual world. The concepts of karma and reincarnation are central to it. It acknowledges Christ as a cosmic being, but its understanding of Him is very different from that of orthodox Christianity," writes Hooper (in Lewis, *Image and Imagination*, 87). For more context, see Lewis, *Image and Imagination*, 87–91.

A definition of anthroposophy in a Wikipedia entry considered accurate by former practitioner Beat Mertz reads: "Anthroposophy is a philosophy founded by Rudolf Steiner that postulates the existence of an objective, intellectually comprehensible spiritual world that is accessible by direct experience through inner development. More specifically, it aims to develop faculties of perceptive imagination, inspiration and intuition through the cultivation of a form of thinking independent of sensory experience, and to present the results thus derived in a manner subject to rational verification. Anthroposophy aims to attain in its study of spiritual experience the precision and clarity attained by the natural sciences in their investigations of the physical world. The philosophy has double roots in German idealism and German mysticism and was initially expressed in language drawn from Theosophy. Anthroposophical ideas have been applied practically in many areas including Steiner/Waldorf education, special education (most prominently through the Camphill Movement), biodynamic agriculture, medicine, ethical banking, organizational development, and the arts. The Anthroposophical Society has its international center at the Goetheanum in Dornach, Switzerland. Modern critics, particularly Michael Shermer, have termed

25, 1927, Lewis writes that he was delighted about a "heart to hearter" of a conversation between Mrs. Moore and Owen Barfield's wife in which Mrs. Barfield told Mrs. Moore that she "hates Barfield's Anthroposophy," and wishes that he had told her about it before they got married.

Lewis's final entry in his diary is dated March 2, 1927. His last reference to his questions about imagination's role in the acquisition of knowledge was made a few weeks earlier, on February 8, in which he denounces some of Steiner notions. Lewis's February entry expresses his frustration:[120]

> A pest on all this nonsense which has spoiled so much wonder for me, degraded pure imagination into pretentious lying, and truths of the spirit into mere matters of fact, slimed everything over with the trail of its infernal mumbo-jumbo! . . . Once you've got it into your head the notion of looking for the wrong sort of truth in imagination (i.e. occult matter of fact), you have lost utterly the truth that is really in imagination (i.e. rightness of feeling—the "affective" side of cognition without the cognition) and made good food into poison. Just to be delighted with the feel of the nymph in the tree is to share emotionally that common life of all living things which you can't fully comprehend intellectually: to believe that by certain ceremonies you can make a girl come out of the tree, is to put yourself a thousand miles further from any spiritual contact with the tree-life that you were before—and a good many miles nearer the asylum.

Lewis packs a lot of information into this statement. He appears to be concerned that entertaining certain notions of spiritualism may be akin to dabbling in the occult. As previously mentioned, he had witnessed the mental deterioration and the eventual institutional confinement of Dr. Askins, Mrs. Moore's brother. In his autobiographical work *Surprised by Joy*, Lewis attributes Askins's mental deterioration, at least in part, to his preoccupation with occultist practises.[121] Lewis is not clear in what he meant by the "'affective' side of cognition without the cognition" as being. His reference to "the truth that is really in imagination" is difficult to ascertain from this diary entry and needs to be explored further.

---

anthroposophy's application in areas such as medicine, biology, and biodynamic agriculture to be pseudoscience. Anthroposophy has also been termed 'the most important esoteric society in European history'" ("Anthroposophy").

120. Lewis, *All My Road*, 449.
121. Lewis, *Surprised by Joy*, 203–4.

Much of Lewis's material about imagination was written after his conversion to Christianity. His earlier writings disclose some insight to his understanding about imagination's role in acquiring knowledge, but it is in his post-conversion writings where significant aspects of imagination's role, not only in acquiring knowledge but also in acquiring belief, can be found. Eventually, Lewis came to the conclusion that reason can take us only so far in matters of religious faith and that imagination, by enhancing our understanding of events, provides insight that is unattainable by reason alone. Lewis later credits imagination's capacity for giving meaning to events as being a significant factor in his coming to Christian faith, and his post-conversion writings offer considerable insight into his understanding of imagination's role.

Although many of his colleagues at Magdalen were either atheists or agnostics, as time went on, Lewis found himself gradually being drawn to the Christians, because to him, they were surprisingly not only more interesting, but their views also appeared to be more substantive. So, too, were many of the Christian authors with whom he came in contact. Sometime after having read Chesterton's *The Everlasting Man*, he "was surprised to find the whole Christian outline of history making sense." When lecturing on philosophical idealists such as Hegel and Bradley, he found their sense of the Absolute to be unclear and unsatisfying, whereas the theistic idealism of Berkeley seemed to be engendered with much more persuasive power.[122]

Adding fuel to Lewis's growing disenchantment with his then-current worldview and his growing awareness that the Christian outline of history made sense was an experience that he characterises in *Surprised by Joy* as "something far more alarming" having happened to him. Lewis writes that "the hardest boiled of all the atheists that I ever knew sat in my room on the other side of the fire and remarked that the evidence for the historicity of the Gospels was really surprisingly good. 'Rum thing,' he went on, 'All that stuff of Frazer's and the Dying God. Rum thing. It almost looks as if it really happened once.'"[123] Lewis considered the speaker to be the toughest of cynics, and the notion that he gave credence to the Gospel narrative had a "shattering impact" on him.[124] He was stunned by what he heard from the man who is now widely believed to have been

---

122. Green and Hooper, *C. S. Lewis*, 100.
123. Lewis, *Surprised by Joy*, 223.
124. Lewis, *Surprised by Joy*, 224.

Thomas Dewar Weldon (1896–1958), a lecturer, fellow, and tutor in philosophy at Magdalen College.[125]

Lewis was likely in his fifties when he wrote the manuscript for *Surprised by Joy*.[126] What might be described as a much earlier unpublished version was written shortly after his conversion to theism. This version consists of a sixty-two-page, handwritten notebook, copies of which are now held at Oxford's Bodleian Library and at Wheaton College's Marion E. Wade Center. Green and Hooper cite this version in their authorized biography, and in 2013, the Wade Center published a copy of the notebook with the title "Early Prose Joy" in the center's journal. It is instructive to read Lewis's reflections, since they were penned shortly after his conversion, which was more than two decades before he published *Surprised by Joy*: "In this book I propose to describe the process by which I came back, like so many of my generation, from materialism to a belief in God . . . I am an empirical Theist.[127] I have arrived at God by induction," he writes.[128] This characterisation of the process by which he came to embrace theism is consistent with what Lewis has written elsewhere; several years earlier, he had told Leo Baker that "to postulate some sort of God" was to him "the least objectionable theory."[129] Alister McGrath, however, thinks that what Lewis describes in *Surprised by Joy* is not a process of logical deduction alone. McGrath thinks that Lewis's account is more like a process of crystallisation whereby things that seem disconnected and unrelated are seen to fit together in a grand scheme that confirms not only their validity but also their connectedness. He likens the process to that of a scientist, who, confronted with a series of seemingly unconnected observations, through a flash of insight, discovers a theory that indicates their interconnectedness.[130] As well, McGrath thinks that Lewis's

---

125. Green and Hooper, *C. S. Lewis*, 100.

126. *Surprised by Joy* was published in 1955, but in a letter to Vera Matthews on September 1948, Lewis mentions that he was busy writing his "autobiography" (Lewis, *Collected Letters*, 1:877).

127. Although Lewis called himself an "empirical Theist," he did not subscribe to the notion as understood by empiricists such as Locke and Hume. He came to believe in the real incarnation and resurrection of Christ. The world external to the mind was real for Lewis; it did not just consist of impressions coming from categories of the mind that tell us nothing about the nature of the actual external world.

128. Lewis, "Early Prose Joy," 13.

129. Lewis, *Collected Letters*, 1:509.

130. This is reminiscent of Thomas Kuhn's notion that "when paradigms change, the world changes with them" (Kuhn, *Structure of Scientific Revolutions*, 111).

correspondence suggests a "dabbling with divinity that has not been fully acknowledged."[131] Lewis's aforementioned statement about "the least objectionable theory" seemingly supports McGrath's suggestion.

Whatever the exact process was by which Lewis came to be a theist, it seems clear that he was searching for a comprehensive worldview that would encompass his perception of reality and thought that theism offered the best option. His reference to being an "empirical Theist" is instructive, because it implies a desire to find an evidence-based solution and is reminiscent of the comment in his diary just two years earlier about finding himself in a "muddle" and in "danger of falling back into childish superstitions, or of running into dogmatic materialism." Furthermore, he thought that he had come to the decision that he did via a logical process. Lewis in *Surprised by Joy* and McGrath in his biography of Lewis both make reference to additional factors being at work in Lewis's embracement of theism. McGrath thinks that the process, rather than being solely inductive, was more akin to Lewis's having gained insight into the connectedness of his various notions, and Lewis frequently makes reference to a chess game in which he is outmatched by God's intervention in his life. Neither McGrath's notion of a crystallisation whereby Lewis found a much sought-after connectedness in theism nor Lewis's perception of God having intervened from time to time detract from the fact that his search for a comprehensive worldview was highly instrumental in his eventual conversion to theism.

When writing many years later, as he did in *Surprised by Joy*, about his decision to fully embrace theism, he views it as "a moment of wholly free choice." He felt as though he had been "holding something at bay, or shutting something out," and he saw himself as being "given a free choice," not unlike a decision to "open the door or keep it shut." He felt no compulsion to make the choice, nor was it presented "as a duty," and "no threat or punishment was attached to it," he writes. Upon reflection, he remembers that "the choice appeared to be momentous but it was also strangely unemotional," and that he "was moved by no desires or fears." Clearly, Lewis felt that there was a free choice to be made, a choice to view reality from what he perceived to be a well-grounded footing, a theistic worldview.[132]

---

131. McGrath, *C. S. Lewis*, 138.
132. Lewis, *Surprised by Joy*, 224.

Lewis's comments about being unaware of having being moved by any desires or fears are instructive. It's important to note that he thought it one of God's "greatest mercies" that he had embraced theism without having had been influenced by a desire for a future life and that for perhaps as long as a year, he was permitted "to know God and to attempt obedience" without considering the question of an afterlife. From Lewis's now theistic perspective, God was to be obeyed and revered simply because he was God. Lewis likens his experience as having been analogous to that of the ancient Israelites, "to whom He revealed Himself centuries before there was a whisper of anything better (or worse) beyond the grave than shadowy and featureless *Sheol*." Lewis writes that although individuals far better than he had made immortality the central doctrine of their faith, he is happy about having had the opportunity to experience God's goodness apart from any notion of reward.[133] His conversion to Christianity didn't take place until many months later.[134]

Lewis's embrace of theism, variously estimated to be as much as a year and a half prior to his conversion to Christianity, may perhaps be best understood if viewed within the context of his search for a sufficiently comprehensive worldview. As stated previously, he came to believe that the postulation of some notion of God presented the most logical explanation of reality. But he found the notion of Christ's divinity, as well as the rationale for his death and resurrection to be so intellectually and imaginatively challenging, that it seemed incomprehensible. However, a long evening's conversation with friends that lasted until the early morning hours eventually led to a dramatic transformation of Lewis's understanding of the Christian faith. The evening's events took place on September 19, 1931, and on September 28, Lewis and Warnie headed out to the Whipsnade Zoo for a picnic lunch on Warnie's motorcycle, with Lewis in the sidecar. Lewis writes in *Surprised by Joy*: "When we set out I did not believe that Jesus Christ is the Son of God, but when we reached the zoo I did. Yet I had not exactly spent the journey in thought. . . . It was more like when a man, after a long sleep, still lying motionless in bed,

133. Lewis, *Surprised by Joy*, 231.

134. Although Lewis's conversion to theism is frequently cited as having occurred sometime between late April and mid-June of 1929, and his conversion to Christianity in late September of 1931, Alister McGrath thinks that Lewis's conversion to theism may actually have taken place a year later, sometime between March and June of 1930. If this later date is correct, it would mean that there was a considerably shorter interval between Lewis's conversion to theism and his eventual conversion to Christianity (McGrath, *C. S. Lewis*, 142).

becomes aware that he is now awake."[135] On October 1, 1931, Lewis wrote to Arthur Greeves that he "had just passed from believing in God to definitely believing in Christ—in Christianity" and that "the long night talk with Dyson[136] and Tolkien[137] had a good deal to do with it."[138] Greeves was thrilled by this turn of events and asked Lewis for more details, and on October 18, Lewis responded with a much more detailed explanation.

Lewis wrote Greeves that he had been hampered in embracing Christianity for at least the past year, not because of difficulty in believing but because of a lack of understanding of what the Christian doctrines meant. After all, one can't believe something if one is ignorant about what the thing is, he explains. He had been puzzled by the whole doctrine of redemption and had been unable to understand "in what sense the life and death of Christ 'saved' or 'opened salvation' to the world." Although from looking at the state of the world, he could see how salvation might be necessary, but other than serving as an example, he couldn't understand how "Someone Else's death" could help. "And the example business though true and important, is not Christianity," he reminds Greeves. At the heart of Christianity—including the Gospels and the apostle Paul's writings—we find words and phrases such as propitiation, sacrifice, and the blood of the Lamb. Although he had been unable to make sense of these words and phrases in the past, because of his long conversation with Dyson and Tolkien, he was now able to understand their significance, he wrote Greeves.

Certain elements of literature had often made a strong impression on Lewis, and from the late-night and early-morning conversation with his two friends, he had discovered a meaning in the Gospel narrative that had previously eluded him. Although in the past he had often been "mysteriously moved" by the idea of a god sacrificing himself, especially by the likes of "the dying and reviving god" as in "Balder, Adonis and Bacchus," he had never found the Gospel account of Christ to be profound or suggestive of meaning. This all changed, Lewis writes, after

---

135. Lewis, *Surprised by Joy*, 237.

136. Henry Victor (Hugo) Dyson (1896–1975) taught English at Reading University from 1924 to 1945. He came to know Lewis through Neville Coghill, and he and Tolkien played a vital part in Lewis's conversion (Green and Hooper, *C. S. Lewis*, 62).

137. John Ronald Reuel Tolkien (1892–1973) met Lewis in 1926 when Tolkien was professor of Anglo-Saxon at Oxford University. He is perhaps best known for his three volumes of *The Lord of the Rings* (Green and Hooper, *C. S. Lewis*, 62).

138. Lewis, *Collected Letters*, 1:974.

the all-night meeting with his friends. He now saw Christianity as "God expressing Himself through what we call 'real things,'" he tells Greeves. And he now believed the Christ narrative to be true in the sense that it really happened, but more importantly for him, he was finally beginning to understand its import and its meaning. Through the language of the "actual incarnation, crucifixion, and resurrection," God has expressed the truth about himself to us, he writes.[139]

Unlike Lewis's earlier conversion to theism, which, judging from his writings, he considered to be a wholly rational decision, it was through his imagination that he was able to grasp the reality of Christianity. Oxford professor Alister McGrath credits J. R. R. Tolkien, one of McGrath's predecessors at Oxford, as being the key figure in assisting Lewis to look at the Christian faith in a wholly new way. McGrath claims that Tolkien helped Lewis to realize that his difficulties in understanding lay not in Lewis's rational failure but in his "imaginative failure" and that the issue was not primarily about truth but about meaning; and it is through our imagination that meaning is comprehended.[140] Tolkien told Lewis that when engaging the Christian narrative, instead of "opening himself to the deepest intuitions of his imagination, he was limiting himself to reason," writes McGrath.[141]

The conversation with Tolkien enabled Lewis to combine reason and imagination, which helped him to comprehend the divine meaning of the Christian narrative. It was his comprehension of the meaning of Christ's birth, sacrifice, and resurrection that enabled him to see the truth not only of its historicity but also of its meaning. The emotional, intellectual, psychological, and spiritual impact of his new insight was such that he continued with his conversation with Tolkien until 3:00 a.m. and with Dyson for another full hour after Tolkien's departure. In his letter to Greeves, Lewis credits Dyson and Tolkien with helping him to see that "the story of Christ is simply a true myth," a story intended to convey a profound truth, a narrative depicting the reality of the Christian faith.

---

139. Lewis, *Collected Letters*, 1:977.

140. This is consistent with Hume's thesis, which holds that ideas are formulated by exercising our imagination and with Barfield's notion that imagination facilitates our discernment of meaning (Hume, *Enquiry Concerning Human Understanding*; Barfield, *Rediscovery of Meaning*, 13–29).

141. McGrath, *C. S. Lewis*, 149.

Unlike other myths, however, he writes Greeves, the Christian narrative is true, having actually occurred.[142]

Lewis had been attracted to theism as a consequence of his search for a worldview with the requisite explanatory power. His loss of confidence in materialism, his reference to the existence of some form of Spirit in addition to matter, and his acknowledgment that postulating some notion of God as being the most plausible theory serve as markers that indicate the path that he had travelled in his philosophical and spiritual journey. Although the Christian reality is eminently defensible rationally and intellectually, it was his imaginative breakthrough that eventually brought Lewis to Christian faith. He still embraced a theistic worldview, but it was now a theistic worldview with more vibrancy and richness, one in which his considerable imaginative gifts found fertile ground for his apologetics.

Concomitant with his pursuit of a worldview was Lewis's quest to satisfy the seemingly elusive longing that he had felt since his teenage years. Upon reflecting about this longing several decades after his conversion, he writes that this longing, characterised as Joy, had lost much of its importance to him. "To tell you the truth," he writes, "the subject has lost nearly all interest for me since I became a Christian. . . . The old stab, the old bitter-sweet, has come to me as often and as sharply since my conversion as at any time of my life whatever. But I now know that the experience was only a pointer to something other and outer."[143]

Lewis's conversion to Christianity not only offered him a sufficiently comprehensive worldview within which to frame his perception of reality, but it also provided him with an explanation of the almost inexplicable joy-like *Sehnsucht* (German, "wistful yearning") that he had experienced throughout much of his life. In *The Pilgrim's Regress*, a book Lewis wrote shortly after his conversion, he describes this experience as one of "intense longing," the mere wanting of which is "felt to be somehow a delight."[144] As will be discussed in subsequent chapters, Lewis eventually came to characterise this longing as a yearning that is unable to be satisfied in this world.

---

142. Lewis, *Collected Letters*, 1:977.
143. Lewis, *Surprised by Joy*, 238.
144. Lewis, *Pilgirm's Regress*, 12.

Chapter Four

DIMENSIONS *of* LEWIS'S WORLDVIEW
Impact on His Apologetics

4.1 INTRODUCTION

A study of Lewis's philosophical and spiritual journey provides important insight into the formation of his worldview; some philosophers cite biography as a determining factor in one's philosophy.[1] Although this notion is subject to debate, clearly, Lewis's biographical sketch offers important insights into the philosophical and spiritual journey that he took in coming to a Christian worldview, or "world picture," as he referred to it.[2] Judging from his writings, his Christian "world picture" seemingly influenced every aspect of his intellectual life. As mentioned previously,[3] Chad Walsh considers Lewis's conversion exceedingly beneficial, because it provided Lewis with the means by which to unify his many and diverse

---

1. See James, *Pragmatism*, 19; Unamuno, *Tragic Sense of Life*, 2; Nietzsche, *Human, All Too Human*, 513; and Nietzsche, *Beyond Good and Evil*, 8.

2. Lewis, *Essay Collection*, 13. On at least one occasion, however, Lewis uses the term *world view*: in a paper presented to The Socratic Club, he cites *world views* as being capable of yielding poetry for those who believe them (Lewis, *Essay Collection*, 15). As well, in a review of a book written by George Steiner, Lewis used the German word *Weltanschauung* in his reference to the imaginative worldview of dramatists (Lewis, *Image and Imagination*, 76).

3. See Walsh's statement on p. 38.

notions. In a paper that he prepared for the Oxford Socratic Club,[4] Lewis characterises the influence that his Christian faith had on his perception of the world: "I believe in Christianity as I believe that the Sun has risen not only because I see it but because of it I see everything else."[5] Lewis seems to view the Christian worldview as the best explanation for reality as he perceives it.

Robert MacSwain claims that although theologians and specialists in religious studies have, for the most part, kept their distance from Lewis, because of Lewis's wide-ranging influence, academic theology can ill afford to disregard him. Despite not being an academic theologian himself, there is much that he can teach theologians about their own subject, writes MacSwain. He postulates that Lewis's popularity may have something to do with the manner by which Lewis harnessed his reason and imagination in a sustained effort to communicate his convictions to as wide an audience as possible.[6]

4.2 LEWIS AND ROMANTICISM

Lewis's unique version of Romanticism[7] seemingly undergirded his deeply held Christian worldview. Stephen Logan, a member of University of Cambridge's English faculty, characterizes Lewis as a "poetico-philosophical" writer whose orientation is profoundly Romantic.[8] He writes that although Lewis described himself as a rationalist, his writings depict

---

4. The Socratic Club at Oxford was founded by the Oxford Pastorate's Stella Ardwinckle and a group of Oxford undergraduates in 1941 for the purpose of discussing concepts dealing with the intellectual basis for the Christian faith. In 1942, Ardwinckle invited Lewis to be its first president, a position that he held until he left Oxford for Cambridge in 1954.

5. Lewis, *Essay Collection*, 21.

6. MacSwain, "Introduction," 4.

7. Romanticism was a movement that emerged in the late eighteenth and early nineteenth centuries. In the arts, its proponents valued individual experience and intuition rather than the orderly, concrete universe of the classical artists. In philosophy, Romantics had more in common with those who were attracted to a philosophy of idealism rather than with proponents of rationalism or realism. In literature, key figures of Romanticism were Goethe, Shelley, Byron, Keats, Wordsworth, Schiller, and Blake. Romanticism was characterised by a heightened interest in nature and an emphasis on emotion and imagination (*American Heritage Dictionary*, 1511; Humphries et al., *Oxford World Book Encyclopedia*, 574).

8. Logan, "Literary Theorist," 36.

a Christian view of the world replete with "moral preoccupations" and "supernatural expansiveness." He argues that because Lewis is so succinct, orderly, and elegant as a writer, his Romantic affinities may have been obscured, causing readers to be easily persuaded to ignore the depth of his "preoccupation" with the supra-rational and the "trans-rational." Logan cites Lewis's Narnia Chronicles and his autobiographical book *Surprised by Joy* as examples of Lewis's interest "in the world beyond the world" and his sense of "aspects of reality which elude but entice our senses." Logan thinks that virtually everything Lewis wrote was in some respects influenced by what he came to regard as the single most important event in his life—an experience that may be best described by the German word *Sehnsucht*, which is sometimes translated as "yearning." Lewis eventually came to signify this experience as Joy.[9] He had described this experience as "an unsatisfied desire which is itself more desirable than any other satisfaction."[10]

Logan describes Lewis's yearning as "straining beyond the bounds of rationality":[11]

> He seems both clear and elegant. But the elegance of the paradox deflects attention from certain and puzzling stray potentialities of its meaning. The sentence compares neither two desires, nor two satisfactions, but a desire and all other satisfactions. It implies, therefore, that the unsatisfied desire for the world beyond the world is itself more satisfying than any other satisfied desire. But what it says is not that the unsatisfied desire is more satisfying, but is more desirable. The effect of the sentence is to simulate a yearning to transcend the limits of sensory experience, by making us wish for the clarification that lies beyond strict logic. Here, even within the limits of a beautifully chiastic sentence, we see Lewis straining beyond the bounds of rationality.

In Logan's view, Lewis's commitment to Romanticism had significant metaphysical and epistemological implications. He claims that, metaphysically, Lewis's romanticism is expressed in a sacramental view of reality: he sees reality as having within its natural dimension "supernatural inherencies." Logan admonishes readers to understand that Lewis's "world of medieval romance arises from a belief that it remains true,

---

9. Logan, "Literary Theorist," 37.
10. Lewis, *Surprised by Joy*, 17–18.
11. Logan, "Literary Theorist," 37.

despite the coercive materialism of modernity."[12] John Piper claims that Lewis was a Romantic rationalist[13] and that "the essence of his romanticism [was] Lewis's experience of the world that repeatedly awakened in him a sense that there is always more than this created world—something other, something beyond the natural world."[14]

As a member of the English faculty at the University of Cambridge, Logan has a unique perspective on the effect that Lewis intended his writings to have on his reading audience. Whereas other writers have commented on the profound effect that the sensation Lewis characterises as joy had on him, Logan takes his analysis to another level by describing the effect that Lewis intended to have on his readers. According to Logan, Lewis wanted to portray the unsatisfied desire as being highly desirable itself. Even though it was ultimately unsatisfying, Logan claims that Lewis's objective was to "simulate" a yearning in his readers to transcend the very limits of sensory experience. He argues that just as Lewis knows "that there is more to reality than our senses can get at, epistemologically he knows that there is more to the mind than ratiocination" and that "other modes of operation may help us become aware of the supernatural elements of experience."[15] In Logan's view, not only did Lewis want to communicate the notion that there was something beyond the senses, but he also wanted to create a yearning for that in his readers. He wanted to instill in them a desire for the other, a yearning for an awareness of the Absolute, for the God that he had come to know himself.

Lewis held a special affection for the medieval period and became a specialist in medieval literature. His attraction to Romanticism may, in part, explain his love for that period. In that regard, Logan's observations are instructive and correspond with what Lewis has written elsewhere. In *The Discarded Image*, a book about medieval and Renaissance literature based on a series of Lewis's Oxford lectures and published posthumously by Cambridge Press, Lewis provides readers with a unique insight into the medieval worldview. He tells readers that what our ancestors believed to be true about the medieval model, most notably in the sciences, particularly in the field of astronomy, is no longer credible. But he freely

---

12. Logan, "Literary Theorist," 37.
13. Piper, "C. S. Lewis" (2013).
14. Piper, "C. S. Lewis" (2014), 26–27.
15. Logan, "Literary Theorist," 38.

admits that much of the "old Model still delights" him.[16] Lewis claims that many of the pagan philosophers had much in common with the medieval Christian fathers and that today's secular modernists would reject many of the views of both.[17] He thinks that both Christian fathers and pagan philosophers would have embarrassed modernists with "stories of visions, ecstasies, and apparitions."[18][19]

Chad Walsh writes that "Lewis was a man born six hundred years late."[20] He claims that "he lovingly depicted the medieval worldview" and that "he would have been more at home in medieval Paris . . . than he was at Oxford." Lewis's love of the medieval worldview did not influence him to embrace it uncritically, however, because he was well aware of its shortcomings, such as its notion of Ptolemaic astronomy, for example.[21]

"No Model is a catalogue of ultimate realities," writes Lewis. He fully expected the contemporary worldview to be replaced with a "new Model" when new evidence was discovered which would create "far-reaching changes in the mental temper" of future generations.[22] He makes no secret about his objections to some elements within the prevailing worldview of his day. The naturalism that he had embraced in his youth had been found wanting. It was discarded in favour of theism, and he may have expected its inadequacies to become increasingly manifest. Because naturalism failed to account for his perception of reality, Lewis likely felt that there were good reasons to believe that its shortcomings would eventually become manifest to the larger society, thereby creating a revision to the existing worldview.[23]

Walsh thinks that the medieval model was appealing to Lewis in large part due to the manner by which it "was satisfying to the imagination" in

16. Lewis, *Discarded Image*, 216.
17. Lewis, *Discarded Image*, 219, 222.
18. Lewis, *Discarded Image*, 216–22.
19. Lewis, *Discarded Image*, 47.
20. Walsh, *Literary Legacy*, 18.
21. Walsh, *Literary Legacy*, 19. "If the medieval approach is alien, that of the Renaissance seems to me sometimes repellant," Lewis writes (Lewis, *Selected Literary Essays*, 129).
22. Lewis, *Discarded Image*, 222.
23. This is consistent with Thomas Kuhn's notion of new understandings resulting in paradigm changes. Kuhn writes: "The decision to reject one paradigm is always simultaneously to accept another, and the judgment leading to that decision involves the comparison of both paradigms" (Kuhn, *Structure of Scientific Revolutions*, 78).

a way that other models had not been and that it had "made man feel at home in the universe." He writes that Lewis "does not claim literal truth for the model, but he contends that such a claim cannot be made for the modern model either" and that "it too will yield to a yet newer model."[24] Lewis had reservations about the continued acceptability of the current worldview. In *The Discarded Image*, he writes: "The new Model will not be set up without evidence, but the evidence will turn up when the inner need for it becomes sufficiently great."[25]

In his *C. S. Lewis Handbook*, Colin Duriez claims that although people have identified such models with reality, "Lewis came to the conclusion that a world model is not meant to represent reality itself." Duriez writes: "Our world model will eventually change, like others before it. Lewis suggested that the change was more likely to come from a change in the mental temper of a future age than from some dramatic discovery about the physical universe."[26]

Lewis was convinced that ultimate understanding of true reality was just as unattainable as was ultimate satisfaction. His quest for a worldview or model that encompassed his perception of reality had eventually led him to embrace theism, a belief from which he never deviated. Although theism left some questions unanswered, it was not burdened with what he perceived to be the many shortcomings embedded within modernity. It was his awareness of modernity's inherent failings that likely persuaded him that modernity's viability would eventually be challenged, thereby initiating a change in the model of the world. The medieval model's imaginative appeal and its acceptance of some elements of the supernatural likely contributed to the attraction it had for Lewis.

Chad Walsh opines that insufficient attention has been paid to Lewis's theory of Romanticism:[27]

> He does not lean upon it as heavily as he does upon Reason, but it offers a complementary road to religious commitment. When two roads lead to the same city you suspect that the city is worth reaching. . . . The concept of 'Romanticism' makes it possible for the individual better to understand a strange variety of experiences which seem at first glance so subjective that they cannot be communicated to others. 'Romanticism' is a clue to their

---

24. Walsh, *Literary Legacy*, 194.
25. Lewis, *Discarded Image*, 223.
26. Duriez, *C. S. Lewis Handbook*, 51–52.
27. Walsh, *C. S. Lewis*, 118–19.

meaning, and the key to unlocking the hidden meaning of much that is otherwise bewildering and almost meaningless in poetry and the arts. . . . I can think of many passages in Wordsworth's poetry that suddenly become fraught with meaning in the light of Lewis's explanation."

Walsh claims that understanding Lewis's notion of Romanticism helps readers in "understanding the truths that were once perceived in flashes, and fitting the fragments of truth together."[28] As is referenced below, Lewis had given Romanticism his own private meaning. Walsh thinks this was unintentional for Lewis and that he likely defaulted to this word in order to describe his unique and repeated experiences otherwise characterised as Joy. According to Walsh, "Romanticism, as he uses the word, is an experience of intense longing, which differs from other desires in two ways: the yearning is in itself a sort of delight, and a peculiar mystery engulfs the object of desire."[29] In Wash's view, the identities of Lewis's desired objects could be as varied as a "distant hill, or a moment in the remote past."[30]

In the preface to the third edition of *The Pilgrim's Regress*, Lewis comments on the various uses of Romanticism and the definition within which he used it. He lists a range of meanings that had become associated with Romanticism, including dangerous adventures, stories of magicians and nymphs, indulgences in the abnormal, subjectivism, revolts against existing civilization, and hypersensibility to the natural world. Although he liked some of the usages, he detested others, he writes. In his opinion, the word had acquired so many usages with varying meanings that it had become useless,[31] which led him to give it a private meaning and use it in a way that was totally unique.[32]

---

28. Walsh, *C. S. Lewis*, 119.

29. Walsh, *C. S. Lewis*, 119.

30. Walsh, *C. S. Lewis*, 116.

31. Corbin Carnell, professor of English at the University of Florida, writes that the word *Sehnsucht* is relatively unknown because it has been subsumed in Romanticism. He claims that it is referred to as being nebulous, not because it involves metaphysical concepts, but because it "has been asked to include so many different tendencies." Carnell refers to an address by Arthur Lovejoy before the *Modern Language Association* in 1923 during which Lovejoy cited the usage of 'Romanticism' as an example of words losing their meaning because of the wide range of meanings associated with a given word. Lovejoy's remedy, writes Carnell, was "that we should all stop talking about Romanticism" (Carnell, 1999:24).

32. Lewis, *Pilgrim's Regress*, 9–11.

Eventually, for Lewis, the word Romanticism came to represent an oft-recurring experience, an experience that has been mentioned in the previous chapter, and which he had characterised as Joy. In his preface to *Pilgrim's Regress*, Lewis expands on the experience that he came to identify with his own private meaning of Romanticism:[33]

> What I meant was a particular recurrent experience which dominated my childhood and adolescence and which I hastily called 'Romantic' because inanimate nature and marvellous literature were among the things that evoked it. I still believe that the experience is common, commonly misunderstood, and of immense importance: but I now know that in other minds it arises under other stimuli and is entangled with other irrelevances and that to bring it into the forefront is not so easy as I once supposed. I will now try to describe it sufficiently to make the following pages intelligible. The experience is one of intense longing. It is distinguished from other longings by two things. In the first place, though the sense of want is acute and often painful, yet the mere wanting is somehow a delight. Other desires are felt as pleasures only if satisfaction is expected in the near future: hunger is pleasant only if we know (or believe) that we are soon going to eat. But this desire, if when there is no hope of possible satisfaction, continues to be prized, and even preferred to anything else in the world, by those who have once felt it. This hunger is better than any other fullness; this poverty better than all other wealth. And thus, it comes about, that if the desire is long absent, it may itself be desired, and that new desiring becomes a new instance of the original desire, though the subject may not at once recognise and thus cries out for his lost youth of soul at the very moment in which he is being rejuvenated. This sounds complicated, but it is simple when we live it. 'Oh to feel as I did then!' we cry; not noticing that even while we say the words the very feeling whose loss we lament is rising again in all its bitter-sweetness. For this sweet Desire cuts across our ordinary distinctions between wanting and having. To have it is, by definition, a want; to want it, we find, is to have it.

As mentioned in his preface to *Pilgrim's Regress*, Lewis's usage of the word Romanticism represents a bitter-sweet longing. This longing has been characterised elsewhere as Joy. It is variously described as yearning, desire, hunger, intense longing, acute wanting, or simply delighting in the sensation that is being created. Lewis finds the object of this desire

---

33. Lewis, *Pilgrim's Regress*, 12–13.

to be elusive, a peculiar mystery, not fully attainable. He considers this longing to be indicative of a future beyond our present spatial-temporal experiences:[34]

> It appeared to me therefore that if a man diligently followed this desire, pursuing the false objects until their falsity appeared and then resolutely abandoning them, he must come out at last into the clear knowledge that the human soul was made to enjoy some object that is never fully given—nay, cannot even be imagined as given—in our present mode of subjective and spatio-temporal experience.

Lewis saw this yearning desire as having been divinely inspired—as a marker put within human consciousness that was designed to serve as a guidepost to lead humanity to its God, the God of creation. He compares this desire to the Siege Perilous, the knight's chair in the Arthurian legend "in which only one could sit." Therefore "if nature makes nothing in vain, the One who can sit in this chair must exist," writes Lewis.[35] A fair interpretation of the preceding statement seems to indicate that Lewis believed that the best inference for the existence of the yearning for something beyond the natural world within human consciousness is the existence of God.

Carnell sees the yearning desire described by Lewis as a universal experience. He writes that there is a sense of *Sehnsucht* even within certain elements of Hinduism. He thinks that "it is significant that writers like Aldous Huxley and Christopher Isherwood should turn to the religions of the East," especially that branch of Hinduism known as Vendantism. "In fact, one might interpret Vendantism as an attempt to face *Sehnsucht* honestly. What the Vendantist seeks to do, of course, is to renounce longing," he writes.[36] Having studied and temporarily embraced some elements of pantheism, Lewis had likely also observed this phenomenon within certain elements of Eastern religions.

Although Lewis had written about the respective philosophies that he had adopted prior to embracing theism and had become a strong advocate for the Christian faith, he was reluctant to speak publicly about the details of his personal spirituality or about his conversion. In May 1943, in response to a request to publicize an account of his spiritual

---

34. Lewis, *Pilgrim's Regress*, 15.
35. Lewis, *Pilgrim's Regress*, 15.
36. Carnell, *Bright Shadow of Reality*, 157n37.

journey to the Christian faith, he wrote that the details of his conversion were too "technically philosophical" and "intimate" for general publication, and that his talents did not "run in that direction."[37] In an address to the C. S. Lewis Society in 1985, Owen Barfield stated that during one of their walking tours shortly after Lewis's conversion, he had tried to get him to talk about it, but that "as soon as the conversation took that direction, he broke it off sharply" and "simply refused to talk at that sort of depth at all." Barfield claimed that he could remember Lewis saying with "more emotion than I ever heard him express: 'I can't bear it.'" Barfield was surprised by Lewis's reaction and stated that he found himself "also feeling deeply distressed—indeed agitated—on that occasion."[38] When asked about the reason for Lewis's emotional reaction to his conversion experience and his reluctance to speak about it, Barfield answered that he did not know but noted that prior to his conversion Lewis had "talked rather glibly about identity with the Absolute." Barfield theorized that perhaps Lewis had come to the realization "that that was all talk," that the "relation of the individual to the Absolute" was in fact "the relationship of man to God," and that he may have been overwhelmed by this acute realization.[39]

Barfield's observation is instructive and provides insight into the emotional impact that Lewis's conversion and his relationship with the Being that he had called the Absolute had on him. Upon reflecting on his earliest memories of Lewis, he writes that "if the first thing you thought about Lewis was poetry, the second thing was 'The Absolute.'"[40] Lewis's belief in the reality of the Christian faith seems to have been overpowering. He remained indefatigable in his support and defense of Christianity. His strong emotional reaction may help to explain his enduring passion for defending the truth claims of the faith of which he had become a believer.

Lewis's yearning desire for an elusive quality to which he had given the name Romanticism remained unsatisfied but had seemingly helped lead him to the profound realization that the One identified by the Christian faith was indeed the object of his relentless yearning. Lewis's training in philosophy and the power of reason had led him to embrace

37. Lewis, *Collected Letters*, 2:575.
38. Barfield, *Owen Barfield*, 111.
39. Barfield, *Owen Barfield*, 116.
40. Barfield, *Owen Barfield*, 6–7.

theism, but it was his understanding of what he called "a true myth"—the birth, death, and resurrection of Jesus—that resulted in his conversion to Christianity. His unique notion of Romanticism was a significant factor in his spiritual and intellectual journey, a journey that eventually led him to an acute realization of the One who was the object of his yearning. And this realization undergirded the defense of his Christian worldview.

4.3 REASON AND IMAGINATION IN LEWIS'S WORLDVIEW

Reason and imagination were key factors in Lewis's conversion to theism and eventually to Christianity. Reason had led him to theism. "I am an empirical Theist.... Like so many of my generation, ... I came back, from materialism to a belief in God.... I have arrived at God by induction," he wrote in his autobiographical notebook shortly after his conversion.[41] Through Kirkpatrick's tutelage, Lewis had become a skilled logician, and he saw logic as the lens through which to gain an accurate perception of reality. In his view, logic was a "real insight into the way in which real things have to exist." For Lewis, "the laws of thought are also the laws of things."[42] And it was his logical reasoning that had led him to embrace theism.[43] His reasoning skills had failed him, however, in coming to an understanding and a belief in the truth claims of Christianity.

It was the power of his imagination that enabled him to comprehend the profound meaning underlying the birth, death, and resurrection of Jesus. His embracement of the Christian faith was propelled by his realization of the logical truth of the gospel narrative; and by exercising the power of his imagination, he was able to discern the profound meaning behind the narrative. Reason provided him with Christianity's logical underpinnings, the meaning and import of which eluded him until he came to understand its importance by viewing it through the lens of his imagination. In a letter explaining his newly gained insight to Arthur Greeves shortly after his conversion, he wrote that "the Christian story is full of meaning" and that "Christianity is to be understood as God

---

41. Lewis, *Image and Imagination*, 13.

42. Lewis, *Christian Reflections* (2014), 78.

43. By declaring himself an empirical theist, Lewis seems to imply that theism was intellectually defensible as the worldview that best represents reality.

expressing Himself through real things . . . in a language more adequate, namely the actual incarnation, crucifixion, and resurrection."[44]

The meaning of Christianity had seemingly confounded him until he came to understand the Christian story as encapsulated within the incarnation, crucifixion, and resurrection, as that of a loving God revealing himself to mankind. His friends and Oxford colleagues J. R. R. Tolkien and Hugo Dyson had been instrumental in helping Lewis gain the necessary insight by advising him to use his considerable imaginative ability in order to be able to discern the Christian story's powerful import. Tolkien and Dyson "convinced Lewis that the death and resurrection of Christ was a real event that also reverberated with meanings beyond what he was able to grasp or express," writes Bowling Green State University's Marvin Hinten. According to Hinten, "this concept of multiple meanings in events beyond what reason can express became a key factor not only in Lewis's conversion, but also in his whole understanding and expression of Christianity."[45] It was becoming aware of the truth, as well as the meaning, of the Christian narrative that led Lewis to embrace a Christian worldview.

Lewis's notion of meaning and imagination's role in discerning meaning were frequent topics in his lectures at Oxford's Socratic Club. In a paper that he read at a meeting of the club in May 1946, Lewis stated: "My conversion, very largely, depended on recognizing Christianity as the completion, the actualization of the entelechy,[46] of something that had never been wholly absent from the mind of man."[47] This Socratic Club statement reinforces what he had stated at the same club about a year earlier: "I believe in Christianity as I believe that the Sun has risen not only because I see it but because of it I see everything else."[48] Although Lewis doesn't expound on the import of his statements in the published versions, when read within the context of the two lectures, they have significant implications. His characterisation of Christianity as

---

44. Lewis, *Collected Letters*, 1:977.

45. Hinten, "Metaphor," 273.

46. Entelechy is the real existence of a thing, not merely its theoretical existence, and is derived from the Greek *entelecheia*, in philosophy, that which realizes or makes actual what is otherwise merely potential. The concept is intimately connected with Aristotle's distinction between matter and form, or the potential and the actual (Britannica, "Entelechy").

47. Lewis, *Essay Collection*, 165–66.

48. Lewis, *Essay Collection*, 21.

the completion, the actualization of the entelechy implies that a full understanding of the Christian faith is tantamount to a full understanding of reality. His reference to Christianity as being analogous to sunlight's illuminating effect on everything would seem to have enormous implications and accountabilities for Christian believers. For Lewis, Christianity represented the totality of reality, including realities such as the origin of the natural world, the characteristics inherent within that world, the existence of a supernatural sphere, the existence of consciousness, the origin of principles and values, and even the existence of the abstract. Within his Christian worldview, he was seemingly able to accommodate his entire perception of reality. Philip Van der Elst writes that Lewis did not become a Christian or advocate for Christianity "because he thought it was good for society or benefited humanity, or because he thought it comforts strengthens or improves individuals." Writes Van der Elst: "Lewis believed in it and defended its claims because he became convinced that Christianity is *true*—that it, and it alone, presents an accurate picture of reality."[49] Lewis's writings would seem to support Van der Elst's observation: "The Christian and the Materialist hold different beliefs about the universe. They can't both be right. The one who is wrong will act in a way which simply doesn't fit the real universe. Consequently, with the best will in the world, he will be helping his fellow creatures to their destruction."[50]

Lewis's published writings provide a wealth of information about his use of reason and the power of logic in defending the truth claims of the Christian faith. It is in his lectures, many of which have now been published, where we find much significant information on his perception of imagination's role in matters of belief. In a published lecture given at Manchester University in the 1930s, titled "Bluspels and Flalansferes," Lewis argues: "I am a rationalist. For me, reason is the natural organ of truth; but imagination is the organ of meaning."[51] The title for the lecture comes from Lewis's conflation of two phrases. He discussed Kant's idea that "whatever I see next will be blue because I'm wearing blue spectacles," contracted blue spectacles to *bluspels*, and imagined the word eventually becoming a metaphor for the idea of shaping reality through one's perceptions. He then took the phrase "Flatlanders' sphere" from

---

49. Van der Elst, *C. S. Lewis*, 37.
50. Lewis, *God in the Dock*, 110.
51. Lewis, *Selected Literary Essays*, 265.

Edwin Abbott's book *Flatland*, a book featuring inhabitants living within a two dimensional world, contracted Flatlander's sphere to *flalansfere*, and imagined the word becoming a metaphor for limitations imposed by the dimensional limitations of one's environment. According to Lewis, the metaphors would still be operating in people's minds even after the original usage of the phrases had been forgotten. By thus illustrating the power of metaphorical language, Lewis attempted to demonstrate that poets frequently spoke "more meaningfully than philosophers, who cannot really understand the metaphysical things they are discussing."[52] From Lewis's perspective, through the power of metaphor working on the imagination, poets have the ability not only to convey meaning but also to transmit knowledge.

Marvin Hinten claims that "virtually all of Lewis's writings are flooded with brief and extended figures of speech." He writes that "if one were to select the key continuing element of Lewis's style both fiction and nonfiction, it would be the repeated use of allegories, analogies, metaphors and similes."[53] Lewis admired poets's use of literary devices, especially metaphors, and he used them with great effectiveness in many of his writings. He understood reason to be the organ of truth, and imagination the organ of meaning. With the use of metaphors and other literary devices working through the imagination, he sought to illuminate reason's truth and make it understandable to his readers.

Respected literary scholar Chad Walsh writes that Lewis's ability to use Aristotle's tools of logic to maximum effect was a key source of power for the literature that he created. "Only the future will tell if this kind of logic will continue to seem as much a part of the universe as it has long appeared to Western man," he writes. Walsh does not expect that Lewis's works of reason or "argumentative books," as he characterises them, would lose all appeal even if "within the framework of Western philosophy other doubting questions are being raised." However, "the solid core of Lewis's achievement consists of those more imaginative and mythological books in which his ability as a writer and his sensibility as a Christian are fruitfully wedded," he adds. Walsh claims that although Lewis's imaginative skills were most formidable, he used both reason and imagination to good advantage and combined them for maximum effect. It is in these books, claims Walsh, that Lewis "puts to work every

---

52. Hinten, "Bluspels and Flalansferes."
53. Hinten, "Metaphor," 274.

talent that he possesses and raises to a high literary level" the quality of his prose, creating a result by which "the schism between logic and romance is healed, and myth, fact, and truth are revealed as mere interim categories."[54] Carnell writes: "Meaning then for Lewis comes through both reason and imagination. And it this dual approach which makes him unusual in an age when it has been fashionable either to damn reason and live for art or to reject artistic statement as empirically meaningless."[55]

In his 2011 book *Reasoning beyond Reason: Imagination as a Theological Source in the Work of C. S. Lewis*, Dr. Jeff Sellars writes: "Imagination and reason are intertwined in a fundamental way: they are different expressions of a single divine source of truth. But with the work of the imagination there is an ability to grasp truths that might otherwise be unintelligible."[56] Sellars thinks that "reason itself suggests a 'space' to be filled in." He writes that "between the gaps of foundational shortcomings," imagination serves as a vehicle for "the initialization of ideas and concepts," and serves as a stimulus for "inferential leaps."[57]

It is noteworthy that reason and imagination, having helped lead Lewis to embrace the Christian worldview, were also highly instrumental in the manner by which he defended it. This is especially manifested in the manner in which he defended the Christian faith against the notion that it was incompatible with modern science; the relationship between faith and science in Lewis's worldview is the subject of the section following.

4.4 CHRISTIAN FAITH AND SCIENCE IN LEWIS'S WORLDVIEW

The relationship between Christian faith and modern science is a recurring theme in Lewis's writings. This subject is addressed both in his works of fiction such as *That Hideous Strength*, his nonfiction literature such as *Miracles*, and his published essays and public lectures. Two of the challenges frequently addressed by Lewis are the notion that scientific knowledge is superior to and supersedes religious knowledge, and the allegation that Christianity is incompatible with modern science. Although he acknowledges that there was a strong conflict between Christianity

54. Walsh, *Literary Legacy*, 248.
55. Carnell, *Bright Shadow of Reality*, 72.
56. Sellars, *Reasoning beyond Reason*, 17–18.
57. Sellars, *Reasoning beyond Reason*, 18.

and scientism,[58] he argues that there is no conflict between science and Christianity.

Lewis took strong exception to the notion held by some of his contemporaries that there was an inherent conflict between science and elements of the Christian faith. In an address that he gave at Oxford's Magdalen College during the Second World War, he objected to the notion that "scientific thought does put us in touch with reality, whereas moral or metaphysical thought does not."[59] Lewis argued that because the physical sciences relied on inferences from experimental observations, for instance, that they were just as reliant "on the validity of logic as metaphysics or mathematics."[60] In his address, he also took objection to what he considered to be a mischaracterisation of the capabilities of the biological evolutionary process.[61] He drew a sharp distinction between demonstrated biological evolutionary changes, the vast majority of which were degenerative in nature, and the popular notions inherent within biological evolutionism, in which biological changes were understood as being improvements over their predecessor species.[62] In the published version of his Magdalen College lecture, Lewis writes:[63]

> Speaking to a scientifically trained audience I need not labour the point that popular Evolutionism is something quite different from Evolution as the biologists understand it. Biological Evolution is a theory about how organisms change. Some of these changes have made organisms, judged by human standards, 'better'—more flexible, stronger, more conscious. The majority of the changes have not done so. As J. B. S. Haldane says, in evolution progress is the exception and degeneration the rule.

58. Scientism is the belief in the universal applicability of the scientific method and approach, and the view that empirical science constitutes the most authoritative worldview to the exclusion of other viewpoints. Scientism is the view that empirical reality is the only reality, and anything not empirical, not subject to measurement and analysis by the scientific method, is merely subjective or unimportant. Scientism is closely related to rationalism, which posits that only those things that are empirically demonstrable fall within the purview of reason (Miller, "C. S. Lewis," 309).

59. Lewis, "Christian Reflections" (2014), 75.

60. Lewis, "Christian Reflections" (2014), 76.

61. Clyde Kilby writes that although Lewis's "opinion about the Darwinian hypothesis seems to be unsettled," he thought that "the myth of universal evolutionism" to be "immensely implausible, because it makes the general course of nature so very unlike those parts of nature we can observe" (Kilby, *Christian World*, 175).

62. Lewis, "Christian Reflections" (2014), 71, 75-76.

63. Lewis, "Christian Reflections" (2014), 71-72.

> Popular Evolutionism ignores this. For it, 'Evolution' simply means 'improvement.' And it is not confined to organisms, but applied also to moral qualities, institutions, arts, intelligence and the like. There is thus lodged in popular thought the conception that improvement is, somehow, a cosmic law: a conception to which the sciences give no support at all. There is no general tendency even for organisms to improve. There is no evidence that the mental and moral capacities of the human race have been increased since man became man. And there is certainly no tendency for the universe as a whole to move in any direction which we should call 'good.' ... The huge background is filled by quite different principles: entropy, degradation, disorganization.

John Burdon Sanderson Haldane was professor of genetics at University College, London, from 1933 to 1957. Haldane, a materialist/naturalist and lifelong Marxist, objected to Lewis's science fiction novels, and publicly critiqued some of Lewis's works. This caused Lewis to respond to Haldane's challenges. One such response, an essay titled "Reply to Professor Haldane," was not published until after Lewis's death.[64]

Lewis addresses scientism in his "Reply to Professor Haldane":[65]

> I think Professor Haldane himself probably regarded his critique of my science as mere skirmishing; with his second charge (that I traduce scientists) we reach something more serious. . . . It certainly is an attack, if not on scientists, yet on 'scientism'—a certain outlook on the world which is causally connected with the popularization of the sciences, though it is much less common among real scientists than among its readers. It is, in a word, the belief that the supreme moral end is the perpetuation of our own species, and that this is to be pursued even if, in the process of being fitted for survival, our species has to be stripped of all those things for which we value it—of pity, of happiness, and of freedom. I am not sure that you will find this belief formally asserted by any writer: such things creep in as assumed, and unstated, major premises.

A critique of scientism is a recurring theme throughout Lewis's body of work, writes Michael M. Miller. Miller claims that one of the "key intellectual labors of Lewis's life, running through all his work from his scholarly essays and Christian apologetics to his children's stories and

---

64. Lewis, *Collected Letters*, 2:236n40.
65. Lewis, *Of Other Worlds*, 76–77.

science fiction, was a critique of scientism."⁶⁶ Miller writes that Lewis believed that scientism "led to relativism, and, in the process, undermined the foundations of true science." In Miller's view, Lewis considered scientism to be "incoherent at its root" and thought that "if followed to its illogical conclusion would lead to the end of Western civilization."⁶⁷

Lewis's employed the word *scientism* when referring to science as characterised by principles and practises directed toward controlling societal issues, rather than the more traditional form of science, which is typically directed toward researching and investigating the natural world. As James Herrick writes, understanding Lewis's distinction between science and scientism is important when reading Lewis's derisive portrayal of certain characters within his works of fiction, most notably in Lewis's novel *That Hideous Strength*. In this book, Lewis offers a devastatingly satirical critique of unethical scientific methods that are employed for conducting human engineering as directed by a central planning committee. And in his book *The Abolition of Man*, Lewis refers to a "Green Book"⁶⁸ being used by the nation's educational system that influences young students to change their views on the objectivity of their values. Lewis dismisses this practise as blatant indoctrination, designed to advance a subjective view of societal values, a notion that Lewis rejects.⁶⁹

Lewis's *Abolition* was initially conceived as a series of lectures that he gave in Newcastle in 1943. Two of the key subjects covered in this classic work are the subtle manner whereby the validity of objective values can be systematically undermined by the educational system of the day and replaced with a philosophy of subjectivism, and the risks to a society's traditional morality when some version of scientism becomes the prevailing philosophy. Lewis confines his sharpest criticism to his works of fiction. While he supported endeavours that pursued knowledge of the natural world, he was highly sceptical of some scientific projects and suspicious of centralized scientific decision-making. His 1945 novel *That*

---

66. Miller, *C. S. Lewis*, 309–10.

67. Miller, *C. S. Lewis*, 310.

68. In his 2007 book *C. S. Lewis: A Guide to His Theology*, David Clark writes that Lewis never gave the names of the author or the title of the high school textbook that concerned him but simply referred to it as "The Green Book." The book to which Lewis referred was actually *The Control of Language: A Critical Approach to Reading and Writing*, by Alex King and Martin Ketley, published in 1939, by Longman's Green and Co. (Clark, *C. S. Lewis*, 34).

69. Herrick, "C. S. Lewis," 239.

Hideous Strength represents one of his most striking critiques of the inherent dangers of scientism. Similar critiques are also expressed in his 1938 and 1943 novels, *Out of the Silent Planet* and *Perelandra*. Although he masks his devastating critique of scientism within his fictional writings, he expected and faced considerable criticism. As Herrick points out, Lewis's anticipation of a forthcoming response from the academic community was expressed in correspondence with Sir Arthur C. Clarke who was himself a scientist. In a letter during the year that he wrote *The Abolition of Man*, Lewis wrote Clarke about his reservations about the effect that increased, unbridled experimentation may have on the human race. As the exchange with Haldane illustrates, Lewis's expectation of eliciting a response was justified. He tells Clarke that he views indiscriminate experimentation as "a cancer in the universe."[70] Lewis wrote the lectures for *The Abolition of Man* in 1944 and published his book *That Hideous Strength* in 1945; how much was known about the experiments carried out by the Nazis' regime is difficult to ascertain. Nevertheless, in retrospect, there is a sense of prescience in Lewis's fictional works. Judging from what can be gleaned from Lewis's published works, as well as from his correspondence, although he favoured scientific investigation of the natural sciences, he was deeply concerned about social experimentation and social engineering. Such experimentation or engineering being done without the moderating influence of moral constraints heightened his concerns. His concern appears to reflect a traditional Christian (perhaps conservative) worldview, which might be characterised as wise stewardship of man's natural resources, undergirded by a recognition of its Creator.

Lewis's influence on Christian apologetics has led to scrutiny about his views regarding the sufficiency/insufficiency[71] of Darwinian processes to explain the emergence of the bio-system.[72] Supporters of Lewis on both sides of the issue claim that Lewis would likely weigh in on their side. Although as a young atheist Lewis seemed to have adopted the

---

70. A. Clarke and Lewis, *From Narnia*, 40.

71. See *The Magician's Twin: C. S. Lewis on Science, Scientism, and Society* for a selection of essays on Lewis's views regarding Darwinian processes and the alleged conflict between science and religion. Edited by John G. West, the title is inspired by Lewis's book *The Magician's Nephew* (West, "Magician's Twin," 19).

72. An overview of Lewis's notion regarding Darwinian processes is also available in a video of a public debate between Michael Peterson and John West (West, "Evolution and C. S. Lewis").

accepted Darwinian view on biological processes, he also appears to have some reservations about the adequacy of the then-current evolutionary thought for explaining the origins of living systems. In the diary that Lewis kept from 1922 to 1927, he provides a summary of a discussion that he had in August 16, 1925, with the then-teenaged Maureen Moore on Genesis and evolution. When Maureen asks him whether he accepts the Genesis account on origins or the scientific view, Lewis replies that he accepts the scientific view. Maureen implies that one has to choose between believing in God or accepting the scientific view. Lewis, in effect, responds that a person may continue to believe in God without accepting a literal interpretation of every statement in the Old Testament.[73] Two days later, on August 18, 1925, in a letter to his father on the occasion of his election to a tutorial fellowship at Magdalen College, Oxford, he expresses some scepticism about the plausibility that Darwinian processes could generate all that had been ascribed to them.[74] It is important to note that these exchanges took place several years prior to his conversion to theism and his later conversion to Christianity.

Lewis's caution about participating in Darwinian controversies is evident in a series of letters between himself and Royal Navy Captain Bernard Acworth. Acworth was sceptical of some Darwinist claims and wanted to engage Lewis as an advocate for his stance. In a 1944 letter to Acworth, Lewis replied that he was unwilling to become involved in the debate, because he felt that he was not adequately informed about the subject matter and that he couldn't see how his involvement would contribute to his work in Christian apologetics.[75] In a letter in 1951, Lewis again writes to Acworth, telling him that he had nearly finished reading Acworth's 1934 book on evolution,[76] and expresses his appreciation to Acworth for having sent him a copy, stating: "I must confess it has shaken me." Although he hasn't given much thought to evolutionary theory, and his knowledge of it is vague and intermittent, he now has serious doubts about the prominence that the theory has acquired, he writes. Lewis tells Acworth that he wishes that he was younger (presumably with more time for research) and that he is "inclined to . . . regard . . . it [evolutionism] as the central and radical lie in the whole web of falsehoods that now

---

73. Lewis, *All My Road*, 361.
74. Lewis, *Collected Letters*, 1:649.
75. Lewis, *Collected Letters*, 2:632–33.
76. Acworth, *This Progress: The Tragedy of Evolution*.

governs our lives." Lewis writes Acworth that he is "shaken" by the "fanatical and twisted attitude" of the defenders of evolutionary theory.[77]

The following year, in response to a request by Acworth for Lewis to write the preface to a book that he had written, Lewis replies to Acworth and expresses his reluctance to become involved in the debate:[78]

> No one who is in doubt about Darwin wd. be impressed by testimony from me who is known to be no scientist. Many who have been or are being moved toward Christianity by my books wd. be deterred by finding that I was connected with anti-Darwinism. I hope that . . . I would not allow myself to be influenced by this consideration if it were only my personal success as an author that was endangered. But the cause I stand for wd. be endangered too. When a man has become a popular Apologist, he must watch his step. Everyone is on the look out for things that might discredit him.

A letter to Acworth from Lewis in 1960 expresses similar reservations about Darwinian theory. In this letter, Lewis cites a book written in 1955 by Jesuit priest Pierre Teilhard de Chardin, titled *The Phenomenon of Man*.[79] Lewis objects to the book's popularity, because it was "being praised to the skies," and considers the book to be an example of "evolution run mad." Teilhard had postulated that there was something in matter that he had labelled *pre-life*, which Lewis compares to calling the darkness in a cellar as the cellar being in a *pre-light* condition. "Can you see any possible use in such language," he asks Acworth and compliments Teilhard's Jesuit order for rejecting those notions, because in his opinion, Teilhard's theory "ends up in something uncomfortably like Pantheism."[80] This letter was written only three years before Lewis's death in 1963. Clearly, Lewis had longstanding concerns about the exaggerated claims of some advocates of Darwinism. Judging by the comments he made to his father at the beginning of his academic career about Spencer and Darwin's "gigantic assumptions" and by the "irreconcilable contradictions"

77. Lewis, *Collected Letters*, 3:138.

78. Lewis, *Collected Letters*, 3:140–41.

79. *The Phenomenon of Man* was published posthumously; Teilhard de Chardin died in 1955. The book proposed a form of emergent evolution and postulated some notion of reality that Teilhard called pre-life. It is noteworthy that Lewis had filled his own copy of the book, now located at the Marion E. Wade Center, with critical annotations such as "a radically bad book" and "he is quite ignorant" (West, "Darwin in the Dock," 135).

80. Lewis, *Collected Letters*, 3:1137.

mentioned in chapter 3, Lewis appears to have had long-standing misgivings about the ambitious claims made by promoters of Darwinism. Judging from the letters to Acworth in his later years, it appears that Lewis remained skeptical throughout much of his academic career about the ability of Darwinian processes to account for the emergence of the bio-system.

In an essay titled "The Funeral of a Great Myth," which was first published in 1998, Lewis gives what appears to be a broad outline of his views on evolutionary biological processes. Lewis's essay is largely a critique of the transformational powers that have been unjustifiably attributed to the theory of evolution. In Lewis's view, the theory has been transformed into a myth that he labels *evolutionism* or *developmentalism*. In this essay, Lewis cites references to argue that evolutionism as myth was founded many decades prior to the publication of Darwin's *Origin of the Species* and claims that most or all of the characteristics of the myth have gradually, over many decades, been transferred to the theory itself. "Already, before science had spoken, the mythical imagination knew the kind of 'Evolution' it wanted. . . . If science offers instances that satisfy demand, they will be eagerly accepted. If it offers any instances that frustrate it, they will simply be ignored," he writes. Lewis lays out a summary of his case in a single paragraph within his essay:[81]

> Again, for the scientist Evolution is a purely biological theorem. It takes over organic life on this planet as a going concern and tries to explain certain changes within that field. It makes no cosmic statements, no metaphysical statements, no eschatological statements. Granted that we now have minds we can trust, granted that organic life came to exist, it tries to explain, say, how a species that once had wings came to lose them. It explains this by the negative effect of the environment operating on small variations. It does not in itself explain the origin of organic life, nor of the variations, nor does it discuss the origin and the validity of reason. It may tell you how the brain, through which reason now operates, arose, but that is a different matter. Still less does it tell you how the universe as a whole arose, or what it is or whither it is tending. But the Myth knows none of these reticences. Having turned what was a theory of change into a theory of improvement, it then makes this a *cosmic* theory. Not merely terrestrial organisms but *everything* is moving "upwards and onwards." Reason has "evolved" out of instinct, virtue out of

---

81. Lewis, *Essay Collection*, 25–26.

complexes, poetry out of exotic howls and grunts, civilization out of savagery, the organic out of inorganic, the solar system out of some side-real [sic] soup, or traffic block. And conversely, reason, virtue, art and civilization as we now know them are only the crude and embryonic beginnings of far better things—perhaps Deity itself—in the remote future. For in the Myth, "Evolution" (as the Myth understands it) is the formula of *all* existence. To exist means to be moving from the status of "almost zero" to the status of "almost 'infinity.'" To those brought up on the Myth nothing seems more normal, more natural, more plausible, than that chaos should turn into order, death into life, ignorance into knowledge. And with this we reach the full blown Myth. It is one of the most moving and satisfying dramas which have ever been imagined.

Lewis accepted the theoretical concept of what might be characterised as microevolution—incidental changes in the characteristics of individual species over time. However, he considers it highly unlikely that evolutionary processes possess anything close to the transformative powers that have been attributed to them. Lewis writes that he "grew up believing in the Myth," that he still feels "its almost perfect grandeur," and that he could almost find it in his heart "to wish that it was not mythical but true." He claims that what "makes it impossible that it should be true is not so much the lack of evidence . . . as the fatal self-contradiction that runs right through it." He writes that the myth expects him to "treat reason as absolute" and then contradicts itself by asking him "to believe that reason is simply the unforeseen and unintended by-product of a mindless process at one stage of its endless and aimless becoming."[82]

Lewis believed that there were deep underlying reasons for the popularity of the myth. He claims that its basic idea was the notion that "small or chaotic or feeble things perpetually turn themselves into large, strong, ordered things." He thought it an "odd" idea, because "we have never actually seen a pile of rubble turning itself into a house." Lewis credits the myth's wide acceptance and its popularity to the tendency to extrapolate phenomena that one has actually observed, to biological processes that have been postulated to have occurred, and cites acorns becoming oaks, grubs becoming insects, and eggs becoming birds as examples. Furthermore, writes Lewis, "everyone has seen 'Evolution' happening in the history of machines. We all remember when locomotives

---

82. Lewis, *Essay Collection*, 28.

were smaller and less efficient than they are now." He thinks that the myth "commends itself to the imagination" by transposing instances within everyone's experiences into a belief that "evolution in a cosmic sense is the most natural thing in the world."[83] As stated earlier, Lewis grew up believing not only in the occurrence of gradual changes within individual species over time but also in what he called the grand myth. In his opinion, "neither the Greeks nor the Norsemen ever invented a better story."[84]

By the time Lewis wrote "Funeral of a Great Myth," he found it "impossible that it should be true." He writes: "In the science, Evolution is a theory about *changes:* in the Myth, it is a fact about *improvements.*" Lewis claims that even though degenerative changes outweigh improvements by a ratio of ten to one, nevertheless, "in the popular mind the word 'Evolution' conjures up a picture of things moving 'onward and upwards.'" He writes that "before science had spoken, the mythical imagination knew the kind of 'Evolution' it wanted." Furthermore, claims Lewis, "if science offers any instances to satisfy that demand, they will be eagerly accepted. If it offers any instances that frustrate it, they will simply be ignored."[85]

In his 1990 book, biographer A. N. Wilson confirms Lewis's reservations about what he considered to be Darwinism's overreach. Wilson claims that during a dinner conversation at the Kilns in the late 1940s, Oxford English professor Helen Gardener had remarked that if anyone remotely resembling the biblical Adam had indeed been the first human, it would likely have been a "Neanderthal ape-like figure," to which Lewis is said to have responded unapprovingly, "I see we have a Darwinian in our midst." Notably, in *The Discarded Image*, Lewis expresses similar reservations about the continued acceptability of the then-current worldview, of which Darwinism was a core component. He had fully expected the world model to be revised, a revision that he did not expect to take place until it was deemed to be needed. "The new Model will not be set up without evidence, but the evidence will turn up when the inner need for it becomes sufficiently great" writes Lewis.[86]

John G. West, senior fellow at The Center for Science and Culture at the Seattle-based Discovery Institute,[87] claims that Lewis's interest

---

83. Lewis, *Essay Collection*, 29.
84. Lewis, *Essay Collection*, 28.
85. Lewis, *Essay Collection*, 25.
86. Lewis, *Discarded Image*, 223.
87. The Discovery Institute is a nonprofit organization that was founded in 1991 by Bruce Chapman to promote ideas in representative government, the free market,

in the topic of evolution is well documented, because Lewis discussed it repeatedly, although circumspectly, in his books and essays. He notes that although Lewis was interested in evolution, he also understood its cultural dominance and exhibited a certain cageyness when publicly communicating about the subject. West claims that while Lewis "was cautious about how much he criticized Darwinian evolution in public, he was equally careful to distance himself from evolution's uncritical boosters."[88] He advises readers of Lewis to untangle the distinct ways in which Lewis employed the term. West characterises the term as elastic and highly subject to interpretation:[89]

> One of the most challenging things about "evolution" is the term is so elastic, covering everything from "mere change over time" to the development of all living from one-celled organisms to man through an unguided process of natural selection on random variations. Evolution has so many different meanings, in fact, that if one doesn't pay close attention, a conversation on the topic will quickly devolve to people talking past one another.

According to West, Lewis addressed at least three different kinds of evolution in his writings: "(1) evolution as a theory of common descent; (2) evolution as a theory of unguided natural selection acting on random variations (a.k.a. Darwinism); (3) evolution as a cosmic philosophy (a.k.a.) 'evolutionism')."[90]

West summarises Lewis's stance on Darwinian evolution as follows:[91]

> Lewis did not object in principle to evolution in the first sense (common descent), although he sharply limited its application in a way that mainstream proponents of evolution would find

---

and individual liberty. The notion that the emergence of the bio-system has been intelligently designed is promoted at the Discovery Institute's Center for Science and Culture. Intelligent design refers to a scientific research program as well as to a community of scientists, philosophers, and other scholars who seek evidence of design in nature. The theory of intelligent design holds that certain features of the universe and of living things are best explained by an intelligent cause, not an undirected process such as natural selection. Unlike the classic argument from design, which attempts to promote the notion of the existence of a being-like God, intelligent design purports to be a vehicle for research into the origin and emergence of the bio-system ("Intelligent Design").

88. West, "Darwin in the Dock," 111.
89. West, "Darwin in the Dock," 112.
90. West, "Darwin in the Dock," 112–13.
91. West, "Darwin in the Dock," 113.

unacceptable. The case for Lewis as a supporter of evolution in the second sense (Darwinism) is almost non-existent. Lewis was a thoroughgoing skeptic of the creative power of unguided natural selection. As for evolution in the third sense—evolutionism—Lewis respected the poetry and grandeur of what he sometimes called the "myth" of evolution, but he certainly regarded it as untrue.

West's summation of Lewis's doubts about certain characteristics of the evolutionary metanarrative would appear to be consistent with certain views on evolution held by two of Lewis's closest friends, J. R. R. Tolkien and Owen Barfield. In a letter written by Tolkien in 1945 to his son Christopher, Tolkien writes that he doesn't view Eden as having the same historicity as the New Testament but that, nevertheless, Eden really existed. Tolkien writes that Christians "have been hustled and bustled now for some generations by the self-styled scientists, and they've sort of tucked Genesis into a lumber world of their mind as not very fashionable furniture, a bit ashamed to have it about the house."[92] He tells Christopher: "Genesis is separated by we do not know how many sad exiled generations from the Fall, but certainly there was an Eden on this very unhappy earth. We all long for it, and we are constantly glimpsing it: our whole nature at its best and least corrupted, its gentlest and most human, is still soaked with the sense of exile."[93] In his letter, Tolkien tells his son that his views have come about partly as development of his own thought and work, and partly as a result of his "contact with C. S. L."[94]

His reference to Lewis is significant, because it is consistent with what Lewis writes in a chapter titled "The Fall," in his book *The Problem of Pain*: "Many people think that this proposition [the fall] has been proved false by modern science," Lewis writes. In his view, however, this question falls within the purview of theology and philosophy, and science "has nothing to say for or against the doctrine of the Fall."[95] Lewis ends the chapter by stating that its thesis "is simply that man, as a species, spoiled himself, and that good, to us in our present state, must therefore

---

92. Tolkien, *Letters*, 109.
93. Tolkien, *Letters*, 110.
94. Tolkien, *Letters*, 109.
95. Lewis, *Problem of Pain*, 590–91. A thorough analysis of Lewis's notion of the fall is beyond the scope of this paper. For more information on Lewis's perspective on this topic, see ch. 5 in *The Problem of Pain*.

mean primarily remedial or corrective good."⁹⁶ West characterises Lewis as being cautious and cagey about his comments regarding the sufficiency of Darwinian evolution to accomplish all that it's been credited for.

Lewis's friend Owen Barfield, however, was not so cautious. His book *The Rediscovery of Meaning and Other Essays* is highly significant in that regard. In a chapter titled "The Coming Trauma of Materialism," Barfield elaborates on a wide range of viewpoints and presuppositions that were coming under intense scrutiny, some of which were having their legitimacy challenged, thereby endangering their very survival as serious intellectual and philosophical topics. In Barfield's view, ongoing questioning will present challenges to many of the underpinnings of modern society's intellectual framework. "I can only mention one or two of the many implications on which that impression is based," writes Barfield.⁹⁷ The two that he mentions are the metaphysical implications of quantum theory and "congealed Darwinism." Barfield elaborates on his doubts about Darwin's theory: "One has to imagine a twentieth-century biologist being asked to accept that the whole library of textbooks from which a man learned at school and university, from which he has himself been teaching all his life, and to which he has perhaps added an original contribution of his own, is in fact largely irrelevant," he writes. Barfield compares his imaginary evolutionary biologist to a consulting engineer who "has spent his life examining and improving a vast central heating system, and who is now asked to accept that what he was working on was really only a thermostat!"⁹⁸ Elsewhere in the chapter, Barfield states: "For the media, today no less than yesterday, to doubt the Darwinian theory is to be a flat-Earther."⁹⁹ Clearly, Barfield had come to view Darwinism as insufficient for explaining the emergence of the bio-system. It seems highly unlikely that these two close friends would not have periodically discussed their views about the capabilities attributed to Darwinian processes. Barfield's reference to flat-Earthers is instructive when considered in the context of Lewis's reticence about actively supporting Acworth.¹⁰⁰

Although Lewis considered his scientific training inadequate for a full-fledged debate on the details of modern Darwinism's capabilities, he

---

96. Lewis, *Problem of Pain*, 600.
97. Barfield, *Rediscovery of Meaning*, 38.
98. Barfield, *Rediscovery of Meaning*, 197–98.
99. Barfield, *Rediscovery of Meaning*, 196.
100. For an extensive treatment of the sufficiency/insufficiency of neo-Darwinian processes see Behe, *Darwin's Black Box* and *Edge of Evolution*.

was not reluctant to challenge its more ambitious claims. One such challenge that he had titled "Is Theology Poetry?" was read to the Oxford Socratic Club in 1945: "That grand myth which I asked you to admire a few minutes ago is not for me a hostile novelty breaking in on traditional beliefs. On the contrary, that cosmology is what I started from. Deepening distrust and final abandonment of it long preceded my conversion to Christianity," he tells the audience. Lewis leaves no doubt about his opinion on the veracity of the grand myth: "Long before I believed Theology to be true I had already decided that the popular scientific picture at any rate was false," he tells them.[101]

As mentioned in ch. 3, Lewis's pursuit of a worldview that could account for his perception of reality was a significant factor in leading him to embrace theism, which, in turn, eventually led him to become a believer in Christianity. Despite the lure that the evolutionary myth had for him and despite his admiration of its grandeur, Lewis could not ignore its lack of explanatory power and its inherent contradictions. "Christian theology," on the other hand, "can fit in science, art, morality, and the sub-Christian religions," he claims. "The scientific point of view cannot fit in any of these things, not even science itself," writes Lewis.[102]

Although Lewis considered himself ill equipped to engage in debates about alleged limits to what Darwinian processes could accomplish, clearly, he felt confident about defending his Christian worldview. In an essay titled "Dogma and the Universe" that was published in *The Guardian* newspaper in 1943, he wrote:[103]

> It is not Christianity which need fear the giant universe. It is those systems which place the whole meaning of existence in biological or social evolution on our own planet. It is the creative evolutionist, the Bergsonian[104] or Shavian,[105] or the Communist

101. Lewis, *Essay Collection*, 18–19.
102. Lewis, *Essay Collection*, 21.
103. Lewis, *God in the Dock*, 44.

104. Henri Louis Bergson (1859–1941) was a French philosopher who was highly influential in the first half of the twentieth century. His ideas influenced a broad spectrum of artistic, literary, and political movements. Initially a disciple of Spencer, he is reported to have broken with him after a careful examination of Spencer's concept of time and mechanistic positivism. In *Creative Evolution*, his best-known work, Bergson argues against both Lamarck and Darwin, urging that biological evolution is impelled by a vital impetus or *elan vital* that drives life to overcome the downward entropic drift of matter (Gunter, "Bergson").

105. This is a reference to George Bernard Shaw or to his works.

who should tremble when he looks up into the night sky. For he really is committed to a sinking ship. He really is attempting to ignore the discovered nature of things, as though by concentrating on the possible upward trend in a single planet he can make himself forget the inevitable downward trend in the universe as a whole, the trend to low temperatures and the irrevocable disorganization. For entropy is the real cosmic wave, and evolution only a momentary tellurian ripple within it.

Furthermore, Lewis claims: "In one respect, as many Christians have noticed, contemporary science has recently come into line with Christian doctrine, and parted company with the classical form of materialism. If anything emerges clearly from modern physics, it is that nature is not everlasting, the [material] universe had a beginning, and will have an end. But the great materialistic systems of the past all believed in the eternity, and thence the self-existence of matter."[106] Citing Professor Whittaker in his 1942 Riddell lecture series, Lewis writes: "It was never possible to oppose seriously the dogma of the Creation except that the world has existed from all eternity in more or less its present state. This fundamental ground for materialism has now been withdrawn." He cautions Christians, however, against leaning too heavily on this, "for scientific theories change. But at the moment it appears that the burden of proof rests, not on us, but on those who deny that nature has some cause beyond herself."[107]

Lewis communicated a similarly cautious message in a lecture that he gave at a conference for Anglican youth leaders and junior clergy in 1945: "If you know any science, it is very desirable that you should keep it up. We have to answer the current scientific attitude towards Christianity, not the attitude that scientists adopted a hundred years ago. Science is in continual change and we must try to keep abreast of it," he tells the conference attendees. Furthermore, he cautions:[108]

> For the same reason, we must be very cautious of snatching at any scientific theory which, for the moment, seems to be in our favour. We may mention such things, but we must mention them lightly, and without claiming that they are more than "interesting." Sentences beginning, "Science has now proved" should be avoided. If we try to base our apologetic on some

---

106. Lewis, *God in the Dock*, 38–39.
107. Lewis, *God in the Dock*, 39.
108. Lewis, *God in the Dock*, 92.

recent development in science, we shall usually find that just as we have put the finishing touches to our argument science has changed its mind and quietly withdrawn the theory we have been using as our foundation stone. Timeo Danaos et dona ferrentes[109] is a sound principle.

Lewis's book *Miracles* is perhaps where Lewis makes the strongest case for the Christian worldview. It is here that he presents his most extensive case for the inconsistencies within naturalism. In a chapter titled "The Cardinal Difficulty of Naturalism," Lewis writes:[110]

> If Naturalism is true, every finite thing or event must be (in principle) explicable in terms of the Total System. . . . Obviously many things will only be explained when the sciences have made further progress. But if Naturalism is to be accepted we have a right to demand that every single thing should be such that we see, in general, how it could be explained in terms of the Total System. If any one thing exists which is of such a kind that we see in advance the impossibility of ever giving it *that kind* of explanation, then Naturalism would be in ruins. . . . If any one thing makes a good claim to be on its own, to be something more than an expression of the character of Nature as a whole—then we have abandoned Naturalism. For by Naturalism we mean the doctrine that only Nature—the whole interlocked system—exists.

Lewis contends that the survival of naturalism as a viable philosophy is dependent upon nothing existing outside of the natural order. He then cites quantum mechanics as a possible threat to naturalism's viability but writes that while it would be well to notice the "threat," it's something "on which I myself will base no argument."[111] He does, however, make the argument that all possible knowledge "depends on the validity of reasoning" and that "unless human reasoning is valid no science can be true."[112] Lewis then cites Professor Haldane and argues: "Thus a strict materialism refutes itself. . . . If my mental processes are determined wholly by the motions of atoms in my brain, I have no reason to believe that my beliefs

---

109. "I fear the Greeks even when they bear gifts" (cited from Virgil, *Aeneid*, bk. 2, line 49.
110. Lewis, *Miracles*, 17–18.
111. Lewis, *Miracles*, 18.
112. Lewis, *Miracles*, 21.

are true, hence I have no reason to believe that my brains are composed of atoms."[113]

In his book *C. S. Lewis and the Crisis of a Christian*, Gregory Cootsona offers a five-point summary of Lewis's argument in *Miracles*: (1) Naturalism asserts that all that exists is part of the natural, or material, world; (2) Reason, being a part of all that is, must therefore be a component of the natural world; (3) In order for reason to discover truth, it cannot be solely based on natural, or material, cause and effect; (4) Hence, naturalists cannot fit reason into their picture; (5) Therefore, we cannot know whether naturalism is true.[114]

John West writes: "The revised 1960 edition of *Miracles* is generally recognized as presenting Lewis's most mature critique of the ability of naturalism/materialism to account for man's rational faculties. What is less noticed is the challenge Lewis's book raises for Darwinian evolution in particular." West claims that it is Darwinian natural selection and "not plain vanilla naturalism" that is the object of Lewis's attack in *Miracles*.[115]

Excerpts sourced from a wide range of books, essays, and letters representative of Lewis's extensive body of work encapsulate his perspective on the relationship between his Christian faith and modern science.[116] Clearly, Lewis considered naturalism to be inadequate to account for his perception of reality, and he found it lacking the requisite creative powers needed to explain the emergence of the bio-system. He understood that one's metaphysical views directly impact the suppositions that are brought to scientific enquiry; and he was aware that those views, as well as the presuppositions, not only highly influence the perceptions received from the scientific enquiry but also directly affect the enquiry itself, because of the manner in which the enquiry is conducted. Therefore, one's worldview is of paramount importance in any scientific endeavour. Lewis's perceptions about the natural world were framed through the lens of his Christian worldview.[117] Although he was well aware of the limitations

---

113. Lewis, *Miracles*, 22.
114. Cootsona, *C. S. Lewis*, 440.
115. West, "Darwin in the Dock," 130.
116. Lewis is often credited with developing the foundational structure for the arguments challenging the logical inconsistencies within naturalism. Alvin Plantinga has expanded on Lewis's philosophical work. See Plantinga, *Where Conflict Really Lies*.
117. Plantinga emphasizes the need for Christian philosophers to do their work from a Christian perspective when it is relevant. In Plantinga's opinion, relevancy applies "in more places than one might think" (Plantinga, "Christian Life Partly Lived,"

and finitude of human endeavours, nevertheless, since he believed the basic tenets of Christianity to be true, Lewis likely thought it beneficial to engage in scientific enquiries from a Christian perspective.

Having examined the relationship between science and Christian faith in Lewis's worldview, it is instructive to see how Lewis's worldview impacted his understanding and interpretation of literature, which is the topic of the section following.

4.5 LEWIS AND LITERATURE

As a former professor of English at Beloit College, Chad Walsh was in a unique position to assess Lewis's writings. He writes about literature's influence on Lewis from the perspective of a literary scholar. Walsh claims that the literature Lewis read influenced the formulation of his emerging worldview, because he finds evidence for that in Lewis's earliest writings. For instance, he notes that in *Spirits in Bondage*, one of Lewis's earliest engagements with poetry, there is evidence for the development of a fluctuating perception of reality and indications of an emergent philosophy. He claims that the poems indicate a drift away from hard materialism toward the notion that there are spiritual forces at work in the universe.[118]

Lewis's growing doubts about the sufficiency of materialism is supported by Corbin Carnell. He writes that there was an increasing ambivalence in *Spirits in Bondage* because God was pictured as nonexistent or cruelly aloof. He claims that the poems exhibit a preoccupation with "elements of desire and flashes of intuitive insight."[119] In Carnell's opinion, the poems reveal that the writings of G. K. Chesterton, George Macdonald, and Henri Bergson "had begun to make the grim and defiant atheism of his teens look less comprehensive and less honest than it once had." He thinks that by the time the poems were written "foundations of Lewis' atheism were begun to crack." He notes that in *Surprised by Joy*, Lewis had quizzically stated that "a young man who wishes to remain a sound atheist cannot be too careful of his reading."[120]

Notable in Lewis's developing worldview was his admiration for certain elements of the medieval period. Walsh points out that the medieval

---

80).

118. Walsh, *Literary Legacy*, 38–39.
119. Carnell, *Bright Shadow of Reality*, 51.
120. Carnell, *Bright Shadow of Reality*, 53.

model of the universe had unique appeal for Lewis. Even though Lewis didn't claim literal truth for the medieval model, he found it appealing and satisfying to his rich sense of imagination, writes Walsh.[121] This sentiment is evidenced in Lewis's highly esteemed academic work *English Literature in the Sixteenth Century (Excluding Drama)*, in which he writes: "By reducing Nature to her mathematical elements it substituted a mechanical for a genial or animalistic conception of the universe. The world was emptied, first of her indwelling spirits, then of her occult sympathies and antipathies, finally of her colours, smells and tastes." The result of this was the "loss of the old mystical imagination," writes Lewis.[122] Research done by Oxford University's Michael Ward has shed additional light on the appeal that the medieval model had for Lewis.

Ward has written that Lewis modeled the *Chronicles of Narnia* series on the medieval model of the universe. He claims that there is strong evidence that Lewis constructed the series by featuring specific elements of medieval cosmology in each of the Narnia chronicles. The medieval Ptolemaic cosmological model is illustrated in the graphic below.[123]

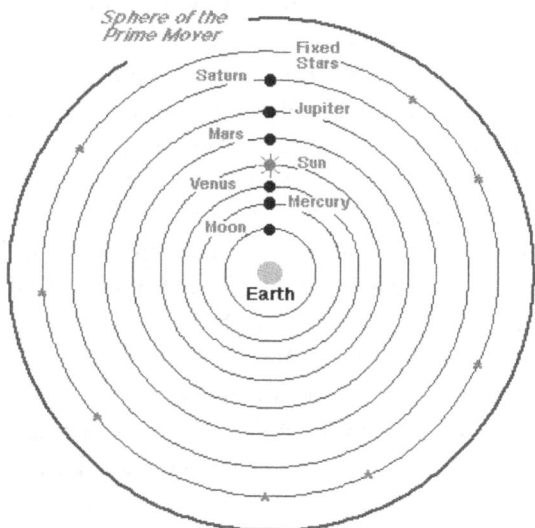

Aristotle's Universe

---

121. Walsh, *Literary Legacy*, 194.

122. Lewis, *English Literature*, 3–4.

123. Graphic courtesy of Dr. Eric Blackman. A pictorial representation of the medieval notion of a seven heavens universe may be viewed in Ward, *Planet Narnia*, and on the official website of the book (Ward, "Seven Heavens").

The medieval cosmological model is based on Ptolemaic astronomy and portrays the moon, Mercury, Venus, the sun, Mars, Jupiter, and Saturn as circling the earth. Ward argues that Lewis arranged his Narnia series within the rubric of the medieval perception of the world. He lays out the evidence for his arguments in two books, *Planet Narnia* and *The Narnia Code*. His thesis represents extensive research, and his arguments are convincing. Ward claims that each of the seven Narnia Chronicles portrays unique characteristics or qualities associated with a particular planet. He claims that the chronicle of *The Lion, the Witch and the Wardrobe* features characteristics associated with Jupiter, that *Prince Caspian* features the qualities traditionally associated with Mars, that *The Horse and His Boy* exhibits qualities associated with Mercury, and so on.[124] Since Lewis was a professor of medieval literature, it is not surprising that the medieval planetary configuration would have played a significant role in how he formulated the Narnia Chronicles. Ward's thesis has gained significant support among Lewis scholars.

In *Christianity Today*, John Wilson describes *Planet Narnia* as a "feat of scholarly detective work that will absorb your attention from start to finish" and that "proposes a heretofore unnoticed structure that unifies the Chronicles of Narnia, based on Lewis's lifelong engagement with medieval astrology."[125] And in a column titled "Welcome to the Real Narnia: The Hidden Medieval Message at the Heart of C. S. Lewis's Classic Chronicles," N. T. Wright writes that although Lewis's book *The Discarded Image* offers a "full-on introduction to the medieval worldview," Wright credits Ward for expounding "the narrative and meaning of each book to show, in outline and detail, how the story in general, and the characterisation of Aslan in particular, fit with the atmosphere of the relevant planet as Lewis has elsewhere expounded it."[126]

There is also credible opposition to Ward's thesis, however. Professor of English Devin Brown[127] writes that although he enjoyed reading Ward's thesis, he remains unconvinced. He argues that "the planet-related imagery does not stay rooted in its 'home' book, but appears scattered randomly in all seven *Chronicles*." He claims that it is impossible for him to believe that Lewis consciously planned for each book to be associated

124. Ward, *Planet Narnia* and *The Narnia Code*.
125. J. Wilson, "Short Reviews."
126. N. Wright, "Welcome to Narnia."
127. Brown is a Lilly scholar and professor of English at Asbury College where, among other duties, he teaches a class on Lewis.

with a distinct planet because of this random scattering. Furthermore, he writes, "if this was Lewis's goal, then he fell far short of achieving it because for every aspect that fits Ward's scheme, we can find one that does not."[128]

In his book *C. S. Lewis: Eccentric Genius, Reluctant Prophet*, which was strategically published in 2013, the fiftieth anniversary of Lewis's death, Alister McGrath offers perhaps the most extensive commentary on Ward's thesis. He makes reference to an Elizabethan classic, Edmund Spencer's *Faerie Queen*, and addresses the notion that Lewis may have created his own work to parallel that of Spencer. McGrath writes:[129]

> Lewis's critics and interpreters have devoted much attention to decoding the significance of the seven Narnia novels. Of the many debates, the most interestingis this: why are there seven models? Speculation has been intense. . . . Perhaps it is an allusion to the seven sacraments? Possibly—but Lewis was an Anglican, not a Catholic, and recognized only two sacraments. Or perhaps there is an allusion to theseven deadly sins? Possibly—but any attempt to assign the novels to individual sins, such as pride and lust, seems hopelessly forced and unnatural. For example, which of the Narnia Chronicles majors on gluttony? Amidst the wreckage of these implausible suggestions, an alternative has recently emerged—that Lewis was shaped by what the great English seventh-century poet, John Donne called "the Heptarchy, the seven kingdoms of the seven planets." And amazingly, this one seems to work.
>
> The idea was first put forward by Oxford Lewis scholar Michael Ward in 2008. Noting the importance that Lewis assigns to the seven planets in his studies of medieval literature, Ward suggests that the Narnia novels reflect and embody the thematic characteristics associated in the "discarded" medieval worldview with the seven planets. In the pre-Copernican worldview, which dominated the Middle Ages, Earth was understood to be stationery; the seven "planets" revolved around Earth. These medieval planets were the Sun, the Moon, Mercury, Venus, Mars, Jupiter and Saturn. Lewis does not include Uranus, Neptune and Pluto, since they were only discovered in the eighteenth, nineteenth centuries, respectively. . . . Ward is not suggesting that Lewis reverts to a pre-Copernican cosmology, nor that he endorses the arcane world of astrology. His point is

---

128. D. Brown, "Planet Narnia Spin."
129. McGrath, *C. S. Lewis*, 297–99.

much more subtle, and has enormous imaginative potential. . . . Lewis regarded the seven planets as being part of a poetically rich and imaginatively satisfying symbolic system. Lewis therefore took the imaginative and emotive characteristics which the Middle Ages associated with each of the planets, and attached these to each of the seven novels.

McGrath's support of Ward's thesis is especially noteworthy in light of McGrath's recent work on Lewis's biography. Ward describes the imaginative characteristics that the Middle Ages had ascribed to the seven planets and lays out the connection of each of Lewis's novels to the respective planets as follows:

- *The Lion, the Witch and the Wardrobe*: Jupiter
- *Prince Caspian*: Mars
- *The Voyage of the Dawn Treader*: the sun
- *The Silver Chair*: the moon
- *The Horse and His Boy*: Mercury
- *The Magician's Nephew*: Venus
- *The Last Battle*: Saturn

Although there is not unanimous support for Ward's notion among Lewis scholars, his thesis does not appear to be implausible. Whatever merit there exists for the case as presented by Ward, there is no doubt that the medieval model held a strong appeal for Lewis. Furthermore, Lewis's references to characteristics within the medieval model are extant throughout the Narnia chronicles. To what extent individual chronicles are focused on any one planet is not germane to this study. What is relevant, however, is the manner by which literature, including elements within medieval literature, impacted Lewis's worldview and his apologetic method.

Lewis had long realized the limits inherent within reason for a person to come to believe the truth claims of the Christian faith. He felt that reason had been instrumental in leading him to embrace theism; he considered himself to have come to that position through the process of induction. A reading of the original draft of his spiritual biography shows that he had considered himself to be an empirical theist, having come to that position through "a process which was largely empirical."[130]

---

130. Lewis, *Image and Imagination*, 13.

As mentioned in chapter 3, he was not converted to Christianity until many months later, at which point he mentions in a subsequent letter to Arthur Greeves that the long talk with Dyson and Tolkien had helped him to realize the meaning of the incarnation. This, in turn, had led him to come to believe that Jesus was the Son of God.[131] Lewis's comments to Greeves would seem to indicate that the imaginative qualities within the literature with which he was familiar helped him to grasp the significance of Jesus's birth, death, and resurrection, which enabled him to embrace the Christian faith.

This is consistent with the account of Lewis's conversion as described by his former pupil and long-time friend Dom Bede Griffiths, who writes that both he and Lewis "came to religion by way of literature" and that even before Lewis's conversion to theism, they were "beginning to discover together the religious values in literature."[132] Griffiths claims that "the turning point in Lewis's conversion had been when his friends Dyson and Tolkien had convinced him that in Christ the myth had become history" and that "the relation between myth and history was the key to Lewis's conversion to Christianity and in a sense to his whole life." Griffiths refers to Lewis's newly gained insight as an "awakening" and considers it to having been a consequence of Lewis having "discovered Siegfried and the Twilight of the Gods, and the world of Norse mythology [which] took possession of his imagination." He records that prior to Lewis's conversion to Christianity, they had "read literature together" and that they "both began to discover more and more of the religious background" of what they were reading.[133] He recalls how Lewis's reading of William Langland's poem[134] *The Vision*

---

131. Lewis, *Collected Letters*, 1:974.

132. Griffiths, "Adventure of Faith," 15.

133. Griffiths, "Adventure of Faith," 16.

134. "*The Vision of Piers Plowman* is a Middle English alliterative poem from the late fourteenth century, attributed to a man named William Langland from the South West Midlands area of England. . . . It is largely an allegorical poem that follows a narrator named Will on his quest for salvation," similar to the form of allegorical narrative in *The Pilgrim's Progress*. "Langland frames the poem as a series of dream visions . . . while he sleeps. It is also a satire of contemporary religious corruption. . . . "There is some evidence to suggest that Langland created" the poem because he was troubled by some of the civil discord in society. . . .

"Will begins to wonder how people can best live 'in the world' and yet still attain eternal salvation. . . .

"Will encounters a plowman named Piers, who becomes for Will a spiritual model: Will even thinks at one point that Jesus and Piers are one and the same. After Will and Piers travel together for some time, Will awakensand, after he falls asleep again,

Concerning Piers Plowman, with Piers Plowman as a figure of Christ, had moved him. Griffiths writes: "Gradually this Christian mythology, as we both would have called it, began to impress us more and more, and the idea that it might after all be true began to dawn on us." He recalls that slowly, progressively, he and Lewis were both becoming theists. "But for both of us the passage from theism to Christianity had to be made, and it was here that Lewis's sense of the value of meaning helped him so much. He was able to reconcile his imagination and reason in Christian faith," Griffiths writes. He claims that the subtitle to Lewis's book *Pilgrim's Regress*, which was written shortly after Lewis's conversion, and is appropriately subtitled *An Allegorical Apology for Christianity, Reason and Romanticism*, "expresses exactly how we both came to accept the Christian faith."[135] Griffiths thinks that Lewis had come to realize that "the meeting of myth and history in the Incarnation was the turning point in the history of religion."[136] He claims that Lewis viewed the incarnation as a turning point in the *history of religion*. It seems likely, however, that Lewis also understood the birth of Christ as a turning point in the course of *human history*. Certainly, his understanding of its meaning represented a personal turning point for Lewis. And it was his recognition of the ability of myth in literary works to convey meaning that enabled him to discern the revelatory power of the incarnation, which, in turn, is highly indicative of how literature influenced his perception of reality. In Griffiths's view, he and Lewis had come to embrace theism at approximately the same time. He writes that for both of them, "the passage from theism to Christianity had to be made."[137] Even though Lewis's breadth and depth of knowledge of literature were superior to his own,[138] nevertheless, Griffiths offers important insights into the process by which Lewis came to believe the truth claims of the Christian faith.

---

continues his journey without the plowman, though Piers is never far from his mind.

"In the most sublime poetry of the English Middle Ages, Langland celebrates the salvation won for humankind by Jesus's death and resurrection, but the poem endswith a disturbing vision of a fallen world," which, for some readers, implies a dark present ("About *Piers Plowman*"). See also Boulay, *Beyond the Darkness*.

135. Griffiths, "Adventure of Faith," 17.
136. Griffiths, "Adventure of Faith," 23.
137. Griffiths, "Adventure of Faith," 17.
138. Commenting on Lewis's capacious memory many years later, Griffiths observes: "Lewis had the most wonderful, accurate, and perceptive mind. They say, and I believe it's true, he could quote from almost any poet in English if you simply opened the quotation. If someone read out a line of poetry, he'd say 'Yes, I've got it' and simply continue the poem. It was a real education to be with him" (Griffiths, *Human Search*, 29).

As mentioned, Lewis credits imagination's capacity for giving meaning to events. Glenn Giokaris contends that Lewis eventually realized that reason also has an impact on how one interprets imaginative events:[139]

> The conversion of C. S. Lewis had been an intellectual pilgrimage. It was a long road along which he had been progressively convinced of the truth of Christianity. The final push had come from the realization that there was reason in imagination; that the great literary themes themselves constituted a rational testimony to the myth of truth. However, for Lewis, the journey did not stop with his attainment of Christianity.
>
> Instead, he used his amazing literary talents to explain what he had found. The literary work most closely related to his journey to Christianity is told through *The Pilgrim's Regress* written in 1933.

Lewis's description of his conversion in *Surprised by Joy* reveals considerable information, but several authors have opined that Lewis intentionally omitted important elements from his biography. In fact, Lewis's friend, biographer, and occasional member of the Inklings George Sayer writes that fellow Inkling member Dr. Humphrey Havard had titled the Lewis biography *Surprised by Joy* as *Suppressed by Jack*, because he thought that Lewis had purposely omitted significant elements from his biography. Sayer thinks that "one would have to know him very well to have penetrated the smoke screen" that Lewis had created.[140] Owen Barfield has also written about Lewis's reluctance to discuss the details of his conversion experience. In his book titled *Owen Barfield on C. S. Lewis*, he recounts a conversation during which he had asked Lewis to expand on that experience, to which Lewis had responded that he couldn't bear to talk about it. Barfield recalls that Lewis had responded to his query with more emotion than he had ever heard him express.[141]

Griffiths's portrayal of Lewis's conversion experience offers significant insight into the breakthrough that Lewis had experienced. A thorough analysis of Griffiths's depiction of the process by which Lewis made the connection between the meaning of myth in literature and its application to the incarnation may have significant potential, because it may be beneficial for contemporary Christian apologetics. In light of the anti-supernatural drift within Western Christianity, in which the notion

---

139. Giokaris, "Philosophical Journey."
140. Sayer, *Jack*, 328.
141. Barfield, *Owen Barfield*, 111.

of Jesus as Son of God is frequently challenged, Christian apologists may well find it productive to fully examine Griffiths's analysis. As we shall see in a subsequent chapter, equally apropos to contemporary apologetics is Lewis's reference to the "Hound of Heaven" in matters of faith.

Griffiths and Lewis have both emphasized the power of myth in enabling Lewis to comprehend the meaning within the incarnation, the result of which was that Lewis ultimately came to embrace Christianity. In his book *The Intellectual World of C. S. Lewis*, which is a later supplement to his Lewis biography, Alister McGrath writes that for Lewis, "a myth weaves together truth and meaning, engaging with both our reason and imagination." His book offers a brief summary of Lewis's notion of the core elements within myths. He claims that "Lewis's analysis of the limits of reason makes it clear that we need more than rational arguments to challenge the spirit of the age" and that Lewis's apologetics can be seen as "commending and offering counter-narrations and counter-arguments against the naturalism and secularism of our age."[142] McGrath credits Lewis's study of English literature for "becoming increasingly aware of the importance of myth, both in generating imaginative appeal and providing a narrative framework for making sense of things, and for holding a more complex vision of reality together as a coherent whole."[143]

In his book *An Experiment in Criticism*, Lewis gives a lengthy description of six core elements in order to explain what he means by myth.[144] The elements may be summarised as follows:[145]

142. McGrath, *Intellectual World*, 73.

143. McGrath, *Intellectual World*, 60.

144. Wheaton College professor of English Wayne Martindale explains that Lewis came to believe that the gospel narrative was true through his understanding of the power of myth. Through "imaginatively experiencing" the myth-like qualities of the incarnation, he came to belief in Jesus as the Son of God. Martindale explains Lewis's experiential breakthrough this way: "Lewis uses 'myth' to mean a story treating the 'permanent and inevitable,' those elements which are always part of a human experience. The greatest truths, like those about God or universal truths about humanity, are not a part of our concrete experience, so we understand them and speak of them as an abstraction. In myth, however, we experience imaginatively, in the concreteness of story, something which would be abstract if translated out. For example, we can't experience love and think reflectively on love at the same time. We either have a single experience in lived reality, or we step back from the experience to think about it; the thought we have in stepping back is abstraction. But when we read a story, like the Gospel account of the Incarnation or even a fictional story which is a shadow of it, we come closest to having an (imaginative) experience which 'incarnates' the abstraction 'God is love'" (Martindale, "Myth," 288).

145. Lewis, *Experiment in Criticism*, 43–44.

- Myth is an extra-literary phenomenon, in that its distinct identity lies in the mythical experience it evokes in its readers.

- Myths have very little to do with suspense or surprise but rather introduce us to a permanent object of contemplation—more like a thing than a narration—which works upon us like a peculiar flavor or quality.

- Myths focus on characters who seem distant to us, like shapes moving in another world, yet whose movements are seen to have a profound relevance to our lives.

- Myth is fantastic, dealing with "impossibles" and "preternaturals."

- Myth allows its readers access to experiences that may be sad or joyful but always grave and never comic.

- Myths have the capacity to inspire awe, on account of their numinous qualities.

Lewis's description of his notion of myths offers important insight into the significance that myths held for him. The feeling that "Northerness" held for him is well represented in this description, as is the sense of awe that has been expressed in many of his writings. His description of myths attests to the importance that literature, especially the meaning of myth in literature, held for Lewis.

Corbin Carnell claims that literature and philosophy played seminal roles in the formulation of Lewis's worldview. He sees Lewis as a Platonist, Aristotelian, and Thomist. Lewis's tough-minded theology finds its "logical sanctions" in "Aristotelian analyses," he writes.[146] Carnell thinks that Lewis's post-conversion thought, however, was most influenced by Macdonald and Williams. From Carnell's perspective, Lewis's worldview was highly influenced by his philosophical training, as well as his literary expertise, of which medieval literature was his specialty.[147]

Not only did Lewis find literature to be enabling in coming to understand and believe the truth claims of Christianity, but he also saw literature as a vehicle that can be employed for advancing the Christian message and for disseminating the Christian worldview. In a lecture to Anglican clergy in 1945, he spoke about the benefits of writing books in which the author's Christianity remains latent. Rather than writing

---

146. Carnell, *Bright Shadow of Reality*, 71.
147. Carnell, *Bright Shadow of Reality*, 71–72.

"little books on Christianity," he urged the authors in attendance to write books on other topics, books in which a Christian worldview is implicit. "It is not the books written in direct defence of Materialism that makes the modern man a materialist; it is the materialistic assumptions in all the other books," he tells his audience.[148] Clearly, Lewis understood the influence that literature, if used effectively, could have for disseminating crucial elements of the Christian worldview.

The breadth of Lewis's literary knowledge[149] was often manifest in his speaking and writing. In a sermon at St. Jude on the Hill Church in London, he demonstrated his considerable range of literary expertise by expounding on the literary background (or lack thereof) of Jesus's audiences. Jesus's listeners were totally oblivious to the parallels that his death and resurrection had within the nature religions expressed in the large body of literature, he tells the congregants. "Or to put it another way, why was it that the only case of the 'dying God' which might conceivably have been historical occurred among a people . . . who had not got any trace of this nature religion, and indeed seem to know nothing about it," he asks rhetorically. His observations had led him to realize how extensive the notion of a dying god had been among ancient cultures. In his opinion, the lack of awareness among Jesus's audiences was unique among the various cultural settings. "When I first, after childhood, read the Gospels, I was full of that stuff about the dying God," Lewis tells the congregation at St. Jude.[150] From his perspective, this lack of awareness about the dying god tradition on the part of Jesus's audiences corroborates the notion that the account of Jesus's death and resurrection should be understood as a true narrative of an actual event, rather than as a myth. In Lewis's view, the cultural setting in early New Testament times was not conducive for the development of a dying God mythology, and therefore, the Gospels are best understood as narratives of actual events. Lewis's 1945 message to Anglican clergy and his sermon at St. Jude's offer valuable insight into the breadth and depth of his knowledge about the various periods of literature and to literature's role in bringing him to Christian faith.

Literature had a critical impact on Lewis throughout his life. It is not an exaggeration to say that Lewis's world was a world of literature.[151] As

148. Lewis, *God in the Dock*, 93.

149. For a broad overview of Lewis and literature, see Lewis, *Image and Imagination*, edited by Walter Hooper.

150. Lewis, *Essay Collection*, 5–6.

151. Hope College professor of English Peter Schakel comments on Lewis's love

discussed in the previous chapter, he had held a fascination for the world of literature since childhood. For Lewis, the world of literature provided much more than information; it also gave him the ability to understand matters that were otherwise seemingly inscrutable. As manifested within the large body of literature that he has written, as well as within the works of Lewis scholars, literature had an enormous influence in shaping his life. It had a profound influence in his conversion to Christianity, his academic life, his apologetic method, and the formulation and proclamation of his worldview.

This worldview also influenced the manner in which he interacted with his surrounding culture, which is the topic of the following section.

4.6 LEWIS AND CULTURE

The relationship between the Christian faith and its surrounding culture has been the subject of much debate throughout the history of Christianity. Lewis's relationship with his cultural environs was multifaceted; examining the manner in which his worldview affected his relationship with his surrounding culture is best done within a structural framework. For this purpose, the underlying structure within Richard Niebuhr's book *Christ and Culture*, which was first published in 1951, would seem to be an ideal framework within which to structure this enquiry. Niebuhr's book has become a classic. It is still being used as a textbook in many seminaries and is an oft-quoted book. In this classic work, Niebuhr lists

---

of books in his book *Imagination and the Arts in C. S. Lewis*. Schakel writes: "Lewis grew up surrounded by books. Both of his parents were educated people and were great readers. In *Surprised by Joy* Lewis calls himself the product of endless books. . . . Lewis learned to read books early in his life, and already as a child he was a voracious reader" (Schakel, *Imagination and the Arts*, 23). "The love of books Lewis displayed in his life is conveyed within his stories, with attention given to the physical qualities of books as well as to their subject matter. Books are referred to frequently in the Chronicles of Narnia. . . . In the magician's house on the Island of Voices, Lucy must go to a large room lined from floor to ceiling with books" (Schakel, *Imagination and the Arts*, 26–27).

This is reminiscent of Lewis's description of his parents' capacious library in *Surprised by Joy*: "My father bought all the books he read and never got rid of any of them. There were books in the study,books in the drawing room, books in the cloak room, books (two deep) in the great bookcase on the landing, books in a bedroom, books piled as high as my shoulder in the cistern attic, books of all kinds reflecting every transient stage of my parents' interest, books readable and unreadable, books suitable fora child and books most emphatically not" (Lewis, *Surprised by Joy*, 10).

five models or categories to describe the manner in which Christians have interacted with their cultural settings. Because culture, like literature, was such an important element in Lewis's apologetics, framing this subject with Niebuhr's structural framework as background serves as a good contour for examining this subject.

In his forward to the 2001 edition of Niebuhr's *Christ and Culture*, University of Chicago's Distinguished Service Professor Emeritus Martin Marty writes that "like most classics," Niebuhr's book "is not an easy work."[152] He opines that although "almost no one" will fit perfectly within any one of the five categories, in his opinion, analysing an author's work with the Niebuhr classic as a backdrop enhances one's understanding of the author's interaction with the culture.[153]

James Gustafson at Yale University's Divinity School writes that Niebuhr's types or categories should be viewed as "heuristic devices to enable readers to understand materials and issues to which they refer."[154] In his preface to the 2001 edition, he recommends that the book should be viewed "as an ideal-typical study of theological ethical ideas drawn from the history of Christian thought."[155] Gustafson cautions against using ideal types strictly as "explanatory devices." He claims that "typologies are heuristic devices; they should help the reader to understand," rather than to explain "structures on which they are brought to bear."[156] Gustafson is aware of the criticism that claims that the inner structure of Niebuhr's book is tilted toward the *Christ Transforming Culture* category and admits to the "plausibility" of Niebuhr's having been drawn to the fifth category, the "transformationist or conversionist type."[157] In his opinion, "the comparative function of the typology in *Christ and Culture* forces any engaged and thoughtful reader to consider the ideal-typical

---

152. Marty, "Forward," xix.
153. Marty, "Forward," xviii.
154. Gustafson, "Preface," xxvi.
155. Gustafson, "Preface," xxxiv.
156. Gustafson, "Preface," xxxi.
157. Gustafson, "Preface," xxxiii. Bruce Guenther mentions that the inner structure of Niebuhr's *Christ and Culture* taxonomy is perceived by some as having been written in a way that favours the fifth category, Christ Transforming Culture (Guenther, "Enduring Problem"). Guenther is a professor of church history at Trinity Western University in British Columbia, Canada.

options in light of each other and ponder the implications of a choice between them."¹⁵⁸

Marty's and Gustafson's recommendations are confirmed in Niebuhr's introduction to the 2001 edition. Niebuhr writes that it is important to be "kept in mind" that "a type is a mental construct to which no individual wholly conforms." He cautions that "it must be used, therefore, only as a means toward understanding the individual and not as a statement of necessary connections."¹⁵⁹

Niebuhr advises against using more than one list of classifications. He recommends that one achieves greater clarity by analysing an author through the lens of a single ideal-typical set of categories. Applying this method in exclusivity would seem to correspond perfectly with Niebuhr's purpose for writing the book. He writes that "these mental constructs, if they are to be useful toward understanding, must be of one sort . . . only one set can be chosen at a time to furnish material for the mental model." He opines that "only confusion results if these categories are mixed."¹⁶⁰ It is with this intent that the Niebuhr classic will be employed; the purpose for engaging it is to utilize the ideal-typical options for providing a structural basis for this enquiry, in order to gain a better understanding of the cultural influences on Lewis's methodology.

Absent any comments about the Niebuhr taxonomy in Lewis's writings, one is left with attempting to discern evidence for characteristics associated with Niebuhr's five models in Lewis's writings without the added advantage of any direct reference to Niebuhr from Lewis himself. Despite the lack of any commentary from Lewis regarding Niebuhr's typology, attempting to assess how Lewis engaged with the culture in which he found himself and how it influenced his apologetic method, viewing it through the Niebuhr lens as part of the process, would seem to be beneficial. Furthermore, judging from Marty's and Gustafson's commentaries regarding the Niebuhr classic, as well as from what Niebuhr has written in his introduction, engaging the book in this fashion is one of its intended functions.

The respective categories within Niebuhr's five-model framework may be summarised as follows:

---

158. Gustafson, "Preface," xxxiii.
159. H. Niebuhr, *Christ and Culture*, xxxviii.
160. H. Niebuhr, *Christ and Culture*, xxxviii.

1. Christ against Culture: the consequence of Christian communities working within this model often results in a withdrawal or separation from their surrounding society.
2. Christ of Culture: this category features Christ as an inspirational standard or model.
3. Christ above Culture: this model aspires to a symmetry between Christianity and culture.
4. Christ and Culture in Paradox: this model implies an enduring tension between Christianity and culture.
5. Christ the Transformer of Culture: an optimistic view of Christianity's potential for cultural renewal is the predominant motif in this model.

Upon reflection, the Niebuhr taxonomy leads one to conclude that whereas several of his five categories or types may be applicable to Lewis, one of Niebuhr's types seems to apply more consistently than any one other type. Judging from Lewis's statements, the "Christ against Culture" type or model would appear to have limited appeal for him. Groups associated with this type are frequently given to withdraw from their cultural environs. Lewis expressed some scepticism upon hearing that three of his friends were attempting to organize their own mini commune. In a letter to Arthur Greeves, Lewis writes: "Their aim is, as far as possible, to use nothing which is a product of the factory system, or of modern industry in general; for they think those things so iniquitous that everyone is more or less partner to a crime in using them. . . . Indeed, whether the whole thing is folly or not, I haven't made up my mind."[161] He did, however, demonstrate a genuine affection and appreciation for members of established religious orders both within and outside of his own denomination, the Anglican Church. Walter Hooper writes that Lewis corresponded regularly with Sister Penelope CSMV, a member of the Anglican Church's Convent of the Community of St. Mary. Lewis referred to her as his "elder sister in the Faith."[162] Father Walter Frederick Adams was another member of an Anglican religious order with whom Lewis had regular contact. Lyle Dorsett claims that Lewis considered Adams to be his spiritual director and held weekly meetings with him.[163]

161. Lewis, *Collected Letters*, 1:908.
162 Lewis, *Collected Letters*, 2:1058.
163. Dorsett, *Seeking the Secret Place*, 87.

"For nearly twelve years Lewis walked the short trek from his rooms at Magdalen College, Oxford, to the adjacent village of Cowley, where the Cowley Fathers lived and ministered," he writes.[164] Lewis also carried on a lifelong correspondence with his former pupil and long-time friend Dom Bede Griffiths, who eventually became a Catholic monk within the Benedictine order. Although Griffiths and Lewis frequently clashed over philosophical and theological matters, Lewis appears to have been generally supportive of Griffiths's decision to dedicate himself to the Catholic monastic order in which he had chosen to become a member.[165] While Lewis valued the unique contributions of the various Christian religious orders, he understood that a Christian's role for the majority of believers was to work and live within and among their respective cultural communities. It is instructive to note that Niebuhr identifies monastic institutions as practitioners of societal withdrawal, and it is therefore difficult to imagine Lewis having a strong affinity for Niebuhr's first category. Ironically, Niebuhr credits monasticism for having been responsible for conserving and transmitting cultural tradition and for having trained not only many of the ecclesiastical leaders within their society but also the political leaders who governed their cultural institutions.[166]

General support for the application of Niebuhr's second category, "Christ of Culture," in which Jesus becomes the embodiment of a desired culture, is also difficult to ascertain from Lewis's writings. Niebuhr uses the example of Thomas Jefferson as someone who personified the "Christ of Culture" type. He quotes Jefferson as having declared himself a Christian "'in the only sense in which he [Jesus Christ] wished any one to be,' but he made that declaration after he had carefully excerpted from the New Testament the sayings of Jesus which commended themselves to him." Niebuhr continues:[167]

> The philosophers, statesmen, reformers, poets and novelists who claim Christ with Jefferson all repeat the same theme: Jesus Christ is the great enlightener, the great teacher, the one who directs all men in culture to the attainment of wisdom, moral perfection and peace. Sometimes he is hailed as the great utilitarian, sometimes the great idealist, sometimes as the man of reason, sometimes as the man of sentiment. But whatever the

164. Dorsett, *Seeking the Secret Place*, 92.
165. Lindskoog, "Dom Bede Griffiths."
166. H. Niebuhr, *Christ and Culture*, 67.
167. H. Niebuhr, *Christ and Culture*, 91–92.

categories are by means of which he is understood, the things for which he stands are fundamentally the same—a peaceful, cooperative society achieved by training.

Niebuhr's characterisation of the "Christ of Culture" category stands in sharp contrast to Lewis's oft-quoted trilemma as stated in his book *Mere Christianity*:[168]

> I am trying here to prevent anyone saying the really foolish thing that people often say about Him: "I'm ready to accept Jesus as a great moral teacher, but I don't accept His claim to be God." That is the one thing we must not say. A man who is merely a man and said the sort of things Jesus said would not be a great moral teacher. He would either be a lunatic—on a level of a man who says he is a poached egg—or else he would be the Devil of Hell. You must make your choice. Either this man was, and is, the Son of God: or else a madman or something worse. You can shut him up for a fool, you can spit at Him and kill Him as a demon; or you can fall at his feet and call Him Lord and God. But let us not come with any patronising nonsense about His being a great human teacher. He has not left that open to us. He did not intend to.

It is difficult to accommodate the Lewis trilemma within the "Christ of Culture" characterisation as portrayed by Niebuhr. Elements of the "Christ of Culture" model are somewhat characteristic of some of the views held by Lewis's friend Dom Bede Griffiths with whom Lewis carried on a lifelong dialogue. In Griffiths's view, Christianity had "developed in a westerly direction, taking on an ever more western character of thought and expression."[169] He thought that in order for the Christian faith to "penetrate deeply into the East," and to "realize its full stature as a genuine Catholicism, that is, as a universal religion of mankind," it would have to discover a correspondingly eastern form and expression.[170] Although Lewis and Griffiths were friends, they frequently clashed on philosophical and religious matters. In an April 1947 letter to Griffiths, Lewis writes that although before they became believers, he, like Griffiths, had come to the conclusion that Christianity or some form of pantheism were the only real options for one's perception of reality, he now believes that "refined, philosophical eastern Pantheism is far further from the true

---

168. Lewis, *Mere Christianity*, 52.
169. Griffiths, *Golden String*, 154.
170. Griffiths, *Golden String*, 155.

Faith than the semi barbarous pagan religions." Furthermore, continues Lewis:[171]

> I am inclined to think that Paganism is the primitive revealed truth corrupted by devils and that Hinduism is neither of divine or diabolical origin but profoundly and hopelessly natural: i.e. it displays the trend of the speculative intellect *sibi relictus*[172]—the line it will always follow when it escapes savagery and does not receive Grace. Hence such parallel systems as Stoicism and Hegelianism. The importance of the Jews, the absolute rightness of the claim made from them in the O.T. becomes clearer every day. But also, there is a penumbra: the almost miraculous avoidance of the Pantheistic swamp by Plato and (still more) by Aristotle. I no longer want to read Eastern books: except good nonreligious philosophers like Confucius.

What Griffiths had expressed appears to represent elements of the "Christ of Culture" category. Lewis evidently did not share Griffiths's views that Christianity should acquire some unique characteristics appropriate to the Eastern cultural framework.[173] In a later letter to Griffiths,

---

171. Lewis, *Collected Letters*, 2:770–71.

172. Latin, "left to itself."

173. Reflecting on his own spiritual journey in an autobiography first published some thirty years after Lewis's death, Griffiths comments on his differences with Lewis: "But I always felt that his Christianity was too limited. For instance, and this is a very simple thing: He never accepted criticism of the New Testament. He had an almost naïve view of the way the gospels were composed. I felt that was a real limitation. I thought that in becoming a Catholic I'd have become much more narrow, but actually it led me on the way to a broader interpretation. So, I feel less near to Lewis now than I did in the early years," he writes (Griffiths, *Human Search*, 31).

Griffiths expands on his differences with Lewis in his contribution to the book titled *C. S. Lewis at the Breakfast Table and other Reminiscences*, edited by James Como: "The question is whether in becoming a Christian Lewis reached the fulfillment of mystical experience. I think that he would have replied in the negative. There is no doubt that he had a profound kind of mystical intuition, which gave him such an extraordinary insight into the mysteries of the Christian faith, and there are times, especially in the *Letters to Malcolm*, when he comes near to a genuine mystical insight. But on the whole, he was so much on his guard against any kind of pantheism and so much inclined, as he confessed, to go as near to dualism as possible that he generally stops short of mysticism. Perhaps his very emphasis on the person of God and the Incarnation made it difficult for him to go beyond 'personality' and experience the presence of God beyond all images and concepts, which is characteristic of mystical experience. . . . I think that he regarded mystical experience as a rare event to which the ordinary Christian (with whom he would have classed himself) need not aspire. I think Lewis's understanding of the place of mystical experience in religious life and

sent in September 1947, Lewis expressed a cautionary note about Eastern pantheism's notion of union with the divine:[174]

> I even feel that the kind of union (with God) wh. they [pantheists] are seeking is precisely the opposite to that which He really intends for us. We all existed potentially in Him and in that sense were not other than He. . . . Thus the whole Indian aim seems to me to be backward toward a unity which God deliberately rejected and not onward to the true one. If mere unity (as opposed to unison) is the aim all Creation seems otiose.[175] As for the Chinese, . . . the transition to truth seems much easier: for Confucius ends up saying "This is the law, but I don't know anyone who has kept it." Doesn't that canal us straight into St. Paul?

Evidently Lewis did not share certain elements of what appears to be Griffiths's version of the "Christ of Culture" notion. Clearly, he did not agree that Christianity needed to be subjected to a major transformation in order to formulate a suitable expression to accommodate the Eastern pantheistic cultural mindset, of which the pantheistic notion of a unique union with the divine is a major component. In fact, as he had mentioned in his April letter to Griffiths, Lewis was then restricting his reading of Eastern books to those of "good philosophers like Confucius."[176]

Although Lewis was justifiably concerned that Griffiths was manifesting elements of syncretism in his beliefs, eventually, in partnership with a Cistercian monk, Griffiths was successful in obtaining Vatican approval for establishing a monastery in India. He went on to author a number of books on Christianity and spirituality and regularly participated in lecture tours throughout Europe and the United States.[177] The excerpts cited above are not to be understood as representative of Griffiths's beliefs but as manifestations of Lewis's dedication to preserve what he considered to be the truth of the Christian faith and as examples of his efforts to defend his notion of objective reality as represented by his Christian worldview.

---

the whole problem of the relation of the Personal God to the absolute Godhead would have grown if he had been able to make a deeper study of Hinduism" (Griffiths, "Adventure of Faith," 23).

174. Lewis, *Collected Letters*, 2:880–81.
175. Serving no useful purpose.
176. Lewis, *Collected Letters*, 2:771.
177. Hooper, *C. S. Lewis*, 673.

The "Christ above Culture" category, third in the *Christ and Culture* taxonomy, is characterised by Niebuhr as culture aspiring for symmetry with Christianity. Niebuhr views the "majority movement in Christianity" as the "church of the center." He thinks that these centrists have refused to accept either the position of the anticultural radicals or that of the accommodators of Christ to culture. Despite their acknowledgment of how prone to sin all human efforts are, these centrists have not regarded their solution of symmetricity as compromising, writes Niebuhr. His notion of symmetricity is not easily understood. He explains his view of the centrists' position as follows:[178]

> One of the theologically stated convictions with which the church of the center approaches the cultural problem is that Jesus Christ is the Son of God, the Father Almighty who created heaven and earth. With that formulation it introduces into the discussion about Christ and culture the conception of nature on which all culture is founded, and which is good and rightly ordered by the One to whom Jesus Christ is obedient and with whom he is inseparably united. Where this conviction rules, Christ and the world cannot be simply opposed to each other. Neither can the "world" as culture be simply regarded as the realm of godlessness; since it is at least founded on the "world" as nature, and cannot exist save as it is upheld by the Creator and Governor of nature.
>
> There is agreement, too, among all the central groups that man is obligated in the nature of his being to be obedient to God—not to a Jesus separated from the Almighty Creator, nor to an author of nature separated from Jesus Christ, but to God-in-Christ and Christ-in-God—and that this obedience must be rendered in the concrete, actual life of the natural, cultural man. In his sex life, in eating and drinking, in commanding and obeying other men, he is in the realm of God by divine ordering under divine orders. Since none of the activities can be carried on without the use of human intelligence and will, on a purely instinctive level, since man as created is endowed and burdened with freedom as he moves among necessities, culture is itself a divine requirement. As created and ordered by God, man must achieve what has not been given him; in obedience to God he must seek many values. There is agreement on this in the central church; though there are varieties of conviction

---

178. H. Niebuhr, *Christ and Culture*, 117–18.

about the extent of asceticism which is mated with such living of the cultural life.

There would seem to be little support for the application of this model in Lewis's literature. For instance, in an essay titled "Christianity and Culture," he writes: "On the whole, the New Testament seemed, if not hostile, yet unmistakably cold to culture. I think we can still believe culture to be innocent after we have read the New Testament; I cannot see that we are encouraged to think it important."[179] Lewis appears to have support for his position among certain members of the academy. For instance, David Clark, professor of New Testament and Greek at Vanguard University, agrees with Lewis. Clark writes: "Collectively, the artistic expression of any group of people who share a common language and homeland form the culture of those people. On this 'higher' level Lewis remains consistent to his Christian principles. Culture is not, in itself, held up as something important in the Scriptures. It must, just as individual expressions of art and literature, be subordinated to God, in whom all values reside."[180] Lewis was exceedingly cautious about ascribing value to creativity and originality as exhibited in art and literature or other aspects of culture. "It is not easy to put into words. The nearest I can come is to say that I find a disquieting contrast between the whole circle of ideas used in modern criticism and certain recurrent ideas in the New Testament," he writes.[181]

Lewis objects to the reverence and near-veneration of qualities such as spontaneity, creativity, and originality associated with conventional cultural elements:[182]

> "Originality" in the New Testament is quite plainly the prerogative of God alone; even within the triune being of God it seems to be associated with the Father. The duty and happiness of every other being is placed in being derivative, reflecting like a mirror. Nothing could be more foreign to the tone of scripture than the language of those who describe a saint as a "moral genius" or a "spiritual genius" thus insinuating that his virtue or spirituality is "creative" or "original." If I have read the New Testament aright, it leaves no room for "creativeness" even in a modified or metaphysical sense. Our whole destiny seems to lie

179. Lewis, *Essay Collection*, 74.
180. Clark, *C. S. Lewis*, 47.
181. Lewis, *Christian Reflections* (2014), 3-4.
182. Lewis, *Christian Reflections* (2014), 8.

in the opposite direction, in being as little as possible ourselves, in acquiring a fragrance that is not our own but borrowed, in becoming clean mirrors filled with a face that is not ours. I am not here supporting the doctrine of total depravity, and I do not say that the New Testament supports it; I am only saying that the highest good of a creature must be creaturely—that is, derivative or reflective—good.

Lewis thinks that Christians should be careful about inordinately elevating the perceived qualities of the cultural rudiments within their environs. He thinks that such qualities should be seen in context—as reflections of the goodness of God as revealed and expressed in the New Testament. Discerning culture as he does, through the theological underpinnings of his worldview, he thinks that culture-centered creativity, originality, and spontaneity should be experienced and expressed through a scriptural lens. His writings convey a cautionary note for practitioners of Eastern spirituality, as well as for "Niebuhrian centrists" within the "Christ of Culture" model of Niebuhr's taxonomy.

Niebuhr titles the fifth category in his taxonomy as "Christ the Transformer of Culture." This model implies the employment of Christianity as an instrument for the transformation of a given culture. In the July 2003 *Mennonite Quarterly Review*, Craig Carter claims that Niebuhr's book actually builds a case for the fifth type by not critiquing the Christ the "Transformer of Culture" category as extensively as the other types and by presenting it at a higher level of abstraction than any of the others. Therefore, readers find this type harder to criticize and are consequently influenced to embrace it. According to Carter, regardless of their denominational backgrounds and predispositions, most students tend to identify with the transforming position after reading Niebuhr's book.[183] As with the first, second, and third categories discussed above, there appears to be limited application for the fifth category in Lewis's body of work.

In an article titled "It Is Time to Take Jesus Back: In Celebration of the Fiftieth Anniversary of H. Richard Niebuhr's *Christ and Culture*," in *The Journal of the Society of Christian Ethics*, Glen Stassen contends that although contemporary culture does have some desired qualities, such as a sense of morality, Christians will be tempted to drift off course by the

---

183. Carter, "Legacy of Inadequate Christology."

forces of accommodation. Stassen describes the task faced by transformationalists as follows:[184]

> We still live in the hangover from Christendom, when churches assumed the culture was Christian, so that all that was needed was to baptize those who had been nurtured by the culture and they would spontaneously do what is Christian. So, evangelicals assume that the task is to convert people, Pentecostals assume the task is to be receptive to the power of the Spirit, spiritualists assume the task is to feel the presence of the divine, and liberals assume the task is to articulate a philosophical principle, and then the desire to be good, combined with the obvious meaning of goodness that we all know in the midst of our reasonable culture, will produce good Christians. Yet the culture is not Christian.

In order to determine what the fifth Niebuhrian type is intended to transform, it is important to understand what is meant by culture in the Niebuhrian context. Niebuhr's notion of culture is everything within one's civilization that is not attributable to nature:[185]

> What we have in view when we deal with Christ and culture is that total process of human activity and that total result of such activity to which now the name culture, now the name civilization, is applied in common speech. Culture is the "artificial, secondary environment" which man superimposes on the natural. It comprises language, habits, ideas, beliefs, customs, social organizations, inherited artifacts, technical processes, and values. This social heritage, this "reality *sui generis*,"[186] which the New Testament writers frequently had in mind when they spoke of "the world," which is represented in many forms but to which Christians like other men are inevitably subject, is what we mean when we speak of culture.... Culture, secondly is human achievement. We distinguish it from nature by noting the evidences of human purposiveness and effort. A river is nature, a canal is culture; a raw piece of quartz is nature, an arrowhead culture; a moan is natural, a word cultural. Culture is the work of men's minds and hands.... Hence it includes speech, education, tradition, myth, science, art, philosophy, government, law, rite, beliefs, inventions, technologies.... These

---

184. Stassen, "It Is Time," 139.
185. H. Niebuhr, *Christ and Culture*, 32–34.
186. Latin, "unique, an entity or reality that cannot be reduced to a lower concept."

human achievements, in the third place, are designed for an end or ends; the world of culture is a world of values.... What men have made and what they make, we must assume, is intended for a purpose; it is designed to serve a good.

Niebuhr identifies Augustine and Calvin as having been advocates of what he perceives to be the transformationalist or "conversionist" solution. He claims that proponents of this solution recognise "that human nature is fallen or perverted, and that this perversion not only appears in culture but is transmitted by it." He notes that "Christ is seen as the converter of man in his culture and society, not apart from these," and that for advocates of this view, "there is no nature without culture and no turning of men from self and from idols to God, save in society."[187]

It is difficult to imagine Lewis fully embracing the transformational motif. For him, embracing the Christian faith meant individual self-surrender. He would likely have viewed any comprehensive undertaking created for the purpose of transforming the prevailing culture with considerable scepticism. Lewis viewed humanity as an amalgam of individual lives, rather than a definable singularity. In this respect, he differed from Barfield who, in his writings, defined humanity as an entity in itself, in the process of evolution. Barfield describes the differences between their respective positions in this manner:[188]

> I will try to enumerate or summarize some of the differences which were undoubtedly there ... [Barfield] does hold that the relation of man to God is something that evolves, continually evolves. I think if you had asked Lewis if he felt the same, he would definitely have said "No," and that leads to another difference, partly connected with it. The very use of the word *man*, if one speaks of the relation of man to God, and does so in terms of evolution or its possibility, implies that one conceives of humanity as a whole constituting an entity, a real being. Now whatever "literary Lewis" has said, "theological Lewis" always writes of the individual *man*, the individual soul. If he used the word *humanity* at all, I think it is clear that he thought of it simply as a numerical aggregate of individual souls. So that anything in the nature of evolution or progress can only occur in the life of some one soul between life and death. There Barfield differs from him: he thinks that man, humanity as a whole, is a spiritual reality and, as I said, that it is evolving and will continue to

187. H. Niebuhr, *Christ and Culture*, 43.
188. Barfield, "Lewis and/or Barfield," 219–20.

evolve. Incidentally, this exclusive emphasis on the individual soul, or individual spirit, as the only reality, is something which appeared earlier in Lewis's life, which was there before his conversion, and was part of his makeup. It is there in the kind of thing that interested him and the kind of thing that didn't. He was never interested in collectivity of any sort. It wasn't real to him. . . . He always came back to the individual soul: a movement might be there in the background, but it was of no particular importance.

Barfield elaborates further on their respective positions and claims that he found a dichotomy between the positions held by what he calls "literary Lewis," and "theological Lewis." He theorizes that "literary Lewis" was likely more sympathetic with his own position than "theological Lewis" was.[189] Barfield's perceived dichotomy notwithstanding, for the purpose of this enquiry, it would seem that Lewisian theological inferences would take precedence over his conception of literary properties. Lyle Dorsett writes that "Lewis's keen ability to translate Scripture into the vernacular grew from a regular and sustained habit of studying the Bible for personal transformation. Convinced that any soul is on a path to Christlikeness, or horrid corruption, he became convinced that Holy Writ was a primary source of spiritual nourishment for the disciple of Jesus Christ."[190] Dorsett's characterisation would seem to suggest that Lewis would have been reluctant to endorse an all-encompassing societal conversionist category. Furthermore, Lewis's account of his wartime experiences and his commentary regarding the human proclivity for decadence, plus the views as expressed in his satirical portrayal of a culture having gone berserk as he did in his novel *That Hideous Strength*, make it doubtful that he would have been optimistic that any comprehensive cultural transformational project would be successful.[191]

Lewis's body of work would seem to best accommodate the "Christ and Culture in Paradox" category, which is the fourth type in the Niebuhrian taxonomy. This model implies the existence of a certain

189. Barfield, "Lewis and/or Barfield," 221–22.

190. Dorsett, *Seeking the Secret Place*, 62.

191. Lewis's letters written during World War II indicate a certain ambivalence, if not outright scepticism, about governments' role in bettering society. In a letter to his brother on March 21, 1940, Lewis writes: "'Dynamic' I think is one of the words invented by this age which sums up what it likes and I abominate. Could one start a Stagnation party—which at General Elections would boast that during its term of office *no* event of the least importance has taken place" (Lewis, *Collected Letters*, 2:368–69).

tension in the relationship between culture and Christianity, and best characterises the Lewisian perspective. It is instructive that in his commentary on the "Paradox" category, Martin Marty writes that this is for those with dialectical imaginations who exhibit "at-homeness with dualism and contradiction."[192] He thinks that individuals in this zone of paradox "never believe that they will truly transform the culture."[193] Reinhold Niebuhr appears to be in agreement with Marty. In his book *Moral Man and Immoral Society: A Study in Ethics and Politics*, he writes: "All men cannot be expected to become spiritual any more than they can be expected to become rational." He opines that "those who achieve excellence will always be a leavening influence in social life, but the political structure of society cannot be built upon this achievement." Niebuhr points out that Augustine had concluded that the "city of this world" was a "compact of injustice" and that "its peace is secured by strife." He claims that Augustine's notion is "a very realistic interpretation of the realities of social life" and contends that this notion "creeps easily into all rigorous religion, with its drift toward dualism." Niebuhr argues that "the injustices of society are placed into such sharp contrast with the absolute moral ideal . . . that the religiously sensitised soul is tempted to despair of society."[194] Although Lewis did not manifest the symptoms of despair expressed in Reinhold Niebuhr's *Moral Man and Immoral Society*, Lewis's writings could be generally characterised as best represented by Reinhold's brother H. Richard's "Paradox" model.

From March to December 1940, a collection of three articles that Lewis had written were published in *Theology*, a British journal, under the title "Christianity and Culture." There is much to be gleaned about Lewis's notion regarding Christian praxis and its relationship with its cultural environs from inferences within Lewis's body of work. These articles represent Lewis's most detailed commentary on the development of his own perspective on the subject of culture and Christian faith or on what

---

192. Marty, "Foreword," xvii. Marty is using the word *dualism* within the context with which it is used in Reinhold Niebuhr's book *Moral Man and Immoral Society: A Study in Ethics and Politics*, in which Niebuhr uses the word to contrast the notion of a transcendent, ideal ethical model with a plausible social reality model.

193. Marty, "Foreword," xviii.

194. R. Niebuhr, *Moral Man*, 48.

Niebuhr has coined the "enduring problem."[195] Lewis begins the series of articles with the following introduction:[196]

> At an early age, I began to believe that the life of culture (that is, of intellectual and aesthetic activity)[197] was very good for its own sake. Or even that it was good for man. After my conversion, which occurred in my later twenties, I continued to hold this belief without consciously asking how it could be reconciled with my new belief that the end [aim] of human life was salvation in Christ and glorifying God. I was awakened from this confused state of mind that the friends of culture seemed to me to be exaggerating. I was driven to the other extreme and began, in my own mind, to belittle the claims of culture. As soon as I did I was faced with the question, "If it is a thing of so little value, how are you justified in spending so much of your life on it?"

Lewis credits Matthew Arnold, Benedetto Croce, and I. A. Richards for contributing to the present elevation of culture, endowing it with a "spiritual" component,[198] and ascribing an "inordinate esteem" to it.[199] Lewis comments on the "kind of soteriological function" that Richards has given to poetry and objects to the "necessary relationship between the quality of the individual's response to art and his general fitness for humane living."[200] Lewis notes that he has a "real problem" with some of these notions. Although he concedes that no one is "maintaining that a fine taste in the arts is a condition for salvation," nevertheless, he objects to the apparent reverence that has been ascribed to art.[201] He also notes,

---

195. H. Niebuhr, *Christ and Culture*, 1.

196. Lewis, *Christian Reflections* (1967), 14.

197. Lewis uses the word *culture* in this series in a narrower sense than Niebuhr does. Niebuhr defines culture as that which is not derived from natural processes, all that is attributable to human influence/activity, including human institutions (H. Niebuhr, *Christ and Culture*, 29–39). For the purpose of this enquiry, examining Lewis's relationship with his cultural environs, culture is understood in the wider sense. Some elements of Lewis's commentary in this series of articles, such as the principle of subordinating "all will and desire to a transcendental Person in whom all values reside," may arguably be extrapolated to apply to entities within the Niebuhrian context (Lewis, *Christian Reflections* [1967], 32).

198. Lewis, *Christian Reflections* (1967), 15.

199. Lewis, *Christian Reflections* (1967), 14.

200. Lewis, *Christian Reflections* (1967), 15.

201. Lewis, *Christian Reflections* (1967), 16.

however, that aesthetic enjoyment of nature was advanced by Jesus. He therefore contends that, on the whole, he finds no justification in the New Testament for art's elevated status. Lewis then cites a range of references from Augustine, Aquinas, and Thomas A. Kempis, and summarises with a quotation from John Henry Newman, stating that "culture has no tendency to make us pleasing to our Maker."[202] He writes that his research has left him "with the impression that there could be no question of restoring to culture the kind of status" that he had given it before his conversion to Christianity.[203] Lewis's objection to art's revered status is based, in part, on his understanding of New Testament principles. He contends that New Testament authors demanded the abandonment of anything that "conflicts with the service of God," and warned against "every kind of superiority."[204]

Lewis argues that, for Christians, even the view of nature itself must be sublimated to the primacy of its Maker. In his book *Miracles*, he notes that his perception of nature changed dramatically after his conversion. He writes that prior to his conversion he found naturalists' notion of the spontaneity of nature exhilarating: "I passionately desired that Nature should exist 'on her own.' The ideas she had been made and altered by God, seemed to take from her all the spontaneity which I found so refreshing. In order to breathe freely I wanted to feel that in Nature one reached at least something that simply was. The thought that she had been . . . 'put there with a purpose' was suffocating," he writes.[205] Lewis points out that his "cure of that mood began years ago" and was not completed until he had done research for his examination of the sufficiency/adequacy of naturalism.[206] Initially, he had imagined that conceiving nature as created was tantamount to reducing her status, he writes. But surprisingly, his admiration of nature has increased. "She has never seemed to me more great or more real than at this moment," he claims.[207] Lewis sees his current view of nature as being analogous to appreciating and admiring the creative powers of Shakespeare or Dickens, as opposed to focusing solely on the talents ascribed to the characters they created. From his

---

202. Lewis, *Christian Reflections* (1967), 23.
203. Lewis, *Christian Reflections* (1967), 23.
204. Lewis, *Christian Reflections* (1967), 17.
205. Lewis, *Miracles*, 100.
206. Lewis, *Miracles*, 101.
207. Lewis, *Miracles*, 102.

perspective, admiring nature while being oblivious to the creative genius of its Creator is tantamount to admiring the qualities of characters within a play while being unaware of the play's author's imaginative prowess. In Lewis's view, Christians should perceive their entire world with an awareness of their Creator and should endeavour to subordinate all that they experience and comprehend to him.[208]

In his book *The Taste of the Other: The Social and Ethical Thought of C. S. Lewis*, Gilbert Meilaender writes that the key to understanding Lewis's attitude to all that God has created is to view created things "as gifts of the Creator meant to be received." Lewis thinks that to treat a created thing as something with infinite value is to destroy its true character, because every created thing will eventually lose the capacity for delighting its recipients, writes Meilaender. He notes that Lewis's novel *Perelandra* conveys a notion similar to that expressed in Lewis's book *Miracles*: attempting to make a gift the object of infinite delight will result in unappealing consequences; any earthly object is only a created thing, and to make of it an object of infinite desire creates a false infinite.[209]

In his preface to *Pilgrim's Regress*, Lewis writes that he has concluded that if a man diligently followed a given desire, "pursuing the false objects until their falsity appeared and then resolutely abandoning them, he must come out at last into the clear knowledge that the human soul was made to enjoy some object that is never fully given ... in our present mode of subjective and spatio-temporal experience."[210] Meilaender refers to Lewis's approach to this unfulfilled desire as "The Dialectic of Enjoyment and Renunciation." He notes that Lewis exhibits this dialectic in his entire body of writing "by placing us, as it were, in a still larger story: the Christian story of creation, fall, incarnation, redemption, and *eschaton*." Meilaender claims that Lewis thinks that humanity "must take up a kind of double attitude toward things—a dialectical movement between enjoyment and renunciation." In his opinion, Lewis views this double movement as being grounded in creation itself, and sees the things of our world as genuine sources of delight, but still as created things that "cannot satisfy the heart which seeks in them a full answer to its longing."[211] He writes that within this Lewisian dialectic movement "we reverence the

---

208. Lewis, *Miracles*, 99–103.
209. Meilaender, *Taste of Other*, 18.
210. Lewis, *Pilgrim's Regress*, 15.
211. Meilaender, *Taste of Other*, 20.

gift of the Creator. . . . [We] receive it with joy and delight in it. Yet from another perspective the thing itself is of little consequence, for our life is directed toward God and not only toward the pleasures of his creation."[212] If Meilaender is correct in his observation (which he appears to be), this would confirm that among the five types within the Niebuhrian taxonomy, Lewis's body of work is best accommodated within the fourth category, "Christ and Culture in Paradox."

In an essay titled "Two Ways with the Self," Lewis writes: "Self-renunciation is thought to be, and indeed is, very near the core of Christian ethics."[213] He notes that the self can be regarded in two ways. On the one hand, the self is God's creature, which is an occasion for rejoicing; on the other hand, the self that puts forward a claim for preferential treatment needs to be "pitied and healed."[214] Meilaender thinks Lewis was "fond of the paradox."[215] He notes that, unlike many intellectuals, Lewis demonstrates a paradoxical relationship "with reference to culture." He writes that Lewis thinks that a Christian is inclined to take culture a "little less seriously than many others, for he knows how easily a supposedly cultural interest can become a sophisticated form of concern for self and how easily this can undermine genuine delight in things."[216]

The relationship between Lewis and culture is a complex one. As someone who exhibited a worldview that included a deep and abiding sense of the supernatural, Lewis was appreciative of the gifts bestowed on humanity by its Creator. He was also profoundly aware of the threats posed by fixating on the gifts themselves at the expense of ignoring the Giver of all gifts. Lewis brought a dialectic approach to his relationship with the gifts, benefits, and features inherent in his cultural environs. In his opinion, these were to be appreciated, but he rejected any inclination to grant them an elevated status. Although Lewis's commentary in his essay on "Christianity and Culture" is aimed at the aesthetic elements in culture, arguably, his sentiments could also be extrapolated to include much of what is included in Niebuhr's more extensive treatment of the term. Four of the models in Niebuhr's taxonomy would seem to have limited application within Lewis's body of work; the Lewisian worldview,

---

212. Meilaender, *Taste of Other*, 21.
213. Lewis, *God in the Dock*, 193.
214. Lewis, *God in the Dock*, 194.
215. Meilaender, *Taste of Other*, 27.
216. Meilaender, *Taste of Other*, 25.

with some qualification, is best accommodated within the "Christ and Culture in Paradox" category, which is underscored by its theological underpinnings and is the subject of the following section.

4.7 LEWIS AND THEOLOGY

In the *Cambridge Companion to C. S. Lewis*, Robert MacSwain writes that Lewis was "both a phenomenon and an anomaly."[217] He views him as a phenomenon because some fifty years since his death, he remains one of the world's most popular authors, and "almost certainly the most influential religious author of the twentieth century."[218] He claims that he is also an anomaly, however, because although he is widely popular, scholars are sharply divided about the value of his work, especially in theology and in religious studies. MacSwain writes that as a literary scholar, Lewis never received any formal theological training, and contends that for over half a century, mainstream academic theologians—including even those within his own denomination, the Anglican Church—have been hoping that Lewis would "quietly go away."[219] Even though Lewis received no formal theological training, he was highly trained in "the study of Greek and Latin language and literature, philosophy, and ancient history, and thus provided a three-fold mental training in precision of language, clarification of concepts and the weighing of historical evidence" McSwain writes.[220] In his opinion, academic theologians can ill afford to disregard Lewis. Because Lewis is so highly influential, academics need to be familiar with his works in order to be in a position to comment on or counteract the content of his books, he claims. In addition, he contends that because Lewis was not an academic theologian himself, he may offer the theological academy a unique insight into their own subject. McSwain cautions academic theologians about an increasing insularity:[221]

> Among other things, this may have to do with the way in which Lewis harnessed his imagination, reason, historical knowledge, wit, and considerable rhetorical gifts in a sustained effort to communicate the substance of his convictions to as wide an

---

217. MacSwain, "Introduction," 1.
218. MacSwain, "Introduction," 3.
219. MacSwain, "Introduction," 4.
220. MacSwain, "Introduction," 4.
221. MacSwain, "Introduction," 4.

audience as possible. In its commendable quest for disciplinary purity and intellectual integrity, academic theology is actually in great danger of sealing itself within a very small, self-enclosed echo chamber in which experts talk to other experts while losing all contact with the outside world. Meanwhile, Lewis continues to sell millions of books a year to shape the religious faith of thousands.

Lewis saw himself as a lay member of the Anglican Church. "I am a very ordinary layman of the Church of England, not especially 'high,' nor especially 'low.' . . . Ever since I became a Christian I have thought that the best, perhaps the only, service I could do for my unbelieving neighbours was to explain and defend the belief that has been common to nearly all Christians at all times," he writes in his preface to *Mere Christianity*.[222] The Anglican Church is a worldwide association of churches that trace their origin back to the Church of England. Lewis's interdenominational appeal is such that although he is one of the Anglican Church's most well-known writers, most readers are unaware of his association with the Church of England. Alister McGrath, an Anglican himself, comments on Lewis's writings as they relate to his Anglicanism:[223]

> Lewis is best seen as a religious writer and apologist who happened to be a member of the Church of England, not someone who intentionally saw himself—or presented himself—as a specifically Anglican religious writer and apologist. Indeed, Lewis would regard the defense of any Christian denomination with suspicion, seeing this as prioritizing or privileging a specific implementation of Christianity over the Christian faith itself. . . . For Lewis, the Church of England represents a distinctly English vision of Christianity, adjusted to the social and cultural realities of this specific region, in much the same way as recent scholarship has emphasized how the Enlightenment—once thought as a universal movement—is known to have adapted to specifics of local contexts. Furthermore, Lewis's own writings suggest a downplaying of any denominational distinctiveness or privilege on his part.

In 1958, Anglican theologian W. Norman Pittenger wrote an article for *The Christian Century* magazine[224] titled "Apologist versus Apologist:

---

222. Lewis, *Mere Christianity*, viii.
223. McGrath, *Intellectual World*, 147–48.
224. George Marsden, emeritus professor of history, Notre Dame, characterises

A Critique of C. S. Lewis as 'Defender of the Faith.'" In his article, Pittenger acknowledges that Lewis was the premier apologist of the day, but he contends that Lewis should not be taken seriously as a theologian. He objects to Lewis accepting the Gospel accounts at face value and argues that rather than taking Jesus's claims literally, as expressed by the Gospel writers, the claims should be examined "in the light of the best critical analysis." In Pittenger's opinion, Lewis was an inept theologian.[225]

Although Lewis had previously considered it a mistake in most cases to counteract criticism, in this instance, he chose to respond, and in the November edition of the *Christian Century* magazine, he submitted a rebuttal, titled "Rejoinder to Dr. Pittenger." Lewis's rejoinder offers insight into the manner in which he differed from the then-current liberal theological interpretations of the Gospel narrative. In his *Christian Century* article, a copy of which is also available in the book *God in the Dock: Essays on Theology and Ethics*, Lewis asks what to make of Pittenger's statement in which he writes about the "validity of our Lord's unique place in Christian faith as that One in whom God was so active and so present that he may be called God-Man."[226] Lewis writes that he is not quite sure what Pittenger means by referring to Jesus as God-Man. If by using the term as he does, Pittenger intends his usage of the word God-Man to convey objective reality (presumably, that in reality, Jesus was fully God and fully man), then he, Lewis, is in full agreement with Pittenger, he states. However, if by God-Man he is simply referring to Jesus in the same way in which Christians often refer to a fellow Christian as someone in whom "God was present and active to a unique degree," then he "must demur," he claims. To avoid any doubt about his own stance, Lewis states: "I think that Jesus Christ is (in fact) the only Son of God, through whom others are enabled 'to become sons of God.'" Furthermore, writes Lewis in *The Christian Century*, if Dr. Pittenger "wishes to attack that doctrine," there are probably any number of "far worthier" opponents for him to contend with.[227]

Lewis's demurral is reminiscent of a sentiment that he had expressed in a letter written to his brother, Warren, many years earlier. Even prior

---

The Christian Century magazine as the "guardian of Progressive Protestantism." W. Norman Pittenger was professor of apologetics at General Theological Seminary in New York (Marsden, *Lewis's Mere Christianity*, 101).

225. Pittenger, "Apologist versus Apologist," 1106.
226. Lewis, *God in the Dock*, 177.
227. Lewis, *God in the Dock*, 178.

to his conversion, Lewis seemingly expected Anglican clergymen to embrace the church's core beliefs or resign from the ministry if unable to do so. In a letter to his brother in 1921, he strongly objected to an Anglican priest, who, although still in the employ of the church, was espousing what he considered to be untenable views. "Strange mortals, these knights of the cloth are, on the divinity of Christ, of which the point is that he was only a man, you can still apparently go on being a parson [by saying] 'We don't worship Jesus Christ, only the Christ THAT WAS in Jesus'—a beautiful distinction," he had written in the letter to his brother.[228] Lewis wrote the letter prior to embracing Christianity; his knowledge about the truth claims of the Christian faith may help explain the interval between his acceptance of theism and his conversion to Christianity.

Lewis's response is also instructive on how he perceived his role as a Christian apologist. In the 1958 article, he writes that he sees himself as that of a "translator" of the Christian faith. In his response to Pittenger, Lewis contends that when he began the BBC broadcast talks, most of his fellow countrymen could not relate to the evangelism that was being offered either by what he considered to be the emotionalism of revivalist preachers nor by the "unintelligible language" of the clergymen of the day. Lewis writes:[229]

> When I began, Christianity came before the great mass of my unbelieving fellow-countrymen either in the highly emotional form offered by revivalists or in the unintelligible language of highly cultured clergymen. Most men were reached by neither. My task was therefore simply that of a translator—one turning Christian, or what he believed to be such, into the vernacular, into language that unscholarly people would attend to and could understand. For this purpose a style more guarded, more *nuanced*, finelier shaded, more rich in fruitful ambiguities—in fact, a style more like Dr. Pittenger's own—would have been worse than useless. It would not only fail to enlighten the common reader's understanding; it would have aroused his opposition. He would have thought, poor soul, that I was facing both ways, sitting on the fence, offering at one moment what I withdrew the next, and generally trying to trick him. I may have made theological errors. My manner may have been defective. Others may do better hereafter. I am ready, if I am young enough, to learn. Dr. Pittenger would be a more helpful critic if he advised a cure

228. Lewis, *Collected Letters*, 1:548.
229. Lewis, "Rejoinder to Dr. Pittenger," 1360–61.

as well as asserting my diseases. How does he himself do such work? What methods, and with what success, does he employ when he is trying to convert the great masses of storekeepers, lawyers, realtors, morticians, policemen and artisans who surround him in his own city? One thing at least is sure. If the real theologians had tackled this laborious work of translation about a hundred years ago, when they began to lose touch with the people (for whom Christ died), there would have been no place for me.

In his response, Lewis concedes some technical points to Pittenger and then reminds him that his (Lewis's) theology was not directed toward a professional audience but rather toward the larger popular audience. Furthermore, Lewis contends that the popular audience has been ill-served by Pittenger and his professional colleagues and that he finds Pittenger's theological claims to be ambiguous. Pittenger's condescending piece warranted a fulsome reply, and Lewis's debating skills are on full display in the Pittenger rebuttal. Lewis usually refrained from directly responding to criticism of his apologetic methods; because of Pittenger's position in academia and the status of *The Christian Century*, he apparently thought it necessary to make an exception.

Richard Purtill, former professor of philosophy at Western Washington University, writes that apologetics is the explanation and defense of the beliefs of religion, and requires an ability to "argue well." He claims that Lewis was exceedingly well trained for this task and considers him to be "one of the greatest prose stylists of this era," with an "ability to use metaphor and analogy" for making Christianity clear to the ordinary listener or reader. He notes that many of his works were honed by his experiences before audiences of the Royal Air Force bases in World War II and his radio broadcasts carried by the BBC in 1941 and 1942.[230]

In the address to an audience of Anglican youth leaders and junior clergy at a conference in Wales in 1945, Lewis supplied clues to his own success as an apologist. He gives his audience a concise description of what the Christian apologist must defend:[231]

> We are to defend Christianity itself—the faith preached by the Apostles, attested by the Martyrs, embodied in the Creeds, expounded by the Fathers. This must be clearly distinguished from the whole of what any one us may think about God and Man.

---

230. Purtill, "Apologetics," 83.
231. Lewis, *God in the Dock*, 90.

> Each of us has his individual emphasis: each holds, in addition to the Faith, many opinions which seem to him to be consistent with it and true and important. And so perhaps they are. But as apologists it is not our business to defend them. We are defending Christianity, not my "religion."

Lewis expands on the importance of making a distinction in the difference between expounding on the faith and expressing personal opinions:[232]

> When we mention our personal opinions, we must always make quite clear the difference between them and the Faith itself. St. Paul has given us the model in I Corinthians 7:25: on a certain point he has "no commandment of the Lord" but gives "his judgment." No one is left in doubt as to the difference in status implied.

Lewis then explains that making a distinction between teaching the faith and expounding on personal opinions has a significant impact on the audience:[233]

> This distinction, which is demanded by honesty, also gives the apologist a great tactical advantage. The great difficulty is to get modern audiences to realize that you are preaching Christianity solely and simply because you happen to think it true; they always assume you are preaching it because you like it or think it good for society or something of that sort. Now a clearly maintained distinction between what the Faith actually says and what you would like it to have said or what you understand or what you personally find helpful or think probable, forces your audience to realize that you are tied to your data just as a scientist is tied by the results of the experiments; that you are not just saying what you like. This immediately helps them to realize that what is being discussed is a question about objective fact—not gas about ideals and points of view.

Moreover, being scrupulous with this distinction also confers an important benefit to the person delivering the message, because it facilitates intellectual and spiritual growth in the messenger himself, he writes:[234]

> Secondly, this scrupulous care to preserve the Christian message as something distinct from one's own ideas, has one very good effect upon the apologist himself. It forces him, again and again, to face up to those elements in original Christianity which he

232. Lewis, *God in the Dock*, 90.
233. Lewis, *God in the Dock*, 90–91.
234. Lewis, *God in the Dock*, 91.

personally finds obscure and repulsive. He is saved from the temptation to skip or slur or ignore what he finds disagreeable. And the man who yields to that temptation will, of course, never progress in Christian knowledge.... It is just the same here as in science. The phenomenon which is troublesome, which doesn't fit in with the current scientific theories, is the phenomenon which compels reconsideration and thus leads to new knowledge. Science progresses because scientists, instead of running away from such troublesome phenomena or hushing them up, are constantly seeking them out. In the same way there will be progress in Christian knowledge only as long as we will accept the challenge of the difficult or repellant doctrines. A "liberal" Christianity which considers itself free to alter the Faith whenever the Faith looks perplexing or repellant must be completely stagnant. Progress is only made into a resisting material.

Clearly, Lewis's presentations to British military personnel regarding the fundamentals of the Christian faith was a critical learning experience for him. In his address to the audience in Wales, Lewis advises the young Anglican clergy to revise their theological vocabulary in order to communicate the Christian Gospel to a contemporary audience. "Our business is to present that which is timeless ... in the particular language of our own age," he tells his listeners. "The bad preacher does exactly the opposite: he takes the ideas of our own age and tricks them out in the traditional language of Christianity. Thus, for example, he may take the *Beveridge Report*[235] and talk about the coming of the Kingdom. The core of his thought is merely contemporary; only the superficies is traditional. But your teaching must be timeless, at its heart," Lewis advises his audience.[236]

Although he was not a professional theologian himself, Lewis advises the clergy who were in attendance at the Wales conference to revise their theological language. "We must learn the language of our

---

235. William Henry Beveridge, first Lord Beveridge (1879–1963), was a social reformer and economist. His Beveridge Plan (1942) became the blueprint for the present welfare system. The *Beveridge Report* was a document submitted to the British Parliament during the 1942–1943 session, which became the plan for the British Social Security system under the auspices of Great Britain's Inter-Departmental Committee on Social Insurance and Allied Services (Humphries et al., *Oxford World Book Encyclopedia*, 83). Lewis appears to object to having church doctrine and biblical teachings being replaced by social and political commentary (Walter Hooper, in Lewis, *Collected Letters*, 2:613n31).

236. Lewis, *God in the Dock*, 93–94.

audience. . . . On this question of language, the best thing I can do is make a list of words which are used by the people in a sense different from ours," he tells them, and offers a list of words for which he would recommend revision, an excerpt of which follows:[237]

> ATONEMENT. Does not really exist in a spoken modern English, though it would be recognized as "a religious word." . . . You must paraphrase.
>
> CATHOLIC. Means Papistical.
>
> CHARITY. Means (a) Alms (b) A "charitable organization."
>
> CHRISTIAN. Has come to include almost no idea of *belief*. Usually a term of approval. . . . A decent chap.
>
> CREATIVE. Now means merely "talented," "original." The idea of creation in the theological sense is absent from their minds.
>
> CRUCIFIXION, CROSS etc. Centuries of hymnody . . . have so exhausted these words . . . that they now . . . convey the idea of execution by torture. It is better to paraphrase.
>
> DOGMA. Used by the people only in a bad sense to mean "unproved assertion delivered in an arrogant manner."
>
> PERSONAL. I discovered that *personal* meant *corporeal*. When they say they don't believe in a "personal" God they may often mean that they are not anthropomorphists.
>
> PRIMITIVE. Means crude, clumsy, unfinished, inefficient. "Primitive Christianity" would not mean to them what it does to you.
>
> SPIRITUAL. Means primarily *immaterial, incorporeal.*

Lewis concludes the section on theology and language by advising the attendees that it is essential that they translate every bit of their theology into the vernacular and that they don't "attempt to water Christianity down." There can be no authentic version of Christianity "with the Supernatural left out," he instructs them. "So far as I can see Christianity is precisely the one religion from which the miraculous cannot be

---

237. Lewis, *God in the Dock*, 96–98.

separated. You must frankly argue for supernaturalism from the very outset," he contends.[238]

Continuing with his message on apologetics, Lewis expounds on some core elements that he considers essential for anyone engaged in Christian apologetics. He notes that while it is "very difficult to produce arguments on the popular level for the existence of God," and while "many of the most popular arguments seem to be invalid," he has found that, fortunately, "people are usually disposed to hear the divinity of Our Lord discussed before going into the existence of God."[239] He tells the conference attendees that when he first began his apologetic work, he would give two lectures and devote the first one to the subject of theism. "But I soon gave up this method because it seemed to arouse little interest [because] the number of clear and determined atheists is apparently not very large," he states. He stresses the importance of focusing on the uniqueness of the incarnation and the reliability and historicity of the Gospels and advises the assembled clergy to remember that they are preaching the Christian faith not because it is good for society or for individuals within their society but because of its truth. "You have to keep forcing them back, and again back, to the real point. . . . One must keep on pointing out that Christianity is a statement which, if false, is of no importance, and if true, is of infinite importance. The one thing it cannot be is moderately important," he tells his audience.[240] In concluding, he advises them not to rest their own faith on the arguments that they make, because it will be no stronger than the weakest pillar of their argument. Lewis closes with this cautionary note: "That is why we apologists take our lives in our hands and can be saved only by falling back continually from the web of our own arguments, as from our intellectual counters, into the Reality—from Christian apologetics into Christ Himself."[241]

Lewis's understanding of Scripture is key to his theology. In his opening comments at the Wales conference, Lewis told the assembly that because his audience was comprised of priests and leaders of Christian youth organizations, he felt that he should be looking to them for spiritual teaching, rather than having them rely on what he had to offer them. However, because he had been requested to appear before them,

---

238. Lewis, *God in the Dock*, 99.
239. Lewis, *God in the Dock*, 100.
240. Lewis, *God in the Dock*, 101.
241. Lewis, *God in the Dock*, 103.

he considered it his duty to comply out of a sense of obedience. In fact, in Lewis's writings is a noticeable dearth of the doctrinal back-and-forth debating that characterises professional theologians.[242] This is likely due to two factors: (1) Lewis had not received professional theological training, and (2) he understood his role to be that of an interdenominational Christian spokesperson and wanted his work to have influence beyond his own denomination. It is noteworthy that some of Lewis's theological views are to be found in his response to letters that individuals had written to him over the years.

One such letter is the one that he wrote in 1959 to Clyde S. Kilby, founder of the Marion E. Wade Center at Wheaton College.[243] Kilby had sent Lewis a copy of the *Wheaton College Statement Concerning Inspiration of the Bible* and asked him a series of questions about his understanding of scriptural inspiration. In response, Lewis tells Kilby that he finds it a "curious thing" that the controversy regarding scriptural authority never arises in his own Bible reading or in his religious life. "Scripture is written for our learning. But learning for what?" he writes Kilby. He thinks that when the Scriptures speak of an event, such as the resurrection, its value depends on whether it really happened, whereas other events may not have the same value in importance. In his letter to Kilby, Lewis begins with some introductory comments and lists six facts or

---

242. In the initial volume of his four-volume series titled *C. S. Lewis: Revelation and the Christ*, theologian and scholar Paul Brazier writes: "Was Lewis a theologian? Many who write on Lewis argue he is not a professional theologian, he was not trained as one, that he wrote no systematic theological treatise. Lewis often referred to himself as a layman and an amateur. Lewis may not have graduated with a project-based theological degree (with no written exams) and pick-and-mix theology and general religious studies, but it may be asserted that he was far more qualified than thousands of theology graduates today. Why? Although he had no formal training in theology, his intellect was confirmed in that he received, within four years of study, two BA Hons degrees, from the University of Oxford, having passed all three required public examinations with first class honors. These degrees were in Greats (Greek and Roman Literature and Classical Philosophy) and in English, and he did not hide behind a supposedly academically disinterested exposition of what other theologians might have said. . . . Lewis sought to return to theology's patristic and biblical roots. Like most patristic theologians, Lewis was a trained philosopher who believed: not a religious professional who did not believe. In addition, Lewis was better read in terms of his patristic and medieval theological heritage than, it may be argued, most theology lecturers today (though not as comprehensively as a patristics expert). Indeed Lewis was in effect a classically trained philosopher theologian" (Brazier, *C. S. Lewis*, 1:125–26).

243. Lewis, *Collected Letters*, 3:1044–46.

rules that he thinks should be understood when formulating one's view on the divine authority of Scripture:[244]

1. Lewis notes the distinction that Paul makes in 1 Cor 7: 10–12 about what Paul considers to be commanded of God versus Paul's opinion on a particular matter.
2. The apparent inconsistencies between the genealogies in Matt 1 and Luke 3, as well as the difference in the accounts of the death of Judas in Matt 26:5 and Acts 1:18–19.
3. Luke's own account of how he obtained/assembled his material in Luke 1:1–4.
4. The universally admitted un-historicity of some narratives such as the parables of Jesus, which may also apply to Jonah and Job.
5. If we believe that "every good and perfect gift comes from the Father of Lights," then all true and edifying writings, whether in Scripture or not, must be *in some sense* inspired.
6. According to John 11:49–52, inspiration may operate in a wicked man without him even knowing it.

In summarising, Lewis writes that items 2 and 4 argue against the view that every statement in Scripture must be *historical* truth and that items 1, 3, 5, and 6 "rule out the view that inspiration is a single thing in the sense that, if present at all, it is always present in the same mode and the same degree." Lewis refutes the view "that any one passage taken in isolation can be assumed to be inerrant in exactly the same way as any other." Not every statement need be taken as historically correct as the resurrection, he tells Kilby. In order for "the over-all operation of Scripture to convey God's word to the reader," it needs to be read in the right spirit, with the assistance of the Holy Spirit, he writes. Without divine inspiration, our own understanding is insufficient, because the reader "also needs His inspiration," he claims. Moreover, writes Lewis, "the very *kind* of truth we are often demanding was, in my opinion, never even envisaged by the Ancients."[245]

Michael Christensen, director of Drew University's doctor of ministry program, writes that although Lewis was not a credentialed theologian and "offers no new religious theory," his contribution is that of "giving

---

244. Lewis, *Collected Letters*, 3:1045.
245. Lewis, *Collected Letters*, 3:1046.

fresh and fluid expression to old ideas." He finds in Lewis "a certain reluctance to systematize his impressions of reality." He thinks that Lewis prefers rather "to embrace the mysteries of religion with intuitive faith." He finds Lewis arguing dogmatically, with his "characteristic either/or logic," for the broad essentials of Christianity, such as God's existence, Christ's divinity, man's immortality, the reality and remedy of sin, and so on. "On doctrinal details," however, he finds Lewis to be "unassuming and tolerant," and frequently confessing to living in the tension of two conflicting points of view.[246]

Scriptural authority has been an oft-disputed subject within Christianity. This disputation has appeared in various forms and has at times emerged as a controversy about biblical or scriptural inerrancy. Christenson writes that both Calvin and Luther affirmed the full authority of Scripture but refused to propose or defend a particular view of scriptural inspiration. He thinks that as the Protestant movement took shape, its leaders seemed to feel that there was a need within Protestantism to find an absolute, infallible authority equal to Catholicism's papacy. Christensen observes that by the seventeenth century, Scripture had come to be viewed as the "paper-Pope of Protestantism." He notes that, judging by their pronouncements, contemporary writers are often "trapped into an effort to do what the Reformers wisely refrained from attempting; namely trying to define precisely the mode, the mechanics, the techniques, by means of which the Bible became the vehicle of revelation God intended."[247]

Based on what he has written, it is hard to imagine Lewis embracing the notion of any form of pope, whether in paper form or in any other. A fair reading of Lewis's address to the assembly of Anglican clergy in Wales would seem to indicate that the teachings "preached by the Apostles, attested by the Martyrs, embodied in the Creeds, [and] expounded by the Fathers" were signposts of his faith leading him to the ultimate reality in Christ. In this regard, it is important to note what he wrote as the concluding thoughts in his book *Surprised by Joy*:[248]

> It [Joy] was valuable only as a pointer to something other and outer. While that other was in doubt, the pointer naturally loomed large in my thoughts. When we are lost in the woods

---

246. Christensen, *C. S. Lewis*, 81.
247. Christensen, *C. S. Lewis*, 85.
248. Lewis, *Surprised by Joy*, 238.

the sight of a signpost is a great matter. He who first sees it cries, "Look!" The whole party gathers round and stares. But when we have found the road and are passing signposts every few miles, we shall not stop and stare. They will encourage us and we should be grateful to the authority that set them up. But we shall not stop and stare, or not much; not on this road, though their pillars are of silver and their letters gold. "We would be at Jerusalem."

The pointer to which Lewis is referring is the Joy or sense of yearning described in previous chapters. This yearning is the *Sehnsucht* (wistful yearning) for something other. Lewis had eventually come to understand that the ultimate fulfillment of this yearning or longing, as he often referred to it, could be found only in the one true reality, in God through Christ. He claims that although he realizes what he sees or experiences are signposts pointing to the reality, nevertheless, on occasion, he still finds himself still focusing on the signposts themselves. Lewis advises his audience not to mistake the signposts for the real objective, because true reality can be found only through Christ.

In an address titled "Inerrancy and the Patron Saint of Evangelicalism," at a National Conference in 2013, Philip Ryken, president of Wheaton College, mentions Lewis's practise of using symbols as teaching devices. He cites an excerpt from one of the Narnia chronicles, *The Silver Chair*, in which one of the main characters in Lewis's novel is given an assignment. In order to be able to complete the assignment, the character is given four signs to which she is required to look for guidance. Whenever she finds herself getting sidetracked, she is reminded that she has been neglecting the signs that were given to her at the outset. He notes that although Lewis doesn't state this, for Ryken, "this story has always illustrated the importance of Holy Scripture in the Christian life." Ryken thinks that if this is what Lewis intended the story to mean, "then it is entirely in keeping with the importance that C. S. Lewis placed on biblical truth for Christian discipleship." Ryken claims: "For Lewis, Holy Scripture was the supreme authority for faith and practice, and reading the Bible had life-giving influence for the Christian."[249] If Ryken's interpretation is correct (as it appears to be), then Lewis's comment in *Surprised by Joy* about not mistaking signposts for the real thing would also apply to reading and understanding Scripture. And that is, that it should not be elevated to the stature of the reality to which Scripture points, which is Christ himself.

249. Ryken, "Inerrancy and Patron Saint," 40.

Ultimate reality can be found only in God, through Christ, the aim and aspiration of the scriptural pointers.

In a chapter titled "Scripture" in his book *Reflections on the Psalms*, which was published in 1958, Lewis provides a commentary on biblical inspiration. As Ryken points out, even though Lewis maintains an exceedingly high view of Scripture in *Reflections*, in the view of some members of the evangelical community of believers, Lewis's stance on biblical inspiration is not entirely satisfactory. In his address at the 2013 conference, Ryken acknowledges that Lewis believed "that the way for us to know God is on the authority of his Word, which provides the data for doing theology." In certain respects, however, he felt that "Lewis's doctrine of Scripture has long been regarded as something less than fully orthodox."[250] In Ryken's opinion, "Lewis placed the inspiration of Scripture on a continuum with other forms of literary inspiration, thus downplaying to some degree the uniqueness of the Bible."[251]

Lewis's book was published in 1958 and predates *The Chicago Statement on Biblical Inerrancy*, which was a doctrinal statement by an assembly of Protestant theologians in 1978. *The Chicago Statement* and its related documents, which were produced by the International Council of Biblical Inerrancy (ICBI), describe the Bible as being infallible and inerrant and describe Scripture as entirely true and trustworthy in all of its assertions. Ryken wishes that Lewis had had more training as a theologian, but it's not entirely clear that this would have benefitted Lewis's work as a Christian apologist. Perhaps there is something to be said for having his understanding of theology framed through the lens of a "lay student of theology," as Lewis referred to himself. As a literary scholar, he brought a unique perspective to theological debates. In keeping with his practise of placing maximal emphasis on Jesus's own words, Lewis may well have responded to Ryken by noting that Jesus did not, at the outset, entrust the Great Commission of preaching the gospel of the kingdom to professional theologians but structured his ministry in such a way so as to guarantee that the earliest messaging was going to be expressed through the voices of nonprofessionals. While professional theologians are most certainly needed, Lewis's literary background has benefitted Christian apologetics immensely.

---

250. Ryken, "Inerrancy and Patron Saint," 40.
251. Ryken, "Inerrancy and Patron Saint," 41.

According to Ryken, although Lewis has received much support within the evangelical Christian community, there is an element of discomfort about some of Lewis's scriptural views among certain Evangelicals. Ryken claims that some of Lewis's views, including his practise of interpreting Scripture in accordance with its respective genres, are considered to be "neoorthodox" or "suborthodox."[252] Ryken writes that "Lewis read the Bible as literature decades before it became fashionable to do so." He thinks, however, that by reading Scripture as literature and emphasising the respective genres in which the Bible was written, Lewis creates discomfort among some Evangelicals. It is important to note that Lewis did not consider the Bible to be merely literature, however; he considered it to be "through and through, a sacred book," Ryken claims. In his address to the 2013 conference, Ryken cites a number of excerpts from Lewis's writings and tells the audience that he considers Lewis's approach in "reading each biblical text according to its literary genre" to be a strength.[253]

In *Reflections on the Psalms*, Lewis writes:[254]

> For us these writings are "holy," or "inspired," or, as St. Paul says, "the Oracles of God." But this has been understood in more than one way, and I must try to explain how I understand it, at least as far as the Old Testament is concerned. I have been suspected of being what is called a Fundamentalist. That is because I never regard any narrative as unhistorical simply on the ground that it includes the miraculous. Some people find the miraculous so hard to believe that they cannot imagine any reason for my acceptance of it other than a prior belief that every sentence of the Old Testament has historical or scientific truth. But this I do not hold, any more than St. Jerome did, when he said that Moses described Creation "after the manner of a popular poet" (as I should say, mythically) or than Calvin did when he doubted whether the story of Job were history or fiction. The real reason why I can accept as historical a story in which a miracle occurs is that I have never found any philosophical grounds for the universal negative proposition that miracles do not happen. I have to decide on quite other grounds (if I decide at all) whether a given narrative is historical or not. The book of Job appears to me unhistorical because it begins about a man quite

---

252. Ryken, "Inerrancy and Patron Saint," 46.
253. Ryken, "Inerrancy and Patron Saint," 59.
254. Lewis, *Reflections on the Psalms*, 127–28.

unconnected with all history or even legend, with no genealogy, living in a country of which the Bible elsewhere has hardly anything to say; because, in fact, the author quite obviously writes as a story-teller not as a chronicler.

This excerpt from *Reflections* offers significant insight into Lewis's understanding of Scripture. He understands the Bible to be the "Oracles of God" and finds no valid reason for considering any narrative to be unhistorical because of its supernatural elements. In his opinion, there are no philosophical grounds for discounting the historicity of the miraculous. His reason for viewing the Job narrative as being unhistorical is instructive. He considers it unhistorical not because of its supernatural components but because of its genre and its lack of reference to any historical setting or geographic background in which it was written. Although Ryken offers no comment on Lewis's reference to Jerome, he critiques Lewis's comment about Calvin. In Ryken's view, "Lewis reveals his limitations in historical theology, since Calvin never denied the historicity of Job."[255]

The Lewisian conception of theology includes the processes whereby the Scriptures were constructed, authenticated, and preserved. Moreover, Lewis views much of Scripture as carrying the word of God rather than being the word of God:[256]

> Generalising this, I take it that the whole Old Testament consists of the same sort of material as any other literature—chronicle (some of it obviously pretty accurate), poems, moral and political diatribe, romances and what not; but all taken onto the service of God's word. Not all, I suppose in the same way. There are prophets who write with the clearest awareness that Divine compulsion is upon them. There are chroniclers whose intention may have been merely to record. There are poets like those in Song of Songs who probably never dreamed of any but a secular and natural purpose in what they composed. There is (and it is no less important) of the work first of the Jewish and then of the Christian Church in preserving and canonising just these books. There is the work of redactors and editors in modifying them. On all of these, I suppose a Divine pressure; of which not by any means all need to have been conscious.
>
> The human qualities of the raw materials show through. Naivety, error, contradiction, even (as in the cursing Psalms)

255. Ryken, "Inerrancy and Patron Saint," 51.
256. Lewis, *Reflections on the Psalms*, 129–30.

wickedness are not removed. The total result is not "the Word of God" in the sense that every passage, in itself, gives impeccable science or history. It carries the Word of God; and we (under grace, with attention to tradition and to interpreters wiser than ourselves, and with the use of such intelligence and learning as we may have) receive that word from it not by using it as an encyclical but by steeping ourselves in its tone or temper and so learning its overall message.

Lewis's overview of scriptural formation in *Reflections* is sometimes at variance with strict evangelical orthodoxy. Ryken thinks that "Lewis comes perilously close to a neoorthodox[257] view of Scripture in which the biblical text is not inherently divine but only becomes the Word of God when the Spirit of God makes it so for the reader."[258]

In his description of the manner by which the Bible has been compiled and preserved as Scripture, Lewis reflects on the human tendency to wish for a more systematic, tidier vehicle for God's word to be revealed to humankind: "We might have expected, we may think we should have preferred, an unrefracted light giving us ultimate truth in systematic form—something we could have tabulated and memorised and relied on like the multiplication table," writes Lewis. He claims that although we can respect the Fundamentalists' view of the Bible and the Roman Catholic's view of the Church, Christians need to be aware of one argument, and that is that God must have had reasons for revealing himself in

---

257. According to Michael Christensen, neoorthodox theologians have adopted some liberal presuppositions and have retained some elements of special revelation and certain traditional doctrines of orthodoxy. Although Søren Kierkegaard is regarded as a forerunner of neoorthodoxy, Karl Barth and Emil Brunner are the two individuals primarily identified as its founders, Barth for formulating some of the key notions and Brunner for introducing Barth's ideas to America. According to Brunner, the Bible is not to be identified as the word of God; the word comes to man as subjective, experienced encounter. The Bible becomes the word of God as God reveals himself through it. In this view, the Bible is not inerrant, but it has the authority of its authors by reason of having experienced the truth about that which they write. In Christensen's view, Lewis comes close to a neoorthodox position when he claims that the Bible carries the word of God. By using the verb carry, however, rather than using becoming or containing, as the neoorthodox theologians do, Christensen thinks that Lewis distances himself from neoorthodoxy. In his opinion, Lewis differs from neoorthodoxy by recognizing that spiritual truths are being conveyed through the words of Scripture. He writes that, for Lewis, the Bible is "not simply a witness to God's Word, but is, in a literary package, the special revelation of God" (Christensen, *C. S. Lewis*, 88).

258. Ryken, "Inerrancy and Patron Saint," 46.

this manner. Lewis contends that God must have done as he did, because he did what is best.²⁵⁹

"Biblical inspiration has become a 'watershed issue' in the evangelical world," writes Michael Christensen. He claims that although there have been internal feuds over the meaning of inspiration and the question of inerrancy, Evangelicals have generally remained united in their opposition to liberal and neoorthodox views about revelation and Scripture. He thinks that an evangelical position can be distinguished from a liberal theological position, because Evangelicals and liberals approach the Bible from two radically different worldviews. For Evangelicals, the Bible, unlike other ancient books, claims for itself a supernatural origin, whereas liberals generally presuppose a worldview in which the miraculous is improbable, if not impossible, writes Christensen. Accordingly, liberal theologians search for naturalistic causes in instances where miraculous events are described as having occurred, he claims. According to Christensen, accounts of biblical miracles are dismissed, and prophecies are regarded as having been written after the events in question are said to have occurred. Lewisian theology differs, in some respects, from what is generally accepted as evangelical theology, but Lewis has much more in common with the position held by Evangelicals than with that of the neoorthodox or liberal theologians. As Christensen points out, Evangelicals and liberals hold radically different worldviews, and Lewis's worldview is closely aligned with Evangelicals's worldview.²⁶⁰

Kevin Vanhoozer, professor of theology at Wheaton College Graduate School, writes that "Lewis was not terribly troubled over his Evangelical credentials or lack thereof."²⁶¹ Vanhoozer claims that although Lewis "explains how he understands the Bible to be the word of God in a brief chapter in *Reflections on the Psalms*," he "never explicitly set forth a 'doctrine' of scripture in his published works."²⁶² Regarding the Bible's inspiration, and "the manner in which it is both human and divine—Lewis acknowledges some ambivalence," writes Vanhoozer. In his opinion, the primary matter for Lewis was "that of which the Bible speaks." He thinks that, for Lewis, our speaking about the Bible was secondary by comparison. He opines that "though the theory of inspiration may have been a

---

259. Lewis, *Reflections on the Psalms*, 130–31.
260. Christensen, *C. S. Lewis*, 88–90.
261. Vanhoozer, "On Scripture," 75.
262. Vanhoozer, "On Scripture," 80.

matter of some indifference" for Lewis, "the fact of inspiration was not." In Vanhoozer's opinion, Lewis was focused on benefitting from the inspiration of Scripture, rather than on formulating a theory of inspiration. He notes that certain authors "detect quasi-Barthian overtones when Lewis likens biblical inspiration to the incarnation" in his writings.[263]

In the previously cited letter to Clyde Kilby in 1959, Lewis had expressed some of his perceptions regarding biblical inspiration. It was in an earlier letter to Lee Turner in 1958 that Lewis compared the incarnation to Scripture:[264]

> The main difficulty seems to me not the question *whether* the Bible is "inspired," but what exactly we mean by this. Our ancestors, I take it, believed that the Holy Spirit either just replaced the minds of the authors (like the supposed "control" in automatic writing) or at least dictated to them as to secretaries. Scripture itself refutes these ideas. S. Paul distinguishes between what the Lord says and what he says "of himself"—yet both are "Scripture." Similarly the passages in which the prophets describe Theophanies and their own reactions to them wd. be absurd if they were not writing for themselves. Thus, without any modern scholarship, we are driven a long way from the extreme view of inspiration. I myself think of it as analogous to the Incarnation—that, as in Christ a human soul-and-body are taken up and made the vehicle of Deity, so in Scripture, a mass of human legend, history, moral teaching etc. are taken up and made the vehicle of God's word. Errors of minor fact are permitted to remain. (Was Our Lord Himself incapable, qua Man, of such errors? Wd. it be a real human incarnation if He was?) One must remember of course that our modern & western attention to dates, numbers, etc. simply did not exist in the ancient world. No one was looking for *that* sort of truth. (You'd find something of my views about all of this in my forthcoming book on the Psalms.)

A fair reading of Lewis's letter to Turner would seem to indicate that he believed that some form of divine guidance (or Divine pressure, as he called it) had been present in the processes whereby Scripture had been written, authenticated, and preserved. The fact that God had used fallible human instruments to accomplish his work did not undermine its authenticity. He thought that Scripture was analogous to the incarnation;

---

263. Vanhoozer, "On Scripture," 81.
264. Lewis, *Collected Letters*, 3:960–61.

in Lewis's view, just as Jesus's human body had become a vehicle for deity, similarly, through God exercising "Divine pressure," the words of the Bible became the vehicle for conveying the word of God.

Lewis expands on the notion of the incarnation being analogous to Scripture in his book, *Reflections on the Psalms*. He begins by noting that humans, as members of the animal world, were "raised" to "something more than an animal" and "taken up into a new life without relinquishing the old."[265] In a similar manner, contends Lewis, "human life becomes the vehicle for Divine life."[266] He seems to imply by this analogy that God's word is being expressed through literature. What Lewis seems to infer is that rather than dictating transcripts for humans to read, God gives us Scripture by taking up human literature and utilizing it to communicate his divine message to us.

In the chapter titled "Scripture" in *Reflections on the Psalms*, Lewis provides perhaps his most expansive commentary on the subject of biblical inspiration and interpretation:[267]

> For we are taught that the Incarnation itself proceeded "not by the conversion of the god-head into flesh, but by the taking of (the) manhood into God"; in it human life becomes the vehicle of Divine life. If the Scriptures proceed not by conversion of God's word into a literature but by taking up of a literature to be the vehicle of God's word, this is not anomalous. . . .
>
> Because the lower nature, in being taken up and loaded with a new burden and advanced to a new privilege, remains, and is not annihilated, it will always be possible to ignore the up-grading[268] and see nothing but the lower. Thus, men can read the life of Our Lord (because it is a human life) as nothing but a human life. Many, perhaps most, human philosophies read human life merely as an animal life of unusual complexity. The Cartesians read animal life as a mechanism. Just in the same way Scripture can be read as merely human literature. No new discovery, no new method will ever give final victory to

---

265. Lewis, *Reflections on the Psalms*, 134.

266. Lewis, *Reflections on the Psalms*, 135.

267. Lewis, *Reflections on the Psalms*, 135–39.

268. Lewis refers to this up-grading as transposition (Lewis, *Essay Collection*, 267–78). Paul Brazier thinks that Lewis is at his most philosophically theological in invoking the concept of transposition to explain how revelation operates. He writes that in Lewis's view, God communicates and mediates truth and his salvific intentions to us through various modes—from the lower to higher, from the general and incomplete to the particular and perfect (Brazier, "C. S. Lewis"; *C. S. Lewis*, 3.1:249).

either interpretation. For what is required, on all these levels alike, is not merely knowledge but certain insight, getting the focus right. Those who can see in each of these instances only the lower will always be plausible. One who contended that a poem was nothing but black marks on white paper would be unanswerable if he addressed an audience who couldn't read. Look at it through microscopes, analyse the printer's ink and paper, study it (in that way) as long as you like, you will never find something over and above all the products of your analysis wherever you can say "This is the poem." Those who can read, however, will continue to say the poem exists. If the Old Testament is a literature thus "taken up," made the vehicle of what is more than human, we can of course set no limit to the weight or multiplicity of meaning which may have been lain upon it. If any writer may say more than he knows and mean more than he meant, then these writers will be especially likely to do so. And not by accident.

The second reason for accepting the Old Testament in this way can be put more simply and is of course more compulsive. We are committed to it in principle by Our Lord Himself. On that famous journey to Emmaus He found fault with the two disciples for not believing what the prophets had said. They ought to have known from their Bibles that the Anointed One, when He came, would enter his glory through suffering. He then explained from "Moses" (i.e., the Pentateuch) down, all the places in the Old Testament "concerning Himself" (Luke 24:25–27). He clearly identified Himself with a figure often mentioned in the Scriptures; appropriated to Himself many passages where a modern scholar might see no such reference. In the predictions of His Own Passion which He had previously made to the disciples. He was obviously doing the same thing. He accepted—and indeed He claimed to be—the second meaning of Scripture.

We do not know—or anyway I do not know—what all these passages were. We can be pretty sure about one of them. The Ethiopian Eunuch who met Philip (Acts 8:27–38) was reading Isaiah 53. He did not know whether in that passage the prophet was talking about himself or about someone else. Philip, in answering his question, "preached unto him Jesus." The answer, in fact, was "Isaiah is speaking of Jesus." We need have no doubt that Philip's authority for this interpretation was Our Lord.... In Mark 12:10 He implicitly appropriates to Himself the words of Psalm 118:22 about the stone which the builders rejected. "Thou shalt not leave my soul in hell, neither shalt

> thou suffer thine Holy One to see corruption" (16:11) is treated as a prophecy of His Resurrection in acts 2:27, and was doubtless so taken by Himself since we find it so taken in the earliest Christian tradition—that is, by people likely closer to both to the spirit and the letter of His words than any scholarship (I do not say "any sanctity") will bring a modern. Yet it is, perhaps, idle to speak here of spirit and letter. There is almost no "letter" in the words of Jesus. Taken by a literalist, He will always prove the most elusive of teachers. Systems cannot keep up with that darting illumination. No net less wide than a man's whole heart, nor less fine of mesh than love, will hold the sacred Fish.[269]

In the first paragraph of this excerpt, Lewis recaps the analogy mentioned in the Turner letter, in which he compares the word of God being infused into the literature of Scripture similar to the manner by which divinity is incorporated into the body of Jesus via the incarnation. In the second paragraph, he writes that for many individuals the truth of the incarnation is not believed or understood, because of those individuals's apparent inability to see anything more than his humanity in the person of Jesus. In similar manner, although Scripture is composed of a variety of genres of literature and is infused with the divine word of God, many unbelievers fail to see the Bible as anything more than literature, Lewis claims. In the final two paragraphs, Lewis cites the words of Jesus as additional corroboration for the literature of the Old Testament being "taken up," whereby it becomes God's word, and concludes with his observation that a reader's openness to the "spirit" in the message is vital for understanding Scripture.

As stated earlier, Kevin Vanhoozer claims that Lewis never explicitly outlined a doctrine of Scripture in his published works. In his opinion, Lewis was less interested in formulating a doctrine of Scripture than he was in looking through Scripture into the truths and mysteries of the faith. He claims that "Scriptural interpretation for Lewis is a matter of reading the whole Bible with one's whole being." He contends that Lewis "occupies that sparse territory between fundamentalists and modern

---

269. Kevin Vanhoozer opines that "fundamentalism and biblical criticism alike mistakenly talk 'about' scripture, thus keeping it at a safe distance, instead of experiencing from head to toe the reality for which it serves as means and medium.... Each lets the reality, *which truth is about*, slip through his fingers." He considers them to be "two different species of inept readers, each dropping 'the sacred Fish'" (Vanhoozer, "On Scripture," 78).

critics that is contagious but does not coincide with Evangelicalism."[270] Philip Ryken, also at Wheaton College, would revise Vanhoozer's characterisation: "We [Evangelicals] could go further and say that Lewis's doctrine of Scripture is not merely adjacent to, but often overlaps with evangelical theology," he opines.[271]

In a chapter titled "The Question of Inerrancy" in his book *C. S. Lewis on Scripture*, Michael Christensen writes: "The question of biblical inerrancy, like many Christian doctrines, has never been completely resolved within the Church." Men of faith have struggled with the question through the ages, advanced many theories, and held many views, claims Christensen. He writes that the "emphasis of the early church fathers was on the question of canonicity, not the meaning of inspiration."[272] He notes that the "early church, it would appear, required less of Scripture (in terms of inerrancy) than the church requires today."[273] Christensen thinks that Lewis would side with Evangelicals on "two distinctive points—worldview and revelation—but would *qualify* the word inspiration." Many Evangelicals traditionally "subscribe to a verbal view of inspiration in which inerrancy extends to the individual words of Scripture," while others favour a "plenary view of inspiration in which the Bible *taken as a whole*, is affirmed as an infallible authority," he points out. According to Christensen, "Lewis, though he never used the term, holds a literary view of inspiration." Lewis views the Bible as "inspired literature carrying a divine message," he claims.[274] Christensen contends that Lewis's literary view of inspiration separates him from fundamentalism, inasmuch as fundamentalists "believe that unless the Bible is verbally inspired and totally inerrant, it can't be authoritative." He claims that for fundamentalists, "the whole of Scripture stands or falls on the accuracy of its parts. If one part is in error the whole Bible is suspect." According to Christensen, Lewis "stands in sharp contrast to evangelical fundamentalism. His example proves that one can be a dedicated Evangelical, accept the authority of Scripture, yet disbelieve in inerrancy."[275]

270. Vanhoozer, "On Scripture," 84–85.
271. Ryken, "Inerrancy and Patron Saint," 64.
272. Christensen, *C. S. Lewis*, 82.
273. Christensen, *C. S. Lewis*, 83.
274. Christensen, *C. S. Lewis*, 90.
275. Christensen, *C. S. Lewis*, 91. In the second of his four-volume series on Lewis, Paul Brazier writes: "The theologian Keith Ward summarizes well the value of Scripture. There may be errors, flaws, and discrepancies in Scripture, but the truths that

Lewis's view of scriptural inspiration is highly complex and is not easily defined. He views the Bible as a literary work that manifests many of the characteristics of its human authors and as divinely inspired, in order to carry the message of God's revelation. Since its various components are centuries apart in the order of occurrence, it reflects the genres and tenors of their respective historical settings. Although inspired and of godly origin, it also reflects many of the shortcomings of its human authors, including the characteristics and limitations consistent with the various biblical periods. Lewis's theology is best understood within the context of his literary background. He was a widely read nonprofessional theologian. Although he was qualified to tutor in philosophy, he spent most of his academic career teaching literature, and he found the gospel message to be mediated through the literature of the Bible, in all of its diversity. As Michael Christensen has pointed out, Lewis's worldview led him to reject many of modern biblical criticism's anti-supernatural notions and to embrace the underlying truth claims of the Christian faith.[276] Lewis's worldview is also manifested in the manner in which he carried out his apologetic ministry, which is the subject of this chapter's final section.

4.8 LEWIS'S APOLOGETICS AS MINISTRY

In his day, Lewis was arguably the world's foremost authority in his professional field, medieval and Renaissance English literature; he had spent some ten years composing his most famous secular work, *English Literature in the Sixteenth Century Excluding Drama*, but he is best known for his religious writings. Brian Murphy, former professor of English at Rochester's Oakland University, writes: "Lewis has become a major force in Christianity in our time, and he holds a position quite unlike anyone

---

God reveals to humanity, that which is essential for our salvation are 'placed there' without error. This is similar to Lewis's approach to inerrancy: there are no substantial errors; there is no misleading as to the nature of our salvation in Scripture. . . . It is very easy for skeptics working from an atheistic standpoint to dismiss the evidence as tainted, even fabricated" (Brazier, *C S. Lewis*, 2:146–47).

276. According to Oxford professor John Lennox, Lewis's inclusion of the supernatural in his worldview is shared by eminent contemporary scientists. Lennox cites several "eminent scientists" for affirming "their belief in the supernatural and, in particular, the resurrection of Christ, which they regard as the supreme evidence for the truth of the Christian worldview" (Lennox, *God's Undertaker*, 196–97).

ever held at any time."[277] Although Lewis didn't refer to his writings as ministry, nevertheless, his impressive body of literature is distinguished by what he wrote while expounding and defending the Christian faith over many decades.

Peter Kreeft, professor of philosophy at Boston University, claims that there were three elements to Lewis's literature: rationalism, Romanticism, and Christianity.[278] It is noteworthy that Lewis came to theism by rational means and was aided in his conversion to Christianity by his imaginative insight. It is not surprising, therefore, that the elements of his own conversion are evidenced in many of his writings. His remarkable imaginative skills are on full display in his works of fiction, and his nonfiction writings exhibit the intellectual power of his rational/logical prowess. In addition to more than forty major published works, Lewis wrote hundreds of essays and poems. As his popularity increased over the years, Lewis was also kept busy answering the thousands of letters he received from his wide-ranging readership.

Lewis believed that Christians should exercise whatever gifts they had for the furtherance of the Christian faith. He appreciated good poetry and held a long-standing ambition to become a great poet. But gradually, over time, he came to accept the fact that he wasn't sufficiently gifted to create great poetry.[279] Eventually, he turned his attention to prose, and it was there that he made his greatest literary contributions. As mentioned earlier in this chapter, in a lecture to Anglican clergy in 1945, he advised authors who had the necessary skills to write books in which their Christianity remained latent. He urged the writers in the audience to write books on non-Christian topics, books in which a Christian worldview was implicit. Lewis's fictional works are perhaps his best example of that. He resisted any urgings for his own ordination, preferring instead to make his contribution to Christianity as an unordained member of the Anglican Church.

The formation of Lewis's worldview led him through many different philosophies and eventually to Christianity. For Lewis, the Christian faith offered the best explanation for his perception of reality. As mentioned previously, Chad Walsh considers it exceedingly fortuitous that Lewis came to embrace the Christian faith, because it provided him

277. Murphy, *C. S. Lewis*, 20.
278. Kreeft, *C. S. Lewis*, 13.
279. See Lewis's essay "The Alliterative Meter" for a sample of his interest in the technical aspects of poetry (Lewis, *Selected Literary Essays*, 15–26).

with a structural framework for his literature. Peter Kreeft contends that Lewis's Christian faith provided the means by which he could integrate his Romanticism and rationality, because it provided him with a much needed "catalyst" that was "powerful enough to make peace between two diverse powers." In Kreeft's opinion, the "romantic-rational blend was far from automatic."[280] In his depiction of his Romantic/rational dilemma in *Surprised by Joy*, Lewis seems to support Kreeft's notion: "Such then was the state of my imaginative life; over against it stood the life of my intellect. The two hemispheres of my mind were in the sharpest contrast. On the one side a many-islanded sea of poetry and myth: on the other a glib and shallow 'rationalism.' Nearly all that I loved I believed to be imaginary; nearly all that I believed to be real I thought grim and meaningless," he writes.[281]

David Clark contends that "as Lewis matured in the faith and his knowledge of the Scriptures deepened, a great many things about his world troubled him as he looked around at it from a Christian perspective." Clark thinks that Lewis was especially concerned about the "assumption in England that Christianity was passé," that it had been tried, and that "now it was time to move on to something else."[282] Lewis, however, took strong objection to that notion, and began his lifelong work of explaining and defending the Christian faith. Clark thinks that the subject matter of Lewis's letters articles and books falls within three distinct categories: (1) Speaking prophetically to his world, (2) reaching out to nonbelievers, or evangelism, and (3) living the faith while helping others do the same.[283] Peter Kreeft compares the respective genres in Lewis's writings to the strings in a bow: "The three main strings to Lewis's bow, rationalism, romanticism and Christianity, correspond to the three main genres of his writing, literary criticism, imaginative fiction and apologetics," he writes.[284]

As Clark has mentioned, there is a prophetic content in many of Lewis's writings, including the atoning death of Aslan, the lion in Lewis's Narnia chronicles. In his 2016 book titled *C. S. Lewis's Mere Christianity:*

---

280. Kreeft, *C. S. Lewis*, 9.
281. Lewis, *Surprised by Joy*, 170.
282. Clark, *C. S. Lewis*, 22.
283. According to Lewis's stepson, Douglas Gresham, rather than teaching him the doctrines of Christianity, Lewis taught the Christian faith by living it (Gresham, 2005). See the book's DVD enclosure for Gresham's statement.
284. Kreeft, *C. S. Lewis*, 13.

A Biography, historian George Marsden writes that when Lewis accepted the invitation to participate in a series of BBC broadcasts, "he recognized that in the modern world one of the great obstacles of the Christian message was that the culture encouraged the people to think they were already good as they were." Marsden contends that Lewis "attempted to counter that modern conceit" by appealing to the instinctive belief that there is an almost universal sense of right and wrong, which implies an objective moral law, and that the presence of such a law would give probability to the existence of a lawgiver.[285] Prophetic elements are extant throughout many of Lewis's writings. For the purpose of this dissertation, however, this section will focus on the prophetic content in a limited number of key nonfictional and fictional works.

In his book *The Abolition of Man*, Lewis presents a devastating critique of the societal values and morals of his time; in retrospect, it is astonishing to see how relevant the Lewisian depiction is to the current era. James Herrick, professor of communication at Michigan's Hope College, writes that recent developments in biological and psychological research have brought into reality certain policies and procedures that were still in the theoretic stage in Lewis's day. Herrick notes that there has been a long tradition whereby futurist proponents offer recommendations for biotechnical and ethical improvements to the human race. He claims that past intellectual luminaries and theorists such as George Bernard Shaw, J. D. Bernal, H. G. Wells, Olaf Stapledon, and J. B. S Haldane were prone to theorizing about the potential for remaking society via social and biological engineering. Herrick argues that a crucial historical development separates today's advocates from their predecessors and from Lewis, because human technological alterations are no longer a matter of mere speculation but are now "vigorously promoted scientific realities awaiting the political and cultural conditions that will allow their implementation."[286] Herrick's observation is evidenced in a lecture given by Oxford philosopher and bioethicist Julian Savulescu a few years ago. In his talk titled "Unfit for Life: Genetically Enhance Humanity or Face Extinction," at the Festival of Dangerous Ideas at the Sydney Opera House in 2009, Savulescu examined the nature of human beings as products of evolution, in particular their limited altruism, limited cooperative instincts, and limited ability to take account of the future consequences

---

285. Marsden, *C. S. Lewis's Mere Christianity*, 167.
286. Herrick, "C. S. Lewis," 239.

of actions. In his lecture, Savulescu argued that humans's biology and psychology are unfit for contemporary society, and that humanity must either alter its political institutions, severely restrain its technology, and change its nature or face annihilation because of shortcomings within its own design.[287] As well, in an article titled "Moral Transhumanism" in the *Journal of Medicine and Philosophy* published in 2010, Ingmar Persson and Savulescu advocate for the notion of a technologically enhanced posthumanity:[288]

> The exponential growth of advanced technology makes our lives much better or it may afford the means of our destruction. Things might get very much worse than they are today. The embracement of transhumanism[289] and posthumanism[290] offers one potential means of addressing this. And we have no reason to regret changes that would make us nonhuman in a biological sense. There is nothing special or valuable about human beings in the biological sense. To be more "human" in the normative sense of the term, in terms of those capacities that afford members of our species moral status and value, may require an evolution to posthumanism.

As Herrick notes:[291]

> In an almost uncanny fashion, Savulescu's comments reflect key elements of the educational, ethical, and scientific planning that

---

287. Savulesco, "Unfit for the Future."

288. Persson and Savulescu, "Moral Transhumanism."

289. "Transhumanism is both a reason-based philosophy and a cultural movement that affirms the possibility and desirability of fundamentally improving the human condition by means of science and technology. Transhumanists seek the continuation and acceleration of the evolution of intelligent life beyond its currently human form and human limitations by means of science and technology, guided by life-promoting principles and values" (More, "H+").

290. "Humanism is centered on the idea that human needs, values, concerns, and ideals are of the highest importance, or that the human being is the epitome of being. As a development of this idea, posthumanism is based on the notion that humankind can transcend the limitations of the physical human form. In a traditional sense, humans have been considered to be solidly and indisputably classified as high-functioning animals, but animals nonetheless. In this way, the same biological and physical constraints that limit the entire animal kingdom tether humankind to that base level. Posthumanism Theory suggests it is both possible and for the best for humans to attempt to surpass these limitations, often through the use of technology to augment biology" ("About Posthumanism Theory").

291. Herrick, "C. S. Lewis," 239.

Lewis was concerned to answer in the *Abolition of Man* as well as in the fictional work, *That Hideous Strength*. Proposals by Savulescu and others who share his concerns thus provide an opportunity for assessing the prophetic nature of Lewis's concerns about applied technology in the context of ascendant Western science operating outside the limits of widespread traditional values Lewis dubbed the *Tao*.[292]

During a conference on posthumanism in Salt Lake City,[293] Lincoln Cannon delivered a lecture titled, "Trust in Posthumanity and the New God Argument," during which he expressed sentiments and notions similar to Savulescu's:[294]

> We can use science and technology to enhance ourselves and our world. If limits continue to recede, we may radically extend our lives and abundantly expand our resources, such that present notions of poverty and even death would no longer apply. We may engineer new worlds and attain presently unimaginable degrees of flourishing. In so doing, we would change. We would be different than we are now to at least the extent that we are now different from our prehuman ancestors. We would be posthumans.

Oxford professor, futurist, and transhumanist Max More, in a blog post titled "A Letter to Mother Nature: Amendments to the Human Constitution," proposes several amendments to the "human constitution," an excerpt of which follows:

---

292. The *Tao* was Lewis's term for the doctrine of objective value. In Lewis's view, there was a common notion of right and wrong and an almost universal basis for considering certain actions and attitudes right and others not. He viewed the *Tao* as "a common human law of action" based on "a dogmatic belief in objective value." In an appendix to *The Abolition of Man*, he gives a list of principles as examples of Tao: respect for human life; fulfillment of obligations to family; the practise of mercy, justice, and truthfulness; and the preference of death to dishonour (Lewis, *Abolition of Man*, 701, 727–38). Lewis's use of the term *Tao* has nothing to do with Taoism. For Lewis, *Tao* designates the natural law, the ethical principles by all civilizations in all times. Doris Myers opines that Lewis uses the term to get away from the associations that the term natural law has with Christian ethics. She thinks that's because he is attempting to write nontheistically rather than from a Christian viewpoint and is using examples from Egyptian, Babylonian, Hindu, and Native American sources, as well as Judeo-Christian, Graeco-Roman, and Teutonic sources (Myers, *C. S. Lewis*, 78).

293. The Mormon Transhumanist Association in Salt Lake City is reputed to be the largest transhumanist chapter.

294. Cannon, "Trust in Posthumanity."

Mother Nature, truly we are grateful for what you have made us. No doubt you did the best you could. However, with all due respect, we must say that you have in many ways done a poor job with the human constitution. You have made us vulnerable to disease and damage. You compel us to age and die—just as we're beginning to attain wisdom. You were miserly in the extent to which you gave us awareness of our somatic, cognitive, and emotional processes. You held out on us by giving the sharpest senses to other animals. You made us functional only under narrow environmental conditions. You gave us limited memory, poor impulse control, and tribalistic, xenophobic urges. And, you forgot to give us the operating manual for ourselves! What you have made us is glorious, yet deeply flawed. You seem to have lost interest in our further evolution some 100,000 years ago. Or perhaps you have been biding your time, waiting for us to take the next step ourselves. Either way, we have reached our childhood's end. We have decided that it is time to amend the human constitution. We do not do this lightly, carelessly, or disrespectfully, but cautiously, intelligently, and in pursuit of excellence. We intend to make you proud of us. Over the coming decades, we will pursue a series of changes to our own constitution, initiated with the tools of biotechnology guided by critical and creative thinking. In particular, we declare the following seven amendments to the human constitution:

Amendment No. 1: We will no longer tolerate the tyranny of aging and death. Through genetic alterations, cellular manipulations, synthetic organs, and any necessary means, we will endow ourselves with enduring vitality and remove our expiration date. We will each decide for ourselves how long we shall live.

Amendment No. 2: We will expand our perceptual range through biotechnological and computational means. We seek to exceed the perceptual abilities of any other creature and to devise novel senses to expand our appreciation and understanding of the world around us.

One is struck by the extent to which the cautionary note in Lewis's *Abolition of Man* is applicable to many of the notions expressed by Savulescu, Cannon, and More. Lewis's book *The Abolition of Man* was first published in 1943 and was a compilation of three lectures that he had given in Newcastle earlier that year. The three lectures were titled "Men without Chests," "The Way," and "The Abolition of Man." The title for the final chapter also became the title for the later publication. The book was a critique of social engineering, biotechnical experimentation, and the abandonment of traditional values. Lewis argued that progressive scientific social engineering, rather than creating an advanced society, would have a dehumanizing effect and lead to the abolishment of traditional humanity. Lewis writes that man's conquest of nature is often used as a description of progress in applied science. This so-called power over Nature often turns out to be "a power exercised by some men over other men with Nature being used as its instrument," he claims.[295] Lewis is concerned that if the dreams of some scientific planners are realized, it will result in a few hundred men exercising control over the lives of "billions and billions of men."[296] He expresses his fears about the result of "Man by eugenics, by pre-natal conditioning, and by an education propaganda based on a perfect applied psychology, [having] obtained full control over himself."[297] Lewis postulates that the "man-moulders of the new age will be armed with the omnicompetent state and an irresistible scientific technique" to produce "a race of conditioners" who can configure society into whatever shape they wish.[298] He expresses concern that these social engineers or conditioners, as he calls them, would find themselves in a position to create an artificial *Tao* of their own choosing. Lewis writes that he is "very doubtful whether history shows us one example of a man who, having stepped outside traditional morality and attained power has used that power benevolently."[299] He is therefore highly sceptical about the likelihood that the power acquired via social engineering will have any societal benefit. He projects that the resulting society would lose its appreciation for sound values by classifying values as nothing more than natural phenomena. Lewis fears that in such a world, humans would be reduced to artifacts, culminating in the abolition of man, the final result of man's conquest of nature. In *The Abolition of Man*, Lewis argues that modern science should exercise caution and restraint before engaging in unbridled adventurist experiments and practises. While he thinks that much of what Western science has accomplished is laudatory, he expresses concern that some of its "triumphs may have been too rapid and

---

295. Lewis, *Abolition of Man*, 719.
296. Lewis, *Abolition of Man*, 720.
297. Lewis, *Abolition of Man*, 720.
298. Lewis, *Abolition of Man*, 721.
299. Lewis, *Abolition of Man*, 724.

purchased at too high a price."[300] Lewis also voices profound concerns in his three lectures about the direction that Western education had taken. James Herrick writes that "Lewis's deep suspicion of modernist educational projects, subjectivism about morality, and progressive scientific planning animates" the Lewis lectures.[301]

These concerns are expressed in even more striking terms in Lewis's 1945 book *That Hideous Strength*. University of Northern Colorado's Doris Myers writes that in the book, Lewis confronts "the modern reverence for science, the fallacy of attempting to apply the scientific method to human beings, and the danger of social control."[302] As mentioned, Lewis voiced his opposition to the undermining of valid objective values by the educational system and to the replacing of those values with subjectivism. While he supported reputable scientific endeavours, he felt that society was at risk when traditional morality was replaced with some version of scientism.

Despite the fact that Lewis masks much of his critique of scientism within his fictional writings, his message is delivered with devastating effect. A key figure in *That Hideous Strength* is Mark Studdock, a professor who is recruited by The National Institute of Coordinated Experiments, a quasi-governmental agency. The National Institute of Coordinated Experiments (N.I.C.E.) is a scientific and social planning agency that exploits nature and devises plans for the modification of humanity, in part, for the purpose of elongating and eventually perpetuating the lifespan of individuals. Studdock was a sociology professor at a local college, who is recruited by N.I.C.E. because of his background in the social sciences and because of his perceived value as a potential propagandist for the furtherance of N.I.C.E.'s objectives. Lewis uses the novel to create a dystopian vision in which a society dominated by scientific materialism as expressed by transhumanism is contrasted with one characterised by traditional Christian beliefs and values. Studdock, upon becoming a staff member, initially supports the agency but eventually joins the opposition, when he discovers N.I.C.E.'s ultimate plans. The plot of *That Hideous Strength* contains elements of historically mythological figures, European Marxism, and Hitlerian notions of central planning. Its depiction of transhumanism reaches a climax when it is revealed that the agency's

---

300. Lewis, *Abolition of Man*, 729.
301. Herrick, "C. S. Lewis," 240.
302. Myers, *C. S. Lewis*, 215.

head is a literal head that is being preserved in perpetuity by seemingly artificial means. Lewis poignantly illustrates the potential disaster that may occur when measures to accrue power are undertaken by a dominating inner circle within society.

Henry Schaefer III at the University of Georgia claims that in *That Hideous Strength*, Lewis is addressing his concern that "some scientists had abandoned the historic Christian view of a rational universe." He thinks that although the language in some of his characters may be a bit overblown, he would "agree with Lewis that science is endangered when it fails to understand why the universe is intelligible."[303] Chad Walsh notes that during one of his meetings with Lewis, he had asked him about some of the content in *That Hideous Strength*:[304]

> Somehow the subject of the N.I.C.E. came up once when I was with Lewis and I asked him whether he was against science. He answered—with unusual warmth—that he was not. "Science is neither an enemy, nor a friend," he said. "Science is not a person!" When I pressed him for some comment on the N.I.C.E. he said that the point had been missed by many readers. The moral is not that science or scientists are launching an attack against humanity, but simply that anyone who is an enemy of humanity would claim the prestige of science.... Lewis added that he had noticed that the "pure sciences" seem to have no dehumanizing effect on those who study them, but that the closer a science approaches to human affairs the more it tends to strip its specialists of their humanity; sociologists and psychologists are in greater peril than chemists and mathematicians.

David Clark thinks that it is in "*That Hideous Strength*, where under guise of fiction he [Lewis] could safely reveal his inner convictions."[305] Clark notes that once Studdock had been drawn into the N.I.C.E. to the point where its leadership felt that they could take them into their confidence, he is introduced to the head of the institute, which turns out to be an actual head that had been removed from its body and ostensibly kept alive through technology. In the storyline, however, the head was actually being sustained and manipulated by fallen angels. Clark thinks that in describing the National Institute of Coordinated Experiments's organizational structure as he does, Lewis is actually revealing some of

303. Schaefer, "C. S. Lewis."
304. Walsh, *C. S. Lewis*, 129.
305. Clark, *C. S. Lewis*, 48.

his own views about the likelihood for demonic influence within some institutions. He thinks that there is Scriptural support for thinking that an organization such as the N.I.C.E. might well be a "devil-led organization" and that indeed "Lewis does have a Scriptural leg to stand on."[306] He notes that the scriptural record in books such as Daniel and Jeremiah would support this notion. As Schaefer, Walsh, and Clark have indicated, Lewis's worldview had a direct impact on the substance of his prophetic messaging.

Alister McGrath claims that apologetics is best described as a principled defense and a commendation of the Christian faith, which is articulated by answering objections raised against the faith and by exploring and explaining its potential attraction to those who haven't yet discovered it. Lewis's apologetic method cannot be easily categorized within any school of apologetics, he writes. There is both a defensive and an evangelistic aspect to Lewis's methodology. McGrath observes that just as historically there are diverse characteristics in the methods employed by notable apologists such as Justin Martyr, Aquinas, and Pascal, so there are also substantial changes in Lewis's methodology as practised during the various periods in which he wrote his body of work.[307] He considers the period between 1940 and 1955 as having been Lewis's Golden Age as a public apologist. Significantly, Lewis first published two of his important works, *The Problem of Pain* and *Surprised by Joy*, in 1940 and 1955, respectively. Many of his classic works, as well as numerous public lectures, were also published during this time. McGrath sees a change in focus in Lewis's apologetics in his later writings. Rather than defending a challenged faith and persuading those outside the church of the truth of the Christian faith, as he had done earlier, McGrath notes that Lewis's messaging shifted to "exploring and appreciating the depths of the Christian faith for the benefit of those who believed, or were close to believing."[308] As McGrath points out, Lewis's *Reflection on the Psalms*, first published in 1958, reflects this change in focus. As Lewis writes in the book's Introduction, *Reflections on the Psalms* is not intended as an apologetic work:[309]

---

306. Clark, *C. S. Lewis*, 49.
307. McGrath, *Intellectual World*, 129.
308. McGrath, *Intellectual World*, 130.
309. Lewis, *Reflections on the Psalms*, 8–9.

> Finally, as will soon be apparent to any reader, this is not what is called an "apologetic work." I am nowhere trying to convince unbelievers that Christianity is true. I address those who already believe it, or those who are ready, while reading, to "suspend their disbelief." A man can't be always defending the truth; there must be a time to feed on it. I have written, too, as a member of the Church of England, but I have avoided controversial questions as much as possible. At one point I had to explain how I differed on a certain matter both from Roman Catholics and from Fundamentalists: I hope I shall not for this forfeit the good will or the prayers of either. Nor do I much fear it. In my experience the bitterest opposition comes neither from them nor from any other thoroughgoing believer, and not from atheists, but from semi-believers of all complexions. There are some enlightened and progressive old gentlemen of this sort whom no courtesy can propitiate and no modesty can disarm. But then I dare say I am a much more annoying person than I know. (Shall we, perhaps in Purgatory, see our faces and hear our voices as they really were?)

McGrath characterises this change in focus as a shift from his public defense of the Christian faith to an exploration of its "spiritual and imaginative dimensions."[310] In his opinion, this shift in focus was also a significant factor in Lewis's continued appeal to his wide-ranging Christian readership. Lewis offered his readers apologetic approaches, which both reassured them about the credibility of their own faith and also enabled them to deal with the stated concerns of others.

Another reason for Lewis's appeal is almost certainly due to the manner in which he communicated the truth claims of Christianity. As noted previously, in his address during a conference for Anglican clergy, Lewis advises the conference attendees about the importance of translating the Christian message into the vernacular, the language of its recipients. This was a capability that he had acquired from his experiences while speaking before his country's military personnel during the war years.

McGrath expresses Lewis's methodology as follows:[311]

> Lewis's approach to apologetics is multi-layered, expressing itself in different ways. *Miracles* offers an essentially rational apologetic; *Mere Christianity* mingles reasoned argument with a much more subjective appeal to the longings of the human

---

310. McGrath, *Intellectual World*, 131.
311. McGrath, *Intellectual World*, 133.

heart; while the *Chronicles of Narnia* set out to captivate the imagination of its readers. It is therefore important to try to disentangle and appreciate the characteristics of these three different apologetic gateways deployed by Lewis: reason, longing, and the imagination. Having mastered the art of popular communication, Lewis had to consider what approaches he might adopt to defend the Christian faith against its critics, and commend it to skeptics.

It is noteworthy that Lewis, in *Mere Christianity* and *Miracles*, assumes little, if any, ecclesiastical knowledge on the part of his audience. Instead, he appeals to the nature of the universe and to the internal self-evident moral law or *Tao* and draws attention to what can be acknowledged "on our own steam":[312]

> We have not yet got as far as the God of any actual religion called Christianity. We have only got as far as a Somebody or Something behind the Moral law. We are not taking anything from the Bible or Churches, we are trying to see what we find out about this Somebody on our own steam. And I want to make it quite clear that what we find out on our own steam is something that gives us a shock. We have two bits of evidence about the Somebody. One is the universe He has made. If we used that as our only clue, then I think we should have to conclude He was a great artist (for the universe is a beautiful place), but also that He is quite merciless and no friend to man (for the universe is a very terrifying and dangerous place). The other bit of evidence is that Moral Law which He has put into our minds. And this is a better bit of evidence than the other, because it is inside information. You find out more about God from the Moral Law than from the universe in general just as you find out more about a man by listening to his conversation than by looking at a house he has built. Now, from this second piece of evidence we conclude that the Being behind the universe is intensely interested in right conduct—in fair play, unselfishness, courage, good faith, honesty and truthfulness. In that sense, we should agree with the account given by Christianity and some other religions, that God is "good." But do not let us go too fast here.

Lewis concludes this section by explicating the nature of the moral law, reasoning about what the implied qualities would be for an Originator of such a law and about the implied problems created by individuals

---

312. Lewis, *Mere Christianity*, 29–30.

who fail to adhere to it. He postulates on the dilemma being created by imputing goodness to an Originator of the moral law, given the apparent consequences wrought by humanity's inevitable shortcomings, and explains the manner in which the Christian faith resolves this dilemma. Rather than attempting to offer unassailable proof of Christianity, Lewis expresses the reasonableness of the Christian faith and demonstrates that although the grounds for Christian belief may not constitute incorrigible proofs, they are, nevertheless, reliably trustworthy indicators of the existence of such a Being as the God of Christianity.

Even prior to his conversion, Lewis was becoming aware of the inadequacy of relying on reason alone for gaining a comprehensive understanding of the nature of reality. Several years before his conversion, in a 1926 letter, he wrote to Cecil Harwood about the limitations of reason:[313]

> About powers other than reason—I would be sorry if you mistook my position. No one is more convinced than I that reason is utterly inadequate to the richness and spirituality of real things: indeed, this is itself a deliverance of reason. Nor do I doubt the presence, even in us, of faculties embryonic and atrophied, that lie in an indefinite margin around the little bit of focus which is intelligence—faculties anticipating or remembering the possession of huge tracts of reality that slip through the meshes of the intellect. And, to be sure, I believe that the symbols presented by imagination at its height are the workings of that fringe and present to us as much of the super-intelligible reality as we can get while we retain our present form of consciousness. My scepticism begins when people offer me explicit accounts of the super-intelligible and in so doing use all the categories of the intellect.

Lewis is dealing with a range of issues here. He tells Harwood that he is well aware of the limits of reason and that he acknowledges the benefit that our imaginative faculty can bring to one's perception of reality. The fringe that he mentions and the scepticism to which he refers are almost certainly related to disagreements that he has with Harwood and Barfield's acceptance of some of Rudolf Steiner's notions about anthroposophy, details of which are mentioned in a previous chapter. Although he is aware of the benefits that may be accrued from intuitive insight and from marshalling one's imaginative capabilities, Lewis is also sceptical about placing undue emphasis on, and about allowing one's intellect to

---

313. Lewis, *Collected Letters*, 1:670–71.

fasten on, those hints that he perceives as having come from the fringe. In his letter, Lewis acknowledges the potential value of imaginative insight but reminds Harwood about reason's capacity for corroborating objectivity and accuracy in matters of human understanding.

Lewis's friend, the philosopher and theologian Austin Farrer, in an essay about Lewis titled "The Christian Apologist," which was published two years after Lewis's death, writes that rational argument, rather than creating belief, helps to foster an intellectual climate that is conducive to fostering belief:[314]

> Rational argument does not create belief, but it maintains a climate in which belief may flourish. . . . Lewis did better. He provided a positive exhibition of the force of Christian ideas, morally, imaginatively, and rationally. The strength of his appeal (as we have said) lies in the many-sidedness of his work. Christian theism, to those who believe it, commends itself as fact, not theory, by the sheer multiplicity of its bearings.

Farrer seems to imply some version of the notion of the "inference to the best explanation" here. Although neither Lewis nor Farrer specifically cite this notion, it involves the acknowledgment of the preponderance of evidence for a situation in which definitive proof is lacking. Notably, Alister McGrath considers inference to the best explanation[315] to be "now widely regarded as the dominant philosophy of the natural sciences."[316] Farrer's observation of Lewis's methodology is instructive. He notes that despite the fact that Lewis had been trained in philosophy, philosophy wasn't Lewis's specialty. Nevertheless, Lewis was "singularly successful" in challenging the prevailing philosophical influences, Farrer writes:[317]

> Philosophy was not Lewis's trade and he had many other irons in the fire. He was singularly successful in so far as challenging philosophical influences current during the thirties as to make a case for Christian beliefs in the minds of university students, and some of them by no means the least intelligent. He was never quite at home in what we may call our post-positivist era; his philosophical commendations of theism cannot be usefully

---

314. Farrer, "Christian Apologist," 26.

315. "Inference to the best explanation" is a form of abductive reasoning, which, unlike deductive reasoning, does not lead to a conclusion as the result of the truth of its premises. See Lipton, *Inference to the Best Explanation*.

316. McGrath, *Intellectual World*, 136.

317. Farrer, "Christian Apologist," 30–31.

recommended to puzzled undergraduate philosophers of the present day. His literary, his moral, and his spiritual development was continuous; his philosophical experience belonged to the time of his conversion. Philosophy is an ever-shifting, never-ending public discussion, and a man who drops out of the game drops out of philosophy. But theological belief is not a philosophical position, it is the exercise of the relation of the most solidly real of all beings; and there are many lights in which it may be placed other than those of philosophical discussion. It does not follow that a Christian apologist who drops out of professional philosophy is left with nothing to say.

Farrer claims that although Lewis's specialty was literature, Lewis contributed to the debate about issues of significance. He notes that many of Lewis's religious writings are not formally apologetic. And he characterises Lewis's *Great Divorce, Screwtape Letters,* and *Mere Christianity* as "plain expositions or imaginative realizations of doctrine," which feature "moral analysis displaying the force of Christian ideas." He thinks that Lewis's autobiographical works, *Pilgrim's Regress* and *Surprised by Joy,* contain the intellectual history of Lewis's conversion rather than straight apologetics. In Farrer's opinion, Lewis's books *Miracles* and *The Problem of Pain,* as well as some of his essays, are the best examples of Lewis's direct approach to apologetics.[318]

Farrer's observation about Lewis's apologetic methodology in dealing with the existence of pain, sometimes characterised as existence of evil, is very informative:[319]

> He recovered from the blow recorded in *A Grief Observed*.... When he wrote *The Problem*, he already had plenty of experimental[320] evidence. His recollections of early life show his feelings to have been alarmingly vulnerable. He had endured the First World War on the Western Front, and been severely wounded. And he had causes of personal grief, some disclosed in his writings, others only hinted at. He who has stood fire may fairly reflect on mortal combat; not, however, while he's dodging the bullets. Some people have no use for reflection; but that's another matter.

---

318. Farrer, "Christian Apologist," 31.
319. Farrer, "Christian Apologist," 32–34.
320. Farrer may have meant experiential.

The first thing to strike us about *The Problem of Pain* is the modesty of its scale. It is a little book, not much more than 40,000 words; and it ranges over a wide area of topics. Its author can never have imagined that he would make a profound contribution to philosophical theology at this rate. . . .

Any academically-minded author attempting Lewis's subject would surely say, "I am writing about the problem which the fact of pain presents to a Christian belief in God." . . . But Lewis's aim is apologetic, and therefore pastoral. He knew his readers. They wrote to him from all over the world; he answered them in unbelievable number, and with unfailing generosity. . . .

Lewis proceeds to give his textbook sketch of the development of religion. It contains no reference to his own evolution into belief; the special themes of *The Pilgrim's Regress* and *Surprised by Joy* are absent. He gives what he regards as the standard answer of the time—*Biblical Revelation* read through Rudolf Otto's spectacles:[321] a world haunted by the supernatural, a conscience haunted by the moral absolute, a history haunted by the divine claim of Christ; such have been the accumulating strata of religious evidence.

Lewis is obliged to put his points so briefly as to be open to every attack. But the protection which his arguments lack in particular is made up to them in general. He concedes that the evidence of religion is not logically compulsive; and compensates for the admission by appealing to the fact that it has so widely prevailed with reasonable men. The chapter, slight as it is, provides an excellent example of the author's good management. Determined as he is to indicate the live sources of belief, he takes the necessary risks; yet he contrives to cover himself from the suspicion of fanaticism or naivete. And that without overloading the page, or saying more than can agreeably be said. So he gives to textbook matter the freshness of a living consideration.

When he turns to the substantial part of his essay, pastoral concern continues to rule his pen.

---

321. Rudolf Otto (1869–1937) was a German Lutheran theologian, and philosopher. He is regarded as one of the most influential scholars of religion in the early twentieth century and is best known for his concept of the numinous, a profound emotional experience he argued was at the heart of the world's religions. He is also known for his book "The Idea of the Holy," which was first published in German in 1911, and favourably referred to by Lewis.

Farrer opines that anyone who attempts to reconcile the stated goodness of God with the natural state of the physical world with all of its apparent evil, disastrous accidents, randomness, and pain, as Lewis does, will find it to be a formidable challenge, no matter what arguments are employed to justify evil's existence. He notes that Lewis cites the corrective effect that it may have on human behaviour or, as Farrer characterises Lewis's method, pressing the overruling of evil for providential ends or viewing incidents of pain/evil as instruments of disciplinary providence.[322] He thinks that anyone attempting this reconciliation will need to make a choice between concentrating on the philosophical side or the theological side of the argument. He notes that Lewis has chosen to structure the argument by favouring its theological aspect, a decision with which Farrer agrees. In Farrer's opinion, the theological approach boldly accepts belief in a particular providence and seeks a setting for the incidents of pains in God's dealing with his human creatures. The advantage of using this approach is that it shows its direct relevance to religion, he claims. Farrer contends that a reader who is concerned to see pain and theism reconciled is presumably concerned with God and with a positive acceptance of his will. He thinks that the theological approach offers general support for a purpose underlying the world-order. He contends that there is a disadvantage in placing a disproportionate amount of weight on the theological approach, however, because "pressed to its logical extreme, it yields revolting paradoxes."[323]

Farrer contends that if pain is the direct instrument of divine purpose, the divine hand is made responsible for afflictions that can have no other effect than the destruction of human personality. He argues that for this and other reasons, no one who knows what he is about can

322. Alister McGrath views some of Lewis's argumentation as a process of abduction. McGrath writes: "We can reframe this approach in terms of the lines of Lewis's main arguments in *Mere Christianity*:
  1. We experience a sense of morality and a 'desire which no experience in this world can satisfy.'
  2. Suppose that the Christian way of thinking is right; if this is so, these resonances or harmonies would be expected.
  3. Therefore there is reason to suspect that Christianity is true.

Abduction is the process by which we observe certain things, and work what intellectual framework mightmake sense of them. Sometimes, . . . abduction comes to us like a flash, as an act of insight. Sometimes, it comes about through slow, methodical reflection, as we try to generate every possibility to make senseof what we observe" (McGrath, Intellectual World, 119–20).

323. Farrer, "Christian Apologist," 35.

really rely on the theological approach alone. And he commends Lewis for strengthening his case by including philosophical argumentation. He notes, however, as an academic, he would have preferred a more extensive treatment of the relationship between the theological and philosophical. Nevertheless, he considers Lewis's treatment of that relationship adequate for Lewis's general readership. And as to the explanation of the apparent paradox of a world such as ours having been created by a benevolent God, Farrer considers Lewis's argument clear, sympathetic, and persuasive. But it also becomes something more, he claims. By responding to the postulated objections, Lewis "discloses the unique transcendent claim of the love of God with a controlled and reasoned passion which is theophanic. . . . We think we are listening to an argument, in fact we are presented with a vision; and it is the vision that carries conviction," he writes.[324]

Farrer endorses most of Lewis's methodology but does not do so without some reservations. For instance, he notes that Lewis sees the primary function of human emotional discomfort or mental pain as a means to draw attention to our misdirectedness, a notion that, in his opinion, "is difficult to deny that it is the distinctively Christian answer."[325] He finds no broad apologetic purpose, however, in what he considers to be Lewis's "tortured speculations" about the future of individuals who remain in a state of "ultimate impenitence."[326]

He thinks that Lewis unnecessarily involves himself in impossible difficulties by articulating some of his speculative notions. Farrer opines that some of these notions may be attributable to the fact that "Lewis was raised in the tradition of an idealist philosophy[327] which hoped to establish the reality of the mental subject independently of, or anyhow in priority to, that of the bodily world."[328] He also takes objection to Lewis's speculative musings about the possibility for the immortality of brutes. He thinks that these musings are a consequence of Lewis's having pushed the notion of morality too far. He thinks that Lewis's imagination, at moments such as these, uncharacteristically slips out of control of the leash imposed by his reason. He notes that this happens despite Lewis's having been gifted with a traditionalist imagination. He commends Lewis,

---

324. Farrer, "Christian Apologist," 37.
325. Farrer, "Christian Apologist," 38.
326. Farrer, "Christian Apologist," 39.
327. See the note X-REF on philosophical idealism in ch. 3.
328. Farrer, "Christian Apologist," 41.

however, "when he solemnly submits such fantasies to the censure of the Church."[329]

As noted earlier, Lewis saw the intellectual world as represented by the Christian faith, and its portrayal of the God of creation as an explanation of reality, as an account of the world as it really is. McGrath points out that Lewis sees God as an intellectual sun lighting up the landscape of reality, allowing us to see things as they really are. He notes that such imagery can be traced back to Plato and Augustine. McGrath thinks that the use of such imagery "suggests that the ability of a worldview or metanarrative to illuminate reality is an important measure of its reliability, and an indicator of its truth."[330] He notes that Lewis's *Mere Christianity* presents the Christian faith as an eminently reasonable account of life, and thinks that helps explain the book's wide acceptance within Western culture, making it "one of the most influential Christian books of the twentieth century."[331] McGrath considers the book to be much more than just rational apologetics, however. He views the book as much more than an appeal from a modernist worldview that privileges rational demonstration. He attributes much of *Mere Christianity*'s success to Lewis's having integrated reason and feelings (emotion) in his apologetic method. McGrath claims that Lewis builds on an argument from desire, drawing from approaches used by historical figures such as Augustine and Aquinas, while giving a distinctly literary focus and identity to the approaches. He notes that Lewis's methodology integrates an appeal to human longings, such as longing for beauty and longing for memories of childhood, and then argues that the Christian worldview accommodates such longings.[332]

As noted in previous references, Lewis's acknowledgment that his own longings and desires remained unfulfilled led him to conclude that ultimate satisfaction was not possible via anything finite and that he was likely made for another world. Clearly, Lewis's methodology was highly influenced by his own spiritual journey. McGrath contends that Lewis's notion of unfulfilled desires is not intended as proof for the truth claims of Christianity but as indicative of being the most likely explanation of our world. In his view, "Lewis's argument is best seen as the commendation of

---

329. Farrer, "Christian Apologist," 42.
330. McGrath, *Intellectual World*, 137.
331. McGrath, *Intellectual World*, 137.
332. McGrath, *Intellectual World*, 137.

a 'big picture,'³³³ an overall way of seeing things which appears to position elements of reality in a plausible manner [in which] . . . it is not the individual components of this picture that provide explanatory persuasion, but the overall capaciousness of the intellectual web."³³⁴ He notes that for Lewis, "Christianity is seen at its best, not in its individual components, but in their combination of the Christian vision of reality."³³⁵ He thinks that helps explain why Lewis has been embraced by modernist and postmodernist apologists alike, and why he was reluctant "to isolate doctrinal statements, or engage in detailed analysis of theories of atonement."³³⁶ McGrath characterizes Lewis's method as a thread of approaches. In a chapter entitled "Lewis's Apologetic Method," McGrath writes:³³⁷

> Lewis's apologetic pallete has a rich range of vibrant colors not often found elsewhere, especially those locked into the rigidities of certain schools of apologetics. As a result Lewis has been embraced by both modernist and postmodernist apologists; by those commending the rational defense of faith, those advocating its imaginative exploration; by those focusing on argument, and those preferring narrative; by those who privilege rationality and those who long for imaginative stimulation. Lewis is able to engage apologetic issues at multiple levels, transcending the limits and dullness of traditional rational defenses of the Christian faith. Rarely has an apologist secured—and retained—such a wide and varied readership.

333. Philosopher Charles Taylor, in his book *A Secular Age*, has referred to the perception of one's world as a *social imaginary*. Whereas Taylor uses the term to represent one's perception of his/her social and cultural world, it contains some of the elements that are included in what Lewis refers to when he uses the term *world picture*. Taylor's social imaginary is representative of how one perceives one's cultural and social environs. Although Taylor's term is more delineated, both terms refer to one's perceived reality (Taylor, *Secular Age*, 171–75).

Ninian Smart, former professor of religious studies at the University of Birmingham and the University of California, Santa Barbara, has advanced the notion of analysing worldviews in a way that uses the term to refer to both traditional religions and ideologies. He perceives the various worldviews as "different pictures of the cosmos," pictures that are conceived as a consequence of the "human search for the truth about what surrounds us" and by a "quest for meaning" (Smart, *Worldviews*, 60–61).

334. McGrath, *Intellectual World*, 120–21.

335. McGrath, *Intellectual World*, 121. It is noteworthy that McGrath credits Austin Farrer, whom he considers to be "one of Lewis's most perceptive interpreters," for the term "Christian vision of reality."

336. McGrath, *Intellectual World*, 121.

337. McGrath, *Intellectual World*, 143.

In addition to speaking prophetically to his world and reaching out to nonbelievers through evangelism, Lewis also lived the faith while helping others do the same. In the introduction to his book on Lewis's theology, David Clark writes that "Lewis not only led people to faith, including Joy Davidman Gresham, the woman who would become his wife, he mentored and encouraged them in their new walk with God." As noted earlier, Lewis's stepson Douglas Gresham has publicly commented on the manner in which Lewis, rather than teaching him about Christian doctrine, taught him the Christian faith by the manner in which he lived it. He also helped hundreds, if not thousands, of people who corresponded with him about religious and personal issues. "Only God knows how many people wrote him with their problems and questions, and Lewis was careful to respond to each, while coping with a very busy schedule, many interruptions in the household, illness, and eventually arthritis in the fingers and other physical problems," writes Clark.[338] Lewis wrote all of his letters by hand, but as the correspondence increased, it became necessary to elicit his brother Warren's assistance for typing some of them in preparation for his signature. Lewis's manifest Christianity was also demonstrated in his participation in and his support of his own denomination, the Anglican Church. Manifestly, he began attending church services regularly immediately after he embraced theism, which occurred perhaps more than a year prior to his conversion to Christianity. Lyle Dorsett notes that Lewis became devoted to community worship and prayer. "He saw community worship in one's particular church as indispensable to spiritual health and growth. In addition to maintaining his routine of regular worship at College Chapel . . . he felt constrained to attend the parish church on Sundays," he writes.[339] In addition to his contributions to apologetics in his written material as well as in his public addresses and church sermons, Lewis is also well known for his extraordinary generosity. In his book titled *Lenten Lands: My Childhood with Joy Davidman and C. S. Lewis*, Douglas Gresham writes: "Mr. Lewis was a man noted for his generosity. He helped with the education of many children by means of a secret charity fund known as 'Araparg' and personified as an imaginary giant of kindly disposition. This fund had been set up by his friend, Owen Barfield. No tramp or beggar would be

---

338. Clark, *C. S. Lewis*, 13.
339. Dorsett, *Seeking the Secret Place*, 40.

turned away empty handed by Jack."³⁴⁰ Cecil Harwood writes that Lewis's "interest was in people, not in institutions. . . . His benefactions, which were very great, were to individuals, not to societies. He had enormous sympathy for the 'little man.'" Harwood comments that on one occasion, when he was deprecating some modern housing estate, Lewis reminded him that if he were to "see not the houses, but the souls of the people in them, it might look very different."³⁴¹

The Lewisian Christian worldview is on full display in the characterisations of Farrer, McGrath, Clark, Gresham, Harwood, and many others who have written about Lewis. Elements of his worldview will be explored more explicitly in Lewis's nonfiction, as well as in his fictional material, in the chapter following.

---

340. Gresham, *Lenten Lands*, 50.
341. Harwood, "Toast to His Memory," 381.

Chapter Five

Lewis's Fusion of Fiction and Apologetics

Weaving Reason with Imagination

5.1 INTRODUCTION

James Sire considers one's worldview to be a commitment to a set of presuppositions that we hold about the basic constitution of reality, presuppositions that provide the foundation on how we perceive our world and how we conduct our lives.[1] Lewis's worldview gradually progressed through a series of changes manifested as materialism, pantheism, and theism, which ultimately led to his conversion to Christianity. The nature of Lewis's Christian faith is well exhibited in his published works. Motivated in part by his desire to appeal to a wide audience, Lewis addressed his writings to the public at large. Even though it was somewhat latent in some of his writings, his Christianity was generally understood by discerning readers. Most of Lewis's written material was not intended for academics and theologians. As mentioned by Robert MacSwain, however, academic theology can ill afford to disregard Lewis, because of Lewis's wide-ranging influence. Nevertheless, theologians and specialists

---

1. Sire, *Universe Next Door*, 20. See also Sire, *Apologetics beyond Reason*; *Naming the Elephant*; *Why Good Arguments often Fail.*

in religious studies, have, for the most part, kept their distance from him, he writes.[2] This chapter will begin by examining the manifestation of Lewis's distinctive Christian worldview in his fictional work, which will be followed by analysing manifestations of his worldview in his nonfictional material.

5.2 WORLDVIEW ELEMENTS IN LEWIS'S FICTIONAL WORKS

Many readers became acquainted with Lewis's fictional writings by reading the Narnia chronicles. His other works of fiction, including his space trilogy (*Out of the Silent Planet, Perelandra,* and *That Hideous Strength*), although popular, have never attracted as wide a readership as Lewis's chronicles have. In the interest of brevity, this section will focus on material from the chronicles. In order to understand Lewis's appreciation for fiction, it is important to consider his views regarding the capacity for imagination to convey meaning. As mentioned in chapters 3 and 4, Coleridge's writings had a profound influence on Lewis's notions of imagination's role in matters of human understanding. Coleridge's views are key to understanding Lewis's perception of imagination's role in one's comprehension of knowledge and meaning.

In the book titled *Coleridge: A Collection of Critical Essays,* which she edited, former Toronto University professor Kathleen Coburn writes that "disagreement with Coleridge's philosophical or literary theories can be shared by those most enthusiastic about him, but it was much too late in the day to refuse to take them seriously. The 'famous theory of the imagination and fancy,' famous with very good reason, has had more serious attention since then."[3] In his book *Faith, Hope and Poetry: Theology and the Poetic Imagination,* Cambridge University's Malcolm Guite claims that Enlightenment philosophers tried to exclude imagination from any right to truth by attempting to divorce reason and imagination. He writes that Coleridge, while living and working in the midst of this process, noted the deadening effect of what he considered to be a falsely materialist philosophy:[4]

---

2. MacSwain, "Introduction," 4.
3. Kathleen Coburn, in Coleridge, *Coleridge, Essay Collection,* 4.
4. Guite, *Faith, Hope and Poetry,* 45.

As a leading figure in the Romantic movement, he was already part of the reaction against the mechanic and materialist view of the world, but unlike most of the other Romantic poets he was concerned with more than creating beautiful fantasies as an alternative to grim reality. He wanted to challenge the philosophers on their own ground and show that the insights of imagination are insights into reality itself. Although Coleridge is best known for a handful of brilliant poems written in the course of a few miraculous years when he was a young man at the end of the eighteenth century, it is well known that he spent the rest of his life, the first thirty-four years of the nineteenth century, reflecting on the meaning of that intense experience—the experience of having been the mind through which great works of imagination had been revealed. In this reflection Coleridge found himself compelled to reject the mechanistic, clockwork cosmos of Newton, to reject the distant and detached clockmaker who passed for God with many of his contemporaries. Instead he discovered for himself the mysterious and suddenly present God who spoke to Moses from the burning bush, the mysterious and all-sustaining Word made flesh at Bethlehem, and the life-giving Holy Spirit through whom the imagination of poets is kindled. After all his preregrinations, Coleridge, like his ancient mariner, found haven and firm footing at last in the Trinity. As we come to the end of the Enlightenment project, whose shortcomings Coleridge so strongly attacked while he was in the midst of it, we may find in his writings very useful guides for the seas we have to navigate in the new "post-modern" era.

Guite and Coburn attest to Coleridge's contribution to the debate about the importance of both reason and imagination in acquiring knowledge about one's world. Coleridge's impact on Lewis is evidenced not only in Lewis's published works but also in his correspondence and diary. Guite credits Coleridge's work in advancing Lewis's theory of imagination for the emergence of certain theology courses at Cambridge. He cites the University of Cambridge's course *Theology through the Arts* as an example of Coleridge's influence. In his opinion, Coleridge should be credited for advancing the notion of imagination being a truth-bearing facility, and he critiques certain Enlightenment figures for impoverishing poetic language by marginalizing imagination's role as a conveyor of meaning and as an authentic truth-bearer. Guite reminds readers that much of the wisdom of the ancient Judeo-Christian, classical world was embodied in myth, story, and song, and commends Coleridge for contributing to its gradual restoration.[5]

Guite uses the term *view of the world* when he writes about the mechanistic, materialist notions that are representative of certain Enlightenment figures. The picture of the world that emerges from his description of Coleridge's ideas represents a much more robust view of the world. Guite's characterisation of the Coleridgean view of the world contains many of the features manifested in Lewis's worldview. Although the supernaturalism in Lewis's distinctive theistic worldview is frequently evidenced in his nonfictional writings, it is most prominently displayed in his fictional works, especially in *The Chronicles of Narnia*. As Jeff Sellars points out, however, Lewis's fictional works are also replete with formal philosophical arguments. "Lewis did not focus on narrative and myth as an act of retreat from the 'hard-nosed' reasoned philosophical attack; rather Lewis focused on narrative and myth because he thought they might move us further along than strict rationalistic reasoning," he writes.[6] Sellars contends that Lewis uses a form of argumentation in his fictional writings known as imaginative arguments or imaginative reasoning. "They may not be 'formal' arguments, but they are imaginative arguments nonetheless," writes Sellars. He claims that this is "a form of reasoning that must be recognised as a special 'imaginative reasoning.'"[7] While Lewis's fictive works are not rationalistic syllogisms or proofs, they are reasoned work, according to Sellars. In addition, even though proofs are not part of imaginative writing in a formal sense, strict argument can and does appear in imaginative writing, Sellars claims. He contends that an argument in real life can be judged strictly on its merits (presumably, regardless of the credibility of its arguer) and that, similarly, an argument in a work of fantasy, or in a dream "can in each case be judged simply on its merits."[8] Sellars notes that Lewis had long understood the limitations of reason's power to persuade and opines that this may have led to his decision to include the imaginative power of fictional narratives to complement his apologetic work.[9]

---

5. Guite, *Faith, Hope and Poetry*, 1–3.
6. Sellars, *Reasoning beyond Reason*, 11.
7. Sellars, *Reasoning beyond Reason*, 35n13.
8. Sellars, *Reasoning beyond Reason*, 35n13.
9. Sellars, *Reasoning beyond Reason*, 33–34.

Lewis's appreciation for the power of imagination is most vividly depicted in the imaginary worlds of Narnia and in his space trilogy. His sense of the supernatural is on full display in both series. In *The Magician's Nephew*, the sixth in the series of the chronicles, Lewis offers a prime example of his ability to stimulate readers' imagination to conceptualize the supernatural. This ability is dramatically portrayed in an event depicted in the eighth chapter of the narrative. Lewis describes a scenario in which everyone within hearing range heard a sound that transfixed everyone who heard it, a sound that seemed to encompass their entire world:[10]

> In the darkness something was happening at last. A voice had begun to sing. It was very far away and Digory found it hard to decide from what direction it was coming. Sometimes it seemed to come from all directions at once. Sometimes he almost thought it was coming out of the earth beneath them. Its lower notes were deep enough to be the voice of the earth herself. There were no words. There was hardly even a tune. But it was, beyond comparison, the most beautiful noise he had ever heard. It was so beautiful he could hardly bear it. The horse seemed to like it too; it gave the sort of whinny a horse would give if, after years of being a cab-horse, it found itself back in the old field where it had played as a foal, and saw someone whom it remembered and loved coming across the field and bring it a lump of sugar.
>
> . . . Then two wonders happened at the same moment. One was that the voice was suddenly joined by other voices; more voices than you could possibly count. They were in harmony with it, but far higher up the scale; cold, tingling, silver voices. The second wonder was that the blackness overhead, all at once, was blazing with stars. They didn't come out gently one by one, as they do on a summer evening. One moment there had been nothing but darkness; next moment a thousand, thousand points of light leaped out—single stars, constellations, and planets, brighter and bigger than any in our world. There were no clouds. The new stars and the new voices began at exactly the same time. If you had seen and heard it as Digory did, you would have felt quite certain that it was the stars themselves which were singing, and that it was the First Voice, the deep one which had made them appear and made them sing. "Glory be," said the Cabby. "I'd ha' been a better man all my life if I'd known there were things like this."

10. Lewis, *Magician's Nephew*, 116.

Lewis packs a wealth of information and meaning into this excerpt. Readers familiar with the early chapters of Genesis or the first chapter of John's Gospel cannot help but notice Lewis's reference to the extraordinary creative and transformative powers of the voice that brings a whole new world into existence. Lewis's narrative is reminiscent of the account in Gen 1:3—"Let there be light, and there was light"—and the statement in John 1:1: "In the beginning was the Word, and the Word was with God, and the Word was God." Lewis adds some additional touches to his narrative by describing the experience through the voice of two of the characters that he has created, young Digory and Cabby (the cabdriver). By giving an overlay to this event through the expressions of the participants, Lewis adds an additional dimension to its dramatic impact. Many of the features of Lewis's worldview are displayed in the above excerpt. This includes its supernatural elements as demonstrated in the voice's creative power, Lewis's own appreciation of the natural world as demonstrated in the beauty of the world of Narnia that is coming into being, and Lewis's sense of morality as expressed by the Cabby, who would have been a better individual had he foreseen such a world coming into existence. As well, the magnificence of God and his creation is manifested in the voice itself when described as being "the most beautiful voice."

In his chapter of the book *The Chronicles of Narnia and Philosophy*, Stephen Webb, professor of religion and philosophy at Wabash College, describes the effect that the Lion's voice had on the surrounding Narnian environment. He notes that with his statement about a voice beginning to sing, Lewis introduces his theory of sound by bringing Aslan the Lion into the narrative:[11]

> Notice, however, that the Lion is heard before he is seen. It is almost as if his voice is what makes the Lion the creature that he is. The form of the Lion is not as significant as his sound, or, better put, the voice of the Lion is able to create or inhabit any form. This is Lewis's way of crediting voice with the property of creativity. When the children, the Cabby, Uncle Andrew, and the Queen first hear the voice, it sounds as if it was coming from all directions simultaneously. The voice wasn't speaking, or even carrying a tune. It was, however, beautiful by comparison. The lower notes of the voice, its deep register, sounded as if it arose from the earth itself, and it called forth other voices higher up in the scales that seemed to come from the sky and the stars.

11. Webb, "Aslan's Voice," 10.

Webb notes that there is something naturally mysterious about sound,[12] in part because it is not visible to the human eye. In fact, even the originator of the sound is at times invisible because of being outside the hearer's field of vision. Sound, as Lewis uses it in *The Magician's Nephew*, "is thus a perfect medium for the supernatural," writes Webb.[13] He claims that Lewis has illustrated the Narnian scenarios in a certain way "in order to have us activate them with our auditory imaginations."[14] He thinks that Lewis "wants us to think about the ways in which sound is the very stuff of our existence." In Webb's opinion, Lewis's chronicles "are a very noisy affair, no matter how quietly we read them to our children at bedtime." He muses that "perhaps we love to read them so much because we are searching for voices that call us home."[15]

Kevin Kinghorn, professor of religion and philosophy at Oxford University, claims that Lewis's own religious commitments didn't merely affect his views on people's notions about their general intellectual duties but that Lewis was also concerned with specific spiritual problems that prevent people from seeing the truth about God.[16] Kinghorn's observation is made evident in the Lewisian narrative immediately following the cabdriver's remark in the earlier quotation:[17]

> The Voice in the earth was now louder and more triumphant; but the voices in the sky, after singing loudly with it for a time, begin to get fainter. And now something else was happening. Far away and down near the horizon, the sky began to turn gray. A light wind, very fresh began to stir. The sky in that one place grew slowly and steadily paler. You could see the shapes of hills standing up sharply against it. All the time the Voice went on singing. There was soon light enough for them to see one another's faces. The Cabby and the two children had open mouths and shining eyes; they were drinking in the sound, and they looked as if it reminded them of something. Uncle Andrew's mouth was

---

12. Alister McGrath claims that while for Martin Luther, "faith arises from hearing the Word of God properly," for Lewis, faith expresses itself in seeing things rightly. He notes, however, that although Lewis's works, "especially the *Chronicles of Narnia*, make reference to all of the human senses: seeing, hearing, smelling, touching and tasting," his clear preference is for metaphors of light (McGrath, *Intellectual World*, 85).

13. Webb, "Aslan's Voice," 12.
14. Webb, "Aslan's Voice," 14.
15. Webb, "Aslan's Voice," 14.
16. Kinghorn, "Virtue Epistemology."
17. Lewis, *Magician's Nephew*, 117–20.

open too, but not open with joy. He looked as if his chin had simply dropped away from the rest of his face. His shoulders were stooped and his knees shook. He was not liking the Voice. If he could have got away from it by crawling into a rat's hole he would have done so. . . .

The eastern sky turned from white to pink and from pink to gold. The Voice rose and rose, till all the air was shaking with it. And just as it swelled to the mightiest and most glorious sound it had produced, the sun rose. Digory had never seen such a sun. The sun above the ruins of Charn had looked older than ours: this looked younger. You could imagine that it laughed for joy as it came up. And as its beams shot across the land the travelers could see for the first time what sort of place they were in. It was a valley through which a broad, swift river wound its way, flowing eastward toward the sun. Southward there were mountains, northward there were hills. But it was a valley of mere earth, rock and water; there was not a tree, nor a bush, nor a blade of grass to be seen. The earth was of many colors; they were fresh, hot and vivid. They made you feel excited; until you saw the Singer himself; and then you forgot everything else. It was a Lion. Huge, shaggy and bright, it stood facing the risen sun. Its mouth was wide open in song and it was about three hundred yards away.

As Lewis gives his description of the Lion, Aslan, literally singing a new world into existence, he describes how the cabdriver and the children stood there in open-mouthed amazement. He describes their excitement at the sight of the newly created world. In his description, they were so excited about what they saw that they forgot about everything else, especially when they caught sight of the Singer himself. He describes the whole scene as having an altogether different effect on the Uncle Andrew character, however:[18]

> We must now go back a bit and explain what the whole scene had looked like from Uncle Andrew's point of view. It had not at all made the same impression on him as on the Cabby and the children. For what you see and hear depends a good deal on where you are standing; it also depends on what sort of person you are. Ever since the animals had first appeared, Uncle Andrew had been shrinking further and further back into the thicket. . . . When the great moment came and the Beasts spoke, he missed the whole point; for a rather interesting reason. When

---

18. Lewis, *Magician's Nephew*, 148–50.

> the Lion had first begun singing, long ago when it was still quite dark, he had realized that the voice was a song. And he had disliked the song very much. It made him think and feel things he did not want to feel. Then when the sun rose and he saw that the singer was a lion ("only a lion," as he said to himself) he tried his hardest to make believe that it wasn't singing and never had been singing—only roaring as any lion might in a zoo in our own world. "Of course, it really can't have been singing," he thought, "I must have imagined it. I've been letting my nerves get out of order. Who ever heard of a lion singing?" and the longer and more beautiful the Lion sang, the harder Uncle Andrew tried to make himself believe that he could hear nothing but roaring. Now the trouble with trying to make yourself stupider than you really are is that you very often succeed. Uncle Andrew did. He soon did hear nothing but roaring in Aslan's song. Soon he couldn't hear anything else even if he wanted to. And at last when the Lion spoke and said, "Narnia awake," he didn't hear any words: he heard only a snarl.

Lewis points out that our understanding is significantly impacted by our perspective or, as he expresses it, as being highly dependent upon "where you are standing." Perception is also heavily dependent on "what sort of person" we are, writes Lewis. Kinghorn describes Lewis's portrayal of the Uncle Andrew character as being "selfish to the bone" and as someone who never reaches a "point of self-discovery." The Lewisian worldview is clearly evident in the above excerpts. The selections chosen exhibit his sense of the supernatural and the significance of Judeo Christian values in matters of understanding. There are also strong hints about society's inclination to be totally oblivious to any influence that God may have in the course of human events. Manifestations of Lewis's notion of the *Tao*, a subject that will be explored in the paragraphs following, is also displayed in the above excerpts.

Tim Mosteller, professor of philosophy at Biola University, notes that Lewis chooses to illustrate his notion of the *Tao* in the chronicles, rather than to argue for it, as he does in *The Abolition of Man*. He views Lewis's notion of the *Tao* as being akin to what philosophers and theologians call natural law. In Mosteller's opinion, if Lewis's notion of the *Tao* is correct, and if there really are natural moral laws that apply to chronicles readers, then there are only three possible responses that readers can have for the *Tao*: accept the *Tao* in whole, accept part of it, or reject it entirely. Mosteller finds examples of all three options in the various characters in Lewis's narratives. He cites several Narnian characters as being representative of individuals who made a commitment to live by the *Tao* in its entirety, as well others who either kept it in part or rejected it altogether.[19] Mosteller thinks that "Lewis wrote the *Chronicles* with a heavy dose of the *Tao* in response to all the moral nonsense he saw being taught in school." He thinks that a similar situation prevails today because "contemporary educators teach our kids that there are no objective truths."[20]

Gayne Anacker, professor of philosophy at California Baptist University, attributes much of the popularity enjoyed by Lewis's chronicles to their moral resonance. "In short, *The Chronicles of Narnia* profoundly engage the moral imagination," he writes.[21] Anacker defines moral imagination as the ability to consider our decisions and our values from a different moral perspective. He cites the phenomenon of having one's imagination aroused by the beauty of a natural event in a manner that inspires a desire for a change in one's moral fabric, as an example of moral imagination. Anacker would likely consider Lewis's account of the cabdriver being overwhelmed by the magnificence of Aslan voicing the Narnia world into being in *The Magician's Nephew* as a prime example of moral imagination. As quoted in the excerpt cited earlier, the Cabby declared that he would have led a better life had he known that such a world could be brought into being. Lewis is describing a sensation in these novels with which he is intimately familiar; on several occasions, Lewis's walking companions commented on Lewis's habit of pausing to admire and reflect on an inspiring natural phenomenon that had seemingly left him speechless and overwhelmed by the effect that the experience had on him. Lewis began writing his Narnia novels in the summer of 1948 and completed them in March of 1954. The first five, written between mid-1948 and the spring of 1951, were completed in fairly rapid succession. This was followed by a fallow period of more than a year. He commenced writing the sixth in the series, *The Last Battle*, in the fall of 1952, and completed the last of the series, *The Magician's Nephew*, in March 1954.[22] In his book *Companion to Narnia*, Paul Ford opines that after finishing *Miracles* and after commencing *Surprised by Joy* in the spring of 1948, Lewis felt sufficiently energized to revisit *The Lion, the Witch and the Wardrobe*, a novel that he

---

19. Mosteller, "Tao of Narnia," 94–96.
20. Mosteller, "Tao of Narnia," 105.
21. Anacker, "Narnia and Moral Imagination," 130.
22. McGrath, *C. S. Lewis*, 266.

had begun to write before the start of World War II.[23] In 1954, the Milton Society of America invited Lewis to attend a meeting that was to be held in New York to honour two contemporary authors, one of whom was to be Lewis. Lewis was in the process of moving from Oxford University to Magdalene College in Cambridge and declined the invitation. When asked to send a description of his books, he used the invitation in December 1954 to explain his reason for using the genre he had employed in the chronicles and in his science fiction. Lewis's letter provides some insight into his usage of fiction:[24]

> Since he [Mr. Hunter] encouraged me to "make a statement" about them, I may point out that there is a guiding thread. The imaginative man in me is a bit older, more continuously operative, and in that sense more basic than either the religious writer or the critic. It was he who made me first attempt (with little success) to be a poet. It was he who, in response to the poetry of others, made me a critic, and, in defence of that response, sometimes a critical controversialist. It was he who, after my conversion led me to embody my religious belief in symbolical or mythopoeic form, ranging from *Screwtape*, to a kind of theologised science-fiction. And it was, of course, he who brought me, in the last few years to write the series of Narnian stories for children; not asking what children want and then endeavouring to adapt myself (this was not needed) but because the fairy-tale was best fitted for what I wanted to say.[25]

Lewis draws Hunter's attention to a common thread in all of his novels. They convey religious convictions via symbolic and mythopoeic imagery in their narratives. He refers to his literary persona as "the imaginative man in me," and the genre that he employed for his *Screwtape* novel and for his space trilogy as "theologised science-fiction." *That Hideous Strength*, as well as his final novel, *Till We Have Faces*, may perhaps also be included in this genre. He refers to the Narnia chronicles

23. Ford, *Companion to Narnia*, 17.
24. Lewis, *Letters of C. S. Lewis*, 443–44.
25. Doris Myers, professor emeritus of English at Northern Colorado University, writes: "Because Lewis did not talk down to children, he did not compose the Chronicles by asking himself what children want in terms of plot and incident, or what they need in terms of a moral. He believed that a writer should instead ask himself what he wants and needs, for children and adults are more alike than different. As he wrote to a child, 'You see, I don't think age matters so much as people think. Parts of me are still 12 and I think parts of me were already 50 when I was 12'" (Myers, *C. S. Lewis*, 118).

as fairy-tales, however. Although the Narnian novels share many of the characteristics of his other fictional works, likely because of the audience to which they were directed, Lewis seems to place them in a separate category. Despite being children's stories, they embody much of the Lewisian worldview, including its sense of morality and its receptivity to notions of the supernatural.

Biographer Andrew Wilson claims that Lewis revised his apologetics by switching from reasoned argumentation to a form of persuasion that elicits an imaginative response. He theorizes that this change was necessitated by Lewis's poor performance in his Socratic Club debate with Elizabeth Anscombe and was influenced by the post-war pressures of his own financial situation and other circumstances. Wilson postulates that Lewis had lost confidence in the validity of Christianity's truth claims after his encounter with Anscombe and that his dissatisfaction was magnified because of a troubled home environment.[26]

Although Lewis had marginally revised one chapter in his book *Miracles*, in order to strengthen the argument that he was making for the veracity of the Christian worldview, his decision to introduce an imaginative component into his apologetic methodology appears to have been inspired by other factors. Lewis's letters during that period give no indication that anything like the scenario that Wilson depicted was being played out in Lewis's home environment. According to the written statements of individuals closest to Lewis, neither Wilson's characterisation of the Lewis/Anscombe debate nor his account of Lewis's reaction to the event appear to be accurate.[27] As mentioned in chapter 4, Lewis is often credited for developing the foundational structure for the arguments challenging the logical inconsistencies within naturalism. Lewis's

---

26. A. Wilson, *C. S. Lewis*, 218.

27. Literary scholar Katherine Harper writes: "Lewis arrived prepared to argue his theory from a theological standpoint, only to find that Professor Anscombe—an expert in the fields of intention and causality—considered it a purely philosophical issue . . . Lewis gamely responded, and, to all accounts, provided solid arguments for his own position; even so he considered himself the loser of the debate. Hugo Dyson and George Sayer have claimed that Lewis was humiliated by his public defeat and resentful of his opponent; Professor Anscombe has disagreed, noting that she and he had dined together with Humphrey Havard only a few weeks later. It is true, however, that Lewis wrote no further apologetics for ten years. Instead, he turned his energies to fiction, an act that gained him a wider audience and recognition as an author as well as a scholar. He may have used the Socratic experience to his advantage . . . In the years since the Socratic Club debate, G. E. M. Anscombe has established herself as the definitive interpreter of Wittgenstein and as an expert translator" (Harper, "Anscombe").

argument has been debated in various venues since his debate with Anscombe. Glendale Community College's Victor Reppert, who holds a PhD in philosophy from the University of Illinois, has written extensively about this subject. Reppert writes that although the argument has taken many forms over the years, in all instances, it argues for the "rejection of all broadly materialistic worldviews."[28] Reppert claims that John Beversluis, author of the book *C. S. Lewis and the Search for Rational Religion*, a book published in 2007 that was highly critical of Lewis's argumentation, was the first to use the phrase "argument from reason" to designate the manner in which Lewis had framed the argument. In 2003, Reppert published his own book, *C. S. Lewis's Dangerous Idea: In Defence of the Argument from Reason*, in which he claimed to have exposed significant difficulties for advocates of a materialist worldview. Reppert cites several notable defenders of Lewis's argument, including Derek Barefoot, Angus Menuge, Michael Rea, and Alvin Plantinga.[29] In the book *The Magician's Twin: C. S. Lewis on Science, Scientism, and Society*, edited by John West, Reppert revises portions of his earlier book in a thirty-four-page chapter titled "C. S. Lewis's Dangerous Idea Revisited," in which he summarises some of the arguments from various contributors in the past few years. In his introduction to the chapter, which serves as a summary, Reppert sums up his chapter as follows:[30]

> I will begin by examining the nature of the argument, identifying the central characteristics of a broadly materialistic worldview, and analyzing the prospects for a genuinely naturalistic alternative to a broadly materialistic worldview. In so doing, I will examine the general problem of materialism, and how the argument from reason points to a single aspect of a broader problem. Second, I will examine the argument's history, including the famous dispute over it, between C. S. Lewis and noted Roman Catholic philosopher Elizabeth Anscombe. In so doing, I will indicate how the argument from reason can surmount Anscombe's objection to it. I will also explain the transcendental structure of the argument. Finally, I will examine some popular objections, and show that these objections do not refute the argument.

28. Reppert, "C. S. Lewis's Dangerous Idea," 199.

29. Barefoot, "Response to Richard Carrier's Review"; Menuge, *Agents under Fire*; Rea, *World without Design*; Plantinga, *Warranted Christian Belief*.

30. Reppert, "C. S. Lewis's Dangerous Idea," 199.

Reppert's scholarly analysis is important, because the Lewis/Anscombe debate has acquired a life of its own. The debate is perhaps more important for what it was not than for any significance it may have had for Lewis's apologetics. In their detailed analysis of four key members of the Inklings, titled *The Fellowship: The Literary Lives of the Inklings*, Philip and Carol Zaleski write:[31]

> Some biographers . . . have advanced the view that Lewis was so devastated by the Anscombe affair that he abandoned apologetics and retreated into children's fantasy. This belief has gained traction in recent years, but there are good reasons to reject it. For one thing, it does not match Anscombe's impression. "My own recollection," she wrote later, "it was an occasion of sober discussion of certain quite definite criticisms, which Lewis's rethinking and rewriting showed he thought were accurate. I am inclined to construe the odd accounts of the matter by some of his friends—who seem to not have been interested in the actual arguments or the subject matter—as an interesting example of the phenomenon called 'projection.'"

The Zaleskis's account counters many of Wilson's notions, including Lewis's decision to redirect his focus from a strict rationality to a more imaginative symbolical and mythopoeic form of apologetics. Rather than initiating a change in focus, as Wilson claims, the preponderance of evidence indicates that the debate merely reinforced a process that was already well underway. Alister McGrath notes that the Anscombe debate "was an uncomfortable encounter for Lewis . . . not because the conclusion was wrong but because the arguments used in the conclusion were not as robust as they ought to have been."[32] He writes: "The problem did not lie with Lewis's rejection of naturalism. Anscombe made it clear from the outset in her presentation of February 1948 that she agreed with Lewis that naturalism was untenable. Yet she did not regard his specific argument, as set out in the first edition of *Miracles*, as being sufficiently rigorous to justify this conclusion."[33] McGrath contends that Anscombe's main concern related to Lewis's insistence that naturalism was irrational. She rightly pointed out to him that most natural processes can be legitimately described as nonrational and that therefore validity is not

---

31. Zaleski and Zaleski, *Fellowship*, 364.
32. McGrath, *C. S. Lewis*, 254.
33. McGrath, *C. S. Lewis*, 253.

an issue, "unless those causes can be shown to predispose it to false or unreasonable beliefs."[34] He, too, challenges the Wilson account:[35]

> Some of Lewis's biographers, primarily A. N. Wilson, have seen this incident as signalling, perhaps even causing, a major shift in Lewis's outlook. Having been defeated in argument, they contend that Lewis lost confidence in the rational basis of his faith, and abandoned his role as a leading apologist. They claim that his shift to fictional works—such as the *Chronicles of Narnia*—reflects a growing realization that rational argument cannot support the Christian faith. However, the substantial body of written evidence concerning this exchange points to a quite different conclusion. A chastised Lewis recognized the weakness of one specific argument he had deployed (a little hastily, it must be said) and worked to improve it. Lewis was an academic writer, and academic books are tested against the criticisms and concerns of colleagues until the arguments and evidence are presented in the best possible way. Lewis was already used to giving and receiving literary criticism in this way, both through the Inklings and through personal discussions with colleagues.... There is no evidence of Lewis retreating into some kind of non-rational fideism or reason-free fantasy as a result of this encounter.

Analyses such as those of McGrath, Reppert, and the Zaleskis about the significance that the Anscombe/Lewis debate may have had in Lewis's shift in focus are important. They demonstrate that Lewis continued to value logic and reason in matters of Christian faith despite his shift in focus, and they help clarify Lewis's view about the influence that an imaginative stimulus may have in bringing individuals to Christian faith. In any event, it is important to remember that Lewis's support of Christian theism and his objections to the arguments for the sufficiency of materialism to account for reality were never in question. It was only the method by which he challenged materialism's adequacy as a metaphysical system that was in question. Lewis did not waver in his commitment to the Christian worldview nor in his belief in that worldview's ability to withstand rational scrutiny. His confidence in the reasonableness of the Christian faith remained unabated. The debate revolved around the method(s) by which he chose to defend it; whether or not it was supported by reason was not in question. Turning to fiction does not

34. McGrath, *C. S. Lewis*, 254.
35. McGrath, *C. S. Lewis*, 254-55.

indicate Lewis having lost confidence in the power of reason as a force in apologetics; it is indicative of a change in genre in which to express the philosophical basis for the Christian faith. McGrath contends that readers "can rightly see Narnia as the imaginative outworking of the core philosophical and theological ideas Lewis had been developing since the mid 1930's, expressed in a narrative rather than a rational manner." He views the Narnia novels as expressing "in the form of a story the same philosophical and theological arguments advanced in *Miracles*." He contends that fiction allows readers to see and enjoy the vision of reality Lewis had already set out in his more apologetic work.[36]

Reppert notes that some form of the "argument from reason" has been around since antiquity. He claims that some version of it can be traced back to Plato and Augustine, both of whom argued that our capacity for discerning eternal and necessary truths supports the existence of God. He contends that Descartes held that the capacity for the higher rational human processes cannot be accounted for in materialistic terms.[37] And he claims that although Kant denied that these considerations provided adequate proof for the immortality of the soul, he believed that they were sufficient to rule out a materialist account of mind. Reppert notes that materialism as a force in Western culture has increased significantly since the publication of Charles Darwin's *Origin of the Species* (Reppert, 2012:210).

Examples of Lewis's use of logic and reason in depicting and defending the Christian worldview, as well as elements of the Lewisian notion of the supernatural, are on full display throughout Lewis's chronicles. Chair of the philosophy department at Covenant College, William Davis writes: "Narnia is clearly enchanted. It is charged with an energy that is both comforting and thrilling. But while it is a world of Deep and Deeper

---

36. McGrath, *C. S. Lewis*, 261. Paul Brazier comments on the Lewis/Anscombe debate in his series of books on Lewis. Brazier notes that this debate marks a slowly developing change in his work, with less of an emphasis on assertive apologetics: "*The Chronicles of Narnia* are foremost in this later period, but also many more devotionally based works such as *Reflections on the Psalms* (1958), and the posthumously published *Letters to Malcolm: Chiefly on Prayer* (1964). There is also a wealth of essays on philosophical theology, and important correspondence that contribute to his doctrine of Scripture, to consider. This later period is characterised essentially as by 'mere' Christology, and by Christlikeness," writes Brazier (Brazier, *C. S. Lewis*, 1:151). He claims that the debate was about "the fundamental philosophical concepts that underpin Christianity" (Brazier, *C. S. Lewis*, 1:207).

37. For a recent treatise on the challenges for materialism to account for mind, see Nagel, *Mind and Cosmos*. Nagel is a professor of philosophy at New York University.

Magic, Narnia enchants us because it is fundamentally a good place. It is a world of characters whose goodness is worth imitating and where goodness is rewarded."[38] Other elements of Lewis's worldview, including Neoplatonism, are also on display: According to theologian-scholar Paul Brazier, "Platonism is fundamental to Lewis's work," especially as it relates to certain doctrinal issues.[39] Michael Christensen, too, sees elements of Platonism in Lewis's body of work: "Lewis's approach to myth, revelation and Scripture presupposes the validity of Platonic Idealism. . . . He perceived, metaphorically, a unified Reality where the 'natural' and the 'supernatural' realms 'co-here,'" he writes.[40] Manifestations of Platonism in Lewis's fictional material demonstrates the extent to which his worldview influenced his apologetic methodology. In the second to last chapter of Lewis's Narnia chronicle *The Last Battle*, one of the novel's characters, Lord Digory, after delivering a rousing address in a voice that "stirred everyone like a trumpet," remarked that the scenario he had just outlined, was "all in Plato, all in Plato."[41]

Gareth Mathews, professor of philosophy at University of Massachusetts Amherst, notes that the Lord Digory in *The Last Battle* was the

---

38. Davis, "Extreme Makeover," 109.

39. Brazier, *C. S. Lewis*, 1:217. Paul Brazier sees a long-term effect of the Anscombe/Lewis debate on Lewis's apologetics: "The issues in the debate were re-examined on several occasions where the conclusions were not always as clear cut as Anscombe had demonstrated and where Lewis failed to press home his case. Reason and imagination now reveal God's purposes and truth through pictures and narrative: revelation revealed through the role of analogy. To this end we must consider a theological concept, a dialectic of sorts, two elements: the *analogia entis-analogia fidei*—the *analogia entis* (the analogy of being) claims we can know of a God from the world, the *analogia fidei* (the analogy of faith) is characterised by faith leading to understanding, faith is then the ground from which reason can work. The aftershock from the debate is that Lewis's championing of apologetics through the *analogia entis* in the 1930s and 1940s takes a more cautious and reflective, a more nuanced line: reason is complemented by wisdom through his use of the *analogia fidei*, given that reason predates creation. Analogical and symbolic narrative methodologically defined by the *analogia fidei* can tell us more of the truth of revelation than assertive philosophical discourse" (Brazier, *C. S. Lewis*, 3.2:81).

40. Christensen, *C. S. Lewis*, 66.

41. Lewis, *Last Battle*, 61. Mark Edwards, lecturer in patristics at the University of Oxford, notes that the professor's expostulation, "It's all in Plato! All in Plato: bless me, what do they teach them at these schools?" alludes to a passage in Plato that foretells the translation of souls after death to a world in which all that is best in ours persists, except that the lines are bolder and the colours more intent (M. Edwards, "Classicist," 66).

professor in Lewis's *The Lion, the Witch and the Wardrobe*, and suggests that Lewis's professor, now known as Lord Digory, may actually have been instructing his students in the teachings of Plato.[42] Matthews's notion would seem to be supported by Digory's understated comment, "What do they teach them at these schools," and by the narrator's comment, "It was exactly like the sort of thing they had heard him say in that other world long ago."[43] Because of its Socratic implication, the questioning nature of Lord Digory's comment adds credence to Matthews's notion. Matthews also finds evidence for Platonic influence in Lewis's novel *The Silver Chair*. He notes the similarity between an image in Lewis's novel and the famous cave allegory in Plato's *Republic*. In presenting the allegory, Socrates relates the story of prisoners who are chained in place inside a cave where a fire is burning. The prisoners are restricted in such a way that only the shadowy figures on the wall of the cave cast by the fire are visible to them. The fire itself remains out of their line of vision, causing the prisoners to believe that the shadowy figures are the true reality. In the account in Plato's *Republic* only those prisoners who get unchained are able to leave the cave and see real objects lighted by the real sun as true reality.[44] In Lewis's novel, rather than a fire casting a shadow, a witch casts a spell on several characters, temporarily convincing them that the world of sunlight and stars didn't actually exist, that it was just a figment of their imagination. The characters were eventually freed of the spell's influence by their determination to recall what they had heard from other sources and by focusing on their previous real-life experiences.[45]

Matthews notes that in *The Silver Chair*, the individuals in the story find their way into Underland, a realm of its own, beneath the Narnian world. Matthews finds parallels between the cave described in the *Republic* and Lewis's depiction of Underland. He thinks Plato is demonstrating the contrast between reality and illusion in his allegory of the cave. In his opinion, Plato thinks the physical world that we experience through our senses is an image or shadow of the real world of eternal realities of the good itself, consisting of beauty, justice, wisdom, or *forms*.[46] Matthews

---

42. Matthews, "Plato in Narnia," 169.
43. Lewis, *Last Battle*, 161.
44. Matthews, "Plato in Narnia," 173.
45. Lewis, *Silver Chair*, 140–45.
46. Professor emeritus John Frame claims that Plato provides distinct roles for reason and sense experience. "Plato's epistemology begins with the observation that we can learn very little from our sense organs," writes Frame. "Our eyes and ears easily

thinks Plato's intent in the allegory is to impress upon his readers that in order to avoid illusion, individuals need to be released from their cave-like ignorance through philosophy and given access to the outside world by reason, thereby enabling them to experience true reality, lighted by the good itself. He notes that the picture in *The Silver Chair* is also a dimly lit world of only partial comprehension. Matthews thinks that he sees a kind of Christian Platonism in Lewis's *The Last Battle*, the final novel of the series. He notes that after the original Narnian world had been destroyed and another one had been brought into being, the survivors had remarked that although the mountains seemed similar, they had more colours, seemed to be further away, and looked more real. He considers this description to be classic Platonism.[47] Matthews notes that although there are many differences between Plato's writings and Lewis's Narnia chronicles, and although there is nothing in Plato similar to Aslan, nevertheless, Lewis's novels are generously endowed with Platonic imagery.[48] The Lewisian worldview similarly influenced Lewis's nonfictional work, which is the subject of the section following.

5.3 WORLDVIEW ELEMENTS IN LEWIS'S NONFICTIONAL WORKS

Lewis's worldview is well manifested in his published nonfictional works, as well as in his works of fiction. Whereas the previous section dealt with the manner in which Lewis's worldview is exhibited in *The Chronicles of Narnia*, this section will focus on the manner in which the Lewisian worldview is manifested in three of his major works, *Mere Christianity*, *Miracles*, and *The Abolition of Man*. *Mere Christianity* is a fairly succinct work about the basic tenets of the Christian faith, *Miracles* is a major critique of metaphysical naturalism, and *The Abolition of Man* is an

---

deceive us. But the remarkable thing is that we have the rational ability to correct these deceptions and thus to find truth. It is by reason also that we form concepts of things ... These concepts Plato calls *Forms* or *Ideas*. Since we cannot find these Forms on earth, they must exist, he says, in another realm, a world of Forms, as opposed to the world of sense" (Frame, "Greeks Bearing Gifts," 18).

47. Andrew Walker, professor emeritus of theology, culture, and education at King's College, opines that Lewis was neither a biblical conservative in the fundamentalist sense, nor a theological liberal, nor a modernist. He thinks that some of Lewis's notions echo classical Platonism and that at times, Lewis habitually idealises concepts beyond their theological usefulness (Walker, "Scripture, Revelation and Platonism").

48. Matthews, "Plato in Narnia," 173–77.

indictment of radical intellectual secularism. The three works are representative of the range and depth of Lewis's apologetic material. There is substantial evidence that *Mere Christianity* represents the Lewisian worldview, that *Miracles*'s challenge to Naturalism has stood the test of time, and that the prophetic elements of *The Abolition of Man* are as relevant today as they were in Lewis's day.

The debate between Lewis and Anscombe at the Oxford Socratic Club took place in February 1948. The first edition of *Miracles* had been published the year before. Alan Jacobs, professor of the humanities at Baylor University, writes that Lewis immediately recognised the cogency of Anscombe's critique and later revised *Miracles* accordingly. He notes that in the summer of 1948, Lewis had told Chad Walsh that he was completing a children's book.[49] Chad Walsh, in his book *C. S. Lewis: Apostle to the Skeptics*, first published in 1949, writes that during an interview with Lewis during the summer of 1948, Lewis had told him that he was completing some projects that were underway. In a brief biographical sketch of Lewis, which comprises the first chapter of his book, Walsh writes: "At present he is writing his memoirs . . . he has reached the end of World War I. He is also doing the volume on English literature of the sixteenth century (exclusive of the dramatists) for the projected Oxford History of English Literature. . . . He talks vaguely of completing a children's book which he has begun."[50] Walsh notes that from Lewis's comments, he felt that Lewis had not written himself out, but that the books he had in mind suggested that he had been thinking about a change in focus and taking a holiday from the kind of writing he had been doing.[51]

As pointed out in the previous chapter, Alister McGrath, too, sees a change in focus in Lewis's apologetics during this period. McGrath notes that Lewis's messaging shifted to exploring and appreciating the depths of the Christian faith for the benefit of those who believed or were close to believing, rather than concentrating on defending a challenged faith and persuading unbelievers of the truth of the Christian faith, as had been his practise. Lewis had a large body of work behind him by this time, including many major works and dozens of published essays and articles. Walsh notes that during the time he spent in Oxford in 1948 interviewing Lewis and doing research for his own book, some bookstore clerks

---

49. Jacobs, "Chronicles of Narnia," 266–67.
50. Walsh, *C. S. Lewis*, 10.
51. Walsh, *C. S. Lewis*, 9–10.

expressed regret that Lewis had not devoted his considerable talents to literary research rather than Christian apologetics. On the other hand, Walsh also encountered members of the clergy and certain laymen who feared that if Lewis resorted to scholarly works and halted his output of apologetic literature, the result would be disastrous for Christianity in England. He also noticed that Lewis was considered to be a formidable enemy by the progressive element of the Oxford faculty.[52] Clearly, by 1948, Lewis's apologetics had had a significant impact.

It is important to remember that Lewis had referred to himself as an empirical theist and that he had considered himself to have arrived at a belief in God "by induction" when he embraced theism.[53] Lewis had begun to attend chapel regularly after becoming a theist, but it was not until many months later, after an all-night session with Tolkien and Dyson, that he converted to Christianity. The power of his imaginative capacity, which enabled him to comprehend the meaning and significance of the incarnation, was not lost on Lewis. His realization of imagination's role in providing meaning to knowledge almost certainly influenced his intention to alter his apologetic method. His own conversion experience was likely instrumental in his decision. From the time Lewis wrote *Pilgrim's Regress* in 1933 until the 1948 debate with Anscombe at the Socratic Club, Lewis had published a large volume of work related to apologetics. Many of his classic works, such as *Mere Christianity* and *Miracles*, although they contained some imaginative elements, were largely reason-based. It is noteworthy that Lewis, in an address to members of the clergy as early as 1945,[54] had recommended that a direct appeal to the reality of the incarnation was often more effective than beginning an address with well-reasoned argumentation about there being an intellectual basis for Christian belief. Coleridge, Wordsworth, and Barfield almost certainly had an important influence on Lewis's epistemology. These factors deserve consideration when analysing the formation of Lewis's worldview. They provide substantive insight into the manner in which his worldview impacted his methodology.

---

52. Walsh, *C. S. Lewis*, 19–20.

53. Lewis, *Image and Imagination*, 13. As mentioned on page 48 in Chapter Three, Alister McGrath thinks that based on Lewis's description of the process by which he had come to embrace theism, it was not a process of deduction, but rather like a process of crystallisation (McGrath, C. S. Lewis:136)

54. Lewis, *God in the Dock*, 100–101.

In *The C. S. Lewis Readers' Encyclopedia*, Mike Perry and Jeffrey Schultz write that *Mere Christianity* is the theological core on which different Christians can agree. They claim that Lewis borrowed the term from the Puritan theologian Richard Baxter (1615–1691) and that it represents Lewis's concept of the common doctrines of Christianity.[55] Perry and Schultz's notion is supported by what Lewis had written in the February 1952 periodical *Church Times*:[56]

> I welcome the letter from the Rural Dean of Gravesend, though I am sorry that anyone should have rendered it necessary by describing the Bishop of Birmingham as an Evangelical. To a layman, it seems obvious that what unites the Evangelical and the Anglo-Catholic against the "Liberal" or "Modernist" is something very clear and momentous, namely, the fact that both are thoroughgoing supernaturalists, who believe in the Creation, the Fall, the Incarnation, the Resurrection, the Second Coming, and the Four Last Things. This unites them not only with one another, but with the Christian religion as understood *ubique et ab omnibus*.[57] The point of view from which this agreement seems less important than their divisions, or than the gulf which separates both from any non-miraculous version of Christianity, is to be unintelligible. Perhaps the trouble is as supernaturalists, whether as "Low" or "High" Church, thus taken altogether, they lack a name. May I suggest "Deep Church"; or, if that fails in humility, Richard Baxter's "mere Christians"?

---

55. Perry and Schultz, "Mere Christianity," 270.

56. Lewis, *Essay Collection*, 421.

57. Latin, "everywhere and by all." "The phrase *ubique et ab omnibus* is from a fifth-century monk by the name of Vincentius of Lérins, who was asserting that we should hold on to that which has been believed by all. Lewis is referring to Vincentius of Lérins key work, *The Commonitory* (written in AD 434), which was written to establish a general or common rule to identify truth from falsity. Vincentius's rule is in essence succinct and simple: it is the authority of Holy Scripture. All questions of doctrine and ethics must be measured against the canon of Scripture, answered from the Bible. But this, Vincentius acknowledges, is problematic because there are so many interpretations of Scripture. The rule of Scripture is then qualified by an appeal to that which has been endorsed universally since the earliest days of the church. The clergy and offices of the church imbue the Bible with this authority, thus: '*quod ubique, quod semper, quod ab omnibus*' ('what has been held always, everywhere, by everybody'). In other words there is a body of doctrine/belief, particularly about Jesus of Nazareth, the Christ, which is non-negotiable, authenticated by scripture, held in faith by all, always" (Brazier, *C. S. Lewis*, 3.2:32).

Lewis questions why Evangelicals and Anglo-Catholics do not embrace their obvious commonality as supernaturalists. He notes that they clearly differ with the stance held by liberals and certain modernists within the Christian church. He thinks that the failure to recognise the gulf between supernaturalistic Christianity and non-supernatural liberalism/modernism is inexplicable and conjectures that it may be a matter of vocabulary. Lewis suggests that Evangelicals and Anglo-Catholics might therefore consider adopting Baxter's term, mere Christians.

In an article titled "C. S. Lewis, Richard Baxter, and 'Mere Christianity,'" Neil Keeble of Scotland's University of Stirling writes that Lewis had read pretty well everything within the scope of his scholarly and critical work, ranging through the literatures of six languages from Homer to modern science fiction. He notes that evidenced both by his habit of quoting from memory in his published articles and by the reminiscences of his friends and colleagues, Lewis seemingly remembered nearly everything he had read. Although Baxter rarely gets attention from literary scholars, Keeble is not surprised that Lewis had read the seventeenth-century Puritan theologian's material and that Lewis had made note of Baxter's phrase "mere Christianity" and used it as a title for his own summary of the Christian faith. Keeble claims that Lewis has nowhere acknowledged the kind of debt to Baxter that he claimed to have owed to George MacDonald, but Keeble finds a kindred spirit in Baxter and Lewis. He notes that in their respective ages, each man was confronted by a significant break with the Christian tradition of the past and a consequent weakening of the authority and influence of the church. Keeble sees a strong similarity in what Baxter faced in the divisiveness and contentiousness of England's protracted Reformation and what Lewis had to confront in the disillusion and apostasy that followed two world wars. He sees Baxter confronting a highly partisan seventeenth-century England, while Lewis had to deal with a materialistic post-Christian England. Despite their challenges, Keeble claims that even though each of them was conspicuously out of sympathy with the prevailing milieu of their respective eras, Baxter and Lewis resisted the pressures to compromise the governing tenets of their faith, in order to accommodate the then-current mores. He notes that Baxter had to counter the deism of the late seventeenth century, whereas Lewis demonstrated a decisive hostility towards the demythologized theology of Rudolf Bultmann and his successors. Keeble credits Baxter for sublimating his strong Presbyterian ties in favour of an interdenominationalist stance, and finds in Lewis a conscious effort to resist accentuating denominational distinctions.[58]

Alister McGrath claims that Baxter believed the religious controversies of his age, including the English Civil War and the execution of Charles I, damaged the Christian faith by causing significant societal matters to be treated as though they were essential to the faith. He thinks, however, that issues that caused despair for Baxter served as wise counsel for Lewis, and notes that although the wartime milieu appears to have increased Lewis's interest in Baxter's nondenominational, core Christianity, his belief in its importance did not wane after the war. McGrath claims that Lewis continued to affirm ecclesiastical distinctiveness and recognised it as being spiritually beneficial for Christian living, while cautioning about keeping distinctions in perspective in order to avoid divisive "denominational triumphalism." He notes that Lewis did not advocate mere Christianity as an idealized abstraction but viewed it as the basic form of Christianity "that underlies all authentic forms of Christian belief and life."[59] McGrath contends that Lewis endeavoured to convey the notion that there is a notional, transdenominational form of Christianity that is to be used as the basis for Christian apologetics and that the actual becoming or being a Christian requires commitment to a *form* of this basic Christianity. He notes that while mere Christianity may take primacy over individual denominations, these denominations are, nevertheless, essential for Christian living. In McGrath's opinion, Lewis was not advocating mere Christianity as the only authentic form, but rather, his argument was "that it underlies and nourishes all those forms."[60] McGrath writes that Lewis's four series of broadcast talks, reworked to retain their basic structure and content and published as *Mere Christianity*, represent "Lewis's finest work of Christian apologetics."[61]

Lewis's *Mere Christianity* has enjoyed an extensive readership not only among members of his own generation and denomination but also among subsequent generations and other denominations. Historian George Marsden notes that Regent College professor Mark Noll claims that the phrase "mere Christianity" has become a widely used code to designate a meaningful body of belief that unites moderate to conservative

---

58. Keeble, "C. S. Lewis."
59. McGrath, *Intellectual World*, 150.
60. McGrath, *C. S. Lewis*, 221.
61. McGrath, *C. S. Lewis*, 213.

Christians from all denominations. Marsden observes that the term mere Christianity has become the name for a concept that has "taken on a life of its own as a way of expressing unity among moderate and conservative believers despite their differing ecclesiastical ties."[62] What Marsden and Noll refer to as "moderate to conservative" Christianity may well be an accurate characterisation of Lewis's Christian worldview. In his broadcast talks, as well as in his book *Mere Christianity*, Lewis endeavoured to communicate the truth claims of the Christian faith as he perceived them. As mentioned in the preceding chapter, during a lecture to Anglican clergy titled "Christian Apologetics," Lewis cautioned the attendees against voicing their own opinions about matters of faith and admonished them to communicate an orthodox Christian faith or consider resigning from the ministry.[63] Evidently, Lewis believed that his apologetic material represented objective truth. It therefore follows that the content of *Mere Christianity* is an accurate representation of the Lewisian worldview. Lewis scholar Paul Brazier seemingly supports this notion:[64]

> Lewis saw Christianity as the worldview, a *Weltanschauung*. This "mere" was the meta-narrative (an all-encompassing story, an over-arching great narrative) above all competing meta-narratives, not because it was easy, fashionable, or a convenient and complimentary lifestyle, but because it was *true*. This *Weltbild* cohered with the situation humanity was in, and related to a lesser or greater degree to all other religions and philosophies... and, as such, contradicts humanity's discredited meta-narratives.

Whereas *Mere Christianity* provides readers with the basics of authentic Christianity, *Miracles* represents Lewis's most comprehensive critique of naturalism. It was his last major apologetic work prior to launching the Narnia chronicles. The rest of his writings consisted largely of fictional works, his memoir, biblical exposition, and devotional literature. Lewis's progression from reason and argumentation to imaginative and devotional literature is not surprising, considering the progression that accompanied his conversion experience from theism via inductive reasoning to accepting the truth claims of Christianity via imaginative insight. Peter Schakel writes that because reason was a significant factor

---

62. Marsden, *C. S. Lewis's Mere Christianity*, 131–32.
63. Lewis, *God in the Dock*, 90.
64. Brazier, *C. S. Lewis*, 1:115.

in drawing Lewis to Christianity, it is not surprising that many of his early writings were reasoned works to demonstrate the truth of what he believed. He claims that in the last decade and a half of his life, Lewis's writings were less argumentative and relied more on experience and imagination. Schakel notes that Lewis's reason was honed to be sharp as a razor under the strict tutelage of William Kirkpatrick. Lewis differed sharply from Kirkpatrick, however, in his love of myth and imagination and, eventually, in his acceptance of Christian faith. Schakel sees Lewis's *Miracles* as a defence of reason itself with its reasoned argument for the possibility of miracles.[65]

Former Bowling Green University English professor Bruce Edwards claims that *Miracles* was directed toward a more sophisticated audience than many of Lewis's other works. He notes that it is comprised of lucid, succinct chapters, complete with appendices, and written with precise definition of terms, with the anticipation that it would be rigorously critiqued by serious readers. Edwards contends that Lewis draws heavily on the assumptions about the primacy of reason and the validity of natural law employed in his other major works, including *Mere Christianity* and *The Abolition of Man*.[66]

In *Miracles*, Lewis argues that reasoned thought is valueless if derived from strictly naturalistic means. He considers the position of naturalists to be self-contradictory if the human mind is deemed to be the result of nonrational causes. In an implied rebuttal to Professor Haldane,[67] with whom he had shared some prior spirited exchanges, Lewis writes: "Thus a strict materialism refutes itself for the reason given long ago by Professor Haldane: 'If my mental processes are determined wholly by the motions of atoms in my brain, I have no reason to believe my beliefs are true . . . and hence I have no reason for supposing my brain to be composed of atoms.'"[68] Gregory Cootsona's five-point outline of Lewis's argument in *Miracles* was quoted in a previous chapter, a summary of which reads as follows: (1) Naturalism asserts that all that exists is part of the natural world; (2) Reason must therefore be a component of the natural

---

65. Schakel, "Reason," 348–49.

66. B. Edwards, "Miracles."

67. As professor of genetics at University College, London, Haldane, a materialist/naturalist, objected to Lewis's science fiction novels and publicly critiqued some of Lewis's works. Lewis uses some of Haldane's statements to challenge the viability of naturalism.

68. Lewis, *Miracles*, 22.

world; (3) In order for reason to discover truth, it cannot be based solely on natural cause and effect; (4) Hence, naturalists cannot fit reason into their argument; (5) Therefore, we cannot know whether naturalism is true.[69] As John West writes: "The revised 1960 edition of *Miracles* is generally recognized as presenting Lewis's most mature critique of the ability of naturalism/materialism to account for man's rational faculties."[70]

Major tenets of the argument from reason have been dealt with in the previous chapter and need not be revisited in entirety. Professor of philosophy Jay Richards adds additional insight into Lewis's contribution, however. He claims that as an elite populist or translator, Lewis's genius was his ability to translate the argument from reason into the vernacular, thereby making it relevant to a much larger audience. He notes that the purpose of the argument is to show that naturalism and reason are incompatible and that believing in naturalism is self-defeating. Richards contends that the cardinal difficulty of naturalism doesn't depend on a "debatable theistic assumption." He claims that the primary shortcoming is the lack of "causal tools in the naturalist toolkit" and that at its core, Lewis's argument, rather than showing the falsity of naturalism, demonstrates that "naturalism can't be rationally believed."[71] As Richards and others have shown, a recognition of the inadequacy of naturalism/materialism to account for reality was a major component in the formation of the Lewisian worldview.

First published in 1944, *The Abolition of Man* was conceived as a series of three lectures when Lewis was asked by the University of Durham to present the Riddell Memorial Lectures at the university's Newcastle campus. The third lecture in the series eventually became the title for the book. John West notes that the main ideas in the book can be found throughout Lewis's other writings and lectures. Lewis's novel *That Hideous Strength* contains some of the most intriguing expressions of those ideas in fictional form, and West recommends that the two books be read together. He characterises Lewis's fictional treatment of those ideas as "the dire social consequences that follow from a Nietzschean science allied with the tools of government bureaucrats."[72] A thirteen-page syn-

---

69. Cootsona, *C. S. Lewis*, 440.
70. West, "Darwin in the Dock," 130.
71. Richards, "Mastering the Vernacular," 185–86.
72. West, "Abolition of Man," 68.

opsis of *The Abolition of Man* is available in Lewis's essay "The Poison of Subjectivism."[73]

The Riddell lectures comprise three essays in Lewis's book. The first essay is titled "Men without Chests." The essay gets its name from Lewis's indictment of the manner whereby objective values are systematically debunked by the educational institutions of his day and replaced with a philosophy of subjectivism. In his essay, Lewis mentions that Plato used the example of a king governing through his executive as a model for individuals to exercise traditional virtues to control and resist undesirable appetites. He notes the ancient tradition that holds that "the head rules the belly through the chest—the seat . . . of emotions organized by trained habit into stable sentiments." This first essay is a devastating critique of the moral relativism as taught in the public school system. He singles out two then-current school textbooks and cites specific examples, without disclosing the names of the books or the identities of the two authors. Lewis deems the public school system a "tragi-comedy" and considers the debunking of objective values as akin to removing a bodily organ from a person and expecting its continuing function. "We make men without chests and expect of them virtue and enterprise. We laugh at honour and are shocked to find traitors in our midst. We castrate and bid the gelding to be fruitful" he writes.[74] He concludes the first essay with an introduction of the objective moral code that he named the *Tao*. Lewis develops the concept of the *Tao* in much greater depth in his second lecture, in which he argues that an extensive survey of ancient cultures indicates the existence of a universal moral code that transcends time.

John West writes that in the book's second essay, which Lewis has titled "The Way,"[75] Lewis makes the point that "the only way for rela-

73. Lewis, *Christian Reflections* (2014), 89–101.

74. Lewis, *Abolition of Man*, 704.

75. The title of the chapter likely has special significance for Lewis. Toward the end of his autobiography *Surprised by Joy*, while describing the final steps in his conversion, Lewis comments on the manner by which two of his friends had disabused him of his shallow frivolity and his acquired Oxfordian idealism. He writes that during a luncheon with his then-student Bede Griffiths and friend Owen Barfield, he had referred to philosophy as a "subject," to which Barfield had responded: "It wasn't a subject to Plato, it was *a way*." Lewis notes that "the quiet but fervent agreement of Griffiths, and the quick understanding between these two" revealed his own "frivolity" and made him decide that "it was about time that something should be done" about his Oxfordian idealism, which was preventing him from embracing the Christian faith. "I thought the business of us finite and half-real souls was to multiply the consciousness of Spirit; to be tied to a particular time and place and set of circumstances,

tivists to escape self-contradiction is to deny the existence of objective truth altogether and to claim we create our own meaning by a sheer act of willpower."[76] In fact, Lewis notes that those who deny the validity of objective moral judgments are usually self-contradictory because they cannot escape making moral judgments themselves:[77]

> However subjective they may be about traditional values, Gaius and Titius[78] have shown by the very act of writing *The Green Book* that there must be some other values about which they are not subjective at all. They write to produce certain states of mind in the rising generation, if not because they think those states of mind intrinsically just or good, yet certainly because they think them to be the means to some state of society which they regard as desirable.

Lewis claims that although it would be a simple matter to ascertain what the real objective is of the two authors he has cited, he doesn't consider it to be necessary; after all, they must either have a purpose for writing or confess to having written a useless book. "In actual fact," writes Lewis, "Gaius and Titius will be found to hold, with complete uncritical dogmatism, the whole system of values which happened to be in vogue among moderately educated young men of professional classes during the period between the two wars."[79] He considers the scepticism about values professed by the two authors to be disingenuous. Lewis claims: "Their scepticism is on the surface: it is for use on other people's values; about the values current in their own set they are not nearly sceptical enough.... A great many of those who 'debunk' traditional (or as they

---

yet there to will and think as Spirit itself does. This was hard, for the very act whereby Spirit projected souls and a world gave those souls different and competitive interests, so that there was a temptation to selfishness. But I thought each of us had in his power to discount the emotional perspective produced by his own particular selfhood, just as we discount the optical perspective produced by our position in space.... Really a young Atheist cannot guard his faith too carefully.... Idealism can be talked, and even felt, it cannot be lived. It became patently absurd to go on thinking 'Spirit' as either ignorant of, or passive to, my approaches," writes Lewis (*Surprised by Joy*, 225–26).

76. West, "Abolition of Man," 68.

77. Lewis, *Abolition of Man*, 705.

78. Gaius and Titius are imaginary names that Lewis had given the authors in order to preserve their anonymity.

79. Lewis, *Abolition of Man*, 706.

would say) 'sentimental' values have in the background values of their own which they believe to be immune from the debunking process."[80]

Lewis observes that the two authors (Gaius and Titius), for all their debunking of traditional values, are not exactly value-free themselves. He opines that they most likely see themselves as bringing a more practical foundation for morality than those who advocate for an old-fashioned and, presumably, out-dated, "sentimental" value system. Lewis then tests various postulates, including instinct, societal preservation, and societal advantageousness for their potential invulnerability and finds them equally susceptible to being debunked.[81]

Lewis characterises proponents of the search for a new morality as innovators. "The truth finally becomes apparent that neither in any operation with factual propositions nor in any appeal to instinct can the Innovator find any basis for a system of values. None of the principles he requires can be found there," he writes.[82] Lewis contends that the principles for objective values are to be found elsewhere. "All the practical principles behind the Innovator's case for posterity, or society, or the species, are from time immemorial in the *Tao*. But they are nowhere else," he claims.[83] Lewis argues that the principles within the *Tao* were held by great moral leaders of the past, including Confucius, certain Stoics, Jesus, and Locke, and that they cannot be reached as conclusions but have to be held as premises. He contends that the values that the innovator uses to attack traditional values are themselves derived from the *Tao*. He notes that innovators advocate values, such as the need for getting people fed, duty to family members, responsibility to posterity and so on but claims that he can find no grounds for their claims to such values.[84] "Whence comes the Innovators authority to pick and choose?" asks Lewis. Because he can see no answer to the question, he draws the following conclusion:[85]

> This thing which I have called, for convenience, the Tao, and which others may call Natural Law or Traditional Morality, or the First Principles of Practical Reason, or the First

---

80. Lewis, *Abolition of Man*, 706.
81. Lewis, *Abolition of Man*, 707–12.
82. Lewis, *Abolition of Man*, 712.
83. Lewis, *Abolition of Man*, 712.
84. Lewis, *Abolition of Man*, 712–13.
85. Lewis, *Abolition of Man*, 713–14.

Platitudes . . . is the source of all value judgements.[86] If it is rejected, all value is rejected. If any value is retained, it is retained. The effort to refute it and raise a new system of value in its place is self-contradictory. There never has been, and never will be, a radically new judgement of value in the history of the world.

After demonstrating the debunkers' proclivity for destabilizing society, Lewis introduces the third chapter of the book, which is appropriately titled "The Abolition of Man." As John West has noted, Lewis's most intriguing treatment of the ideas in *The Abolition of Man* are included as fiction in *That Hideous Strength*. Seemingly outlandish notions such as transhumanism and posthumanism, which have been discussed in the previous chapter, have now become subjects under consideration. West claims that natural law continued to interest Lewis for the rest of his life and finds coverage of it in Lewis's *Discarded Image* and in *English Literature in the Sixteenth Century*, as well as in *The Chronicles of Narnia*.[87] Clearly, Lewis's notion of natural law had a significant impact on his apologetics.

In the final chapter of *The Abolition of Man*, Lewis envisions a future society in which man has subjugated nature and where the dreams of scientific planners are finally realized. He envisages a civilization governed by *Tao*-less conditioners who are commissioned to design what man is to become. In its final stages, Lewis visualizes a scenario whereby through eugenics, prenatal conditioning, education, and propaganda based on perfectly applied psychology, man had achieved total control over himself. Lewis postulates that the result of such an outcome would mean the end of human nature and thereby, ultimately, the end of man. He notes that if eugenics are sufficiently efficient, it is unlikely that there would be a revolt against authorized conditioners.[88]

Cameron Wybrow notes that Lewis warns against a grim future if humanity insists on abandoning the authority of the *Tao* and engaging in unrestrained manipulation, complete with mastery over nature. The result could be a conditioner-induced global tyranny and the abolition

---

86. It is instructive to note Ronald Galloway's observation: "Even developed perceptions of the evil and the good grounded in elaborated theories of knowledge and worldviews seem to owe their beginning to this at least partly intuitive, partly unlearned sense of the evil and the good" (Galloway, *Study in Perception*, 3304).

87. West, "Abolition of Man," 68.

88. Lewis, *Abolition of Man*, 718–20.

of man himself.[89] A professor himself, Wybrow expresses concern about contemporary academia. He sees striking similarities in Lewis's characterisation of the two academics featured above and individuals within modern-day academia. He notes that thousands of academics "operate in a world of pure theory, a world of academic discourse in which the like-minded preach to each other."[90] Wybrow considers significant numbers in academia to be bereft of practical life-changing experiences and living "in an almost completely artificial intellectual environment, protected by tenure, and in no way answerable for the real-life effects of their theories."[91] In contradistinction, University of Pretoria professor Conrad Wethmar writes: "The university system should guard against a pragmatism that would prevent theology from rendering a meaningful service to the academy and society at large. Confessionality and academic freedom are both valid dimensions in the process of theological thinking and should not be isolated from one another, either in terms of a theory of science or institutionally."[92]

Although the series of lectures that comprise the three chapters in *The Abolition of Man* were delivered during the Second World War, they are surprisingly relevant to today's academic environment. John West considers the book to be one of Lewis's most prophetic books. In his opinion, "the moral subjectivism that he predicted in the 1940's has come to pass with a vengeance, not only in Europe, but in America." West notes that "such subjectivism was uncritically adopted by much of the social sciences, and still undergirds much of modern economics, political science, psychology and sociology." He attributes these developments to the abandonment of moral absolutes: "The denial of the old moral absolutes has paralleled a dramatic increase in the authority of government to plan people's lives down to the last detail. It has also led to a moral vacuum in many disciplines, opening the door to the postmodern claim," writes West.[93]

By some measure, many of Lewis's prophetic words may be as applicable to today's generation as they were to his own. Contemporary application for Lewis's apologetics is the subject of the next chapter.

89. Wybrow, "Education of Mark Studdock," 273.
90. Wybrow, "Education of Mark Studdock," 286–87.
91. Wybrow, "Education of Mark Studdock," 287.
92. Wethmar, "Theology between Church, University," 237–38.
93. West, "Abolition of Man," 69.

Chapter Six

C. S. LEWIS'S RELEVANCE *for* PRESENT-DAY CHRISTIAN APOLOGETICS

6.1 INTRODUCTION

In order to understand the manner whereby Lewis came to formulate his worldview and the process by which he eventually came to embrace the Christian faith, it is important to analyse his spiritual journey. As has been shown, Lewis became doubtful about his Christian faith after experiencing a life-changing event, the death of his mother, which was followed by his introduction to alternative notions about the nature of reality. Subsequently, during various periods of his early years, he came to embrace naturalism, atheism, pantheism, certain versions of idealism, and, eventually, theism. Finally, he embraced Christianity as the ultimate worldview, a worldview that he believed to be a true representation of reality. Lewis's early attraction to alternative worldviews provided him with important insight when he encountered them as challengers to his Christian worldview. Michael Ward has written that Lewis is "probably the most influential practitioner of Christian apologetics over the last 100 years."[1] Alister McGrath refers to Lewis as "perhaps the greatest apologist of the twentieth century."[2] This chapter examines how present-day

---

1. Ward, "Good Serves the Better," 59.
2. McGrath, *Mere Apologetics*, 12.

apologetics may benefit from Lewis's methodology when dealing with the current challenges to Christianity.

6.2 CHALLENGES FROM INAUTHENTIC, NON-SUPERNATURAL CHRISTIANITY

There are good reasons to believe that Lewis believed non-supernatural versions of Christianity to be one of the most serious challenges to authentic, salvific Christian faith. As evidenced in his writings, Lewis embraced a Christian faith that had been "preached by the Apostles, attested by the Martyrs, embodied in the Creeds, expounded by the Fathers."[3] It is not difficult to imagine what Lewis's critique would be about certain current versions of Christianity. Lewis told the assembled clergy in Wales during the Second World War that alterations to the Christian faith that are motivated by a desire to make it more acceptable or more appealing to society would render it insipid and would lead to its stagnation: "A 'liberal'[4] Christianity which considers itself free to alter the Faith when-

---

3. Lewis, *God in the Dock*, 90.

4. James Como, professor, editor of *C. S. Lewis at the Breakfast Table and Other Reminiscences*, and president of the New York C. S. Lewis Society, writes: "Culturally conservative and militantly orthodox in his religious beliefs, C. S. Lewis is nevertheless difficult to categorize in terms common to political discourse. Precisely to avoid such categorization (he viewed it as politically inconvenient) he refused an offer of knighthood from Churchill's postwar government. In that light he is best seen as conservatively disposed rather than as a conservative per se. Touchstones of his conservative thought are his trust in the validity of reason, defense of natural law, general reliance upon tradition ('mere Christianity'), objective view of creation (both natural and supernatural) and the legitimacy of its claims upon us (our moral and aesthetic responses are trainable and ought to be ordinate), distrust of emotion as a guide to truth, refusal to equate progress with innovation or to see it as at all inevitable, and a rejection of egalitarianism as dangerous and immoral. . . . He distrusted collectivism (especially mass movements) of any kind, loathed government intrusion into everyday life, and reviled statist presumptuousness. . . . Yet he allowed that a genuinely Christian society would somehow be a socialist one. His unvarying orthodoxy notwithstanding. . . . His allegiance to scriptural inerrancy did not lead to anything resembling biblical literalism or fundamentalism. . . . Thus, his thought must be read within the considerable context he provided, not as lessons or, worse, tricks, but as an organic worldview arising from inherited culture and faith in the Risen Lord. In over forty books, two hundred essays and sermons, and eighty poems, he was one of the greatest Christian apologists ever to have written in English; a formidable religious thinker, psychologist and devotional writer; a philosopher and poet; a fiction writer who arguably produced benchmarks in religious allegory, the first-person novel, children's fantasy and science fiction; and one of the foremost literary historians and critics of the

ever the Faith looks perplexing or repellant must be completely stagnant," Lewis admonished the assembly.[5] He told the conference attendees that from his perspective, salvific Christianity must retain certain doctrines or lose its authenticity and that clergy members should resign from Christian ministry if their abandonment of core beliefs crosses a certain line:[6]

> It is not, of course, for me to define to you what Anglican Christianity is—I am your pupil, not your teacher. But I insist that wherever you draw the lines, bounding lines must exist, beyond which your doctrine will cease to be Anglican or to be Christian: and I suggest also that the lines come a great deal sooner than many modern priests think. I think it is your duty to fix the lines clearly in your own minds: and if you wish to go beyond them you must change your profession.
>
> This is your duty not specifically as Christians or as priests but as honest men. There is a danger here of the clergy developing a special professional conscience which obscures the very plain moral issue. Men who have passed beyond these boundary lines in either direction are apt to protest that they have come by their unorthodox opinions honestly. In defense of these opinions they are prepared to suffer obloquy and to forfeit professional advancement. They thus come to feel like martyrs. But this simply misses the point which so gravely scandalizes the layman. We never doubted that the unorthodox opinions were honestly held: what we complain of is your continuing your ministry after you have come to hold them. We always knew that a man who makes his living as a paid agent of the Conservative party may honestly change his views and honestly become a Communist. What we deny is that he can honestly continue to be a Conservative agent and to receive money from one party while he supports the policy of another.

Lewis insists that the core elements of the faith as preached by the apostles, attested by the martyrs, embodied in the creeds, and expounded by the fathers must be maintained in order for it to be authentic Christian faith. He recognised that the attendees were entitled to hold opinions

---

twentieth century. Withal, he is what he famously called himself, an Old Western Man, and he would consistently remind us that 'anything not eternal is eternally out of date.' In short, his imaginative effusions as radical as nature itself; his reason as conservative as the multiplication table; and his spirit as liberal and as liberated as the open arms of [the Christ of] the Cross [whom] he worshipped" (Como, "Lewis, C. S.").

5. Lewis, *God in the Dock*, 91.
6. Lewis, *God in the Dock*, 89–90.

that were at variance with authentic Christianity. But he also admonished them that just as paid agents of the nation's Conservative party could not continue in their role after having embraced the ideology of, say, the Communist party, so they could not continue as true representatives of Christianity after having abandoned the core tenets of the faith. Lewis considered the Christian faith as taught by the apostles and embodied in the creeds to be authentic Christianity. He believed the Scriptures of the Old and New Testaments to be the word of God and considered them to be the basis on which to determine the difference between authentic and inauthentic Christianity. As discussed in the preceding chapter, *Mere Christianity* expresses Lewis's conception of authentic, supernaturalistic Christianity.

In a letter to Sister Penelope[7] in November 1939, Lewis discusses theological issues, including the subject of high and low forms of Anglicanism: "To me the real distinction is not between high and low but between religion with a real supernaturalism & salvationism on the one hand, and all watered-down and modernist versions on the other," he writes.[8] Lewis had admonished the assembled clergy in Wales that there were certain boundaries to the doctrines of the Christian faith that could not be broken and that they must be careful not to breach those boundaries if they wanted to remain faithful to their profession. For Lewis, belief that the biblical miracles represented actual space-time occurrences was a boundary that could not be breached when teaching, preaching, or practising authentic Christianity. In fact, Lewis was so definitive about the supernaturalistic content of the Christian faith that many of his contemporaries labeled him a fundamentalist. In *Reflections on the Psalms*, Lewis offers insight into his view on the supernatural elements of Scripture:[9]

> I have been suspected of being what is called a Fundamentalist. That is because I never regard any narrative as unhistorical simply on the ground that it includes the miraculous. Some people find the miraculous so hard to believe that they cannot imagine any reason for my acceptance of it other than a prior belief that every sentence of the Old Testament has historical or scientific truth. But this I do not hold.... The real reason why I

---

7. Sister Penelope CSMV was a member of the Anglican Church's Convent of the Community of St Mary. Lewis referred to her as his "elder sister in the Faith" (Lewis, *Collected Letters*, 2:1058).

8. Lewis, *Collected Letters*, 2:285.

9. Lewis, *Reflections on the Psalms*, 127–28.

can accept as historical a story in which a miracle occurs is that I have never found any philosophical grounds for the universal negative proposition that miracles do not happen.

Lewis contended that there was no philosophical basis for rejecting the miraculous in the biblical narratives. Arguments against the miraculous are sometimes incorporated within some form of materialism, which was a notion that Lewis had embraced in his youth but had eventually rejected in favour of theism. Although Lewis believed that parts of the Old Testament were meant to be understood symbolically or allegorically, he came to embrace a Christian faith that considered the Gospels to be accounts of actual events and therefore historically accurate. Lewis argued for the historicity of the Gospel account in an essay titled "Modern Theology and Biblical Criticism, "which he read at Westcott House in Cambridge on May 11, 1959:[10]

> A theology which denies the historicity of nearly everything in the Gospels to which Christian life and affections and thought have been fastened for nearly two millennia—which either denies the miraculous altogether or, more strangely, after swallowing the camel of the Resurrection strains at such gnats as the feeding of the multitudes—if offered to the uneducated man can produce only one or other of two effects. It will make him a Roman Catholic or an atheist. What you offer him he will not recognize as Christianity. If he holds to what he calls Christianity he will leave a church in which it is no longer taught and will look for one where it is. If he agrees with your version he will no longer call himself a Christian and no longer come to church. In his crude, course way, he would respect you more if you did the same.

In Lewis's opinion, it is hazardous to offer a watered-down form of Christianity to a person who has recently embraced the Christian faith. Lewis thought that a form of Christianity that rejects elements of the supernatural out of hand will either cause individuals to reject Christianity altogether or induce them to leave the liberal church where it is being disseminated and join a congregation where biblical Christianity is actually taught.

In his book titled *Letters to Malcolm*, Lewis expresses similar concerns about what he characterises as liberal Christianity. He claims that practitioners of this form of Christianity think it essential for the faith

10. Lewis, *Essay Collection*, 243.

to be demythologised in order to survive. He notes that individuals such as himself, who "proclaim that Christianity essentially involves the supernatural," are considered to be a hindrance to the promulgation of Christianity by those who disseminate a demythologised version. Lewis poses a rhetorical question for the reader: "By the way, did you ever meet, or hear of, anyone who was converted from scepticism to a 'liberal' or 'demythologised' Christianity? I think that when believers come in at all, they come in a good deal further," writes Lewis.[11] Philip Ryken writes: "What he meant by 'a good deal further' was authentic faith in the risen Lord Jesus Christ."[12]

In his *Modern Theology and Biblical Criticism* essay, Lewis held liberal scholars responsible for undercutting authentic Christianity. "The undermining of the old orthodoxy has been mainly the work of divines engaged in New Testament criticism," he writes.[13] Lewis thought it illogical that the opinions of so-called modern-day experts should take precedence over the beliefs of the early church, the church fathers, the Reformers, and nineteenth-century church leaders. Lewis finds a strong commonality in the beliefs in the groups mentioned, a commonality that did not include demythologised Christian faith. He opines that whatever qualifications certain individuals may have as Biblical critics, he distrusts them as critics per se. From his perspective, certain critics seem to lack literary judgment and appear imperceptive about the very quality of the texts they are citing. He finds some critics' commentary that the Gospels are legend or romance to be incongruent. This incongruence leads him to question how many legends and romances the critics's have actually read, how well their palates are trained in detecting a particular flavour in a romance or legend, and how many years the critics have actually spent studying a given Gospel.[14]

Lewis points out notable examples of highly questionable assumptions from Rudolf Bultmann's (1884–1976) *Theology of the New Testament*. He finds instances of a lack of perception in the text in Bultmann's interpretation of Mark's Gospel. He makes reference to Bultmann's claim that there is no personality expressed about Jesus in the New Testament and asks rhetorically: "Through what strange process has this learned

---

11. Lewis, *Letters to Malcolm*, 119.
12. Ryken, "Inerrancy and Patron Saint," 64.
13. Lewis, *Essay Collection*, 243.
14. Lewis, *Essay Collection*, 244.

German gone to make himself blind to what all men except him can see? What evidence have we that he would recognize a personality if he were there? For it is Bultmann *contra mundum*.[15] If anything whatever is common to all believers, and even to many unbelievers, it is the sense that in the Gospels they have met a personality."[16] Lewis notes that there are numerous characters whom we know to be historical but of whom we feel that we have little or no personal information. In Lewis's opinion, Socrates and Jesus[17] are two exceptions, because we not only have historical material about what they did but also much personal information about who they were. Lewis wonders about the Bultmann notion of personality: "Even those passages in the New Testament which superficially, and in intention, are most concerned with the divine, and least with the human nature, bring us face to face with the personality.... I begin to fear that by *personality* Dr. Bultmann means what I should call impersonality: what you'd get in a Dictionary of National Biography article or an obituary."[18]

Lewis also takes exception with liberal scholars's claim that Jesus's teachings and practises were misunderstood and misinterpreted by his earliest followers and that the truth of those teachings and practises have been exhumed by modern scholarship.[19] He claims that similar theories

15. Latin, "against the world."
16. Lewis, *Essay Collection*, 245.
17. For a comprehensive treatment of believing and knowing, see James P. Moreland and William Lane Craig's *Philosophical Foundations for a Christian Worldview*. Moreland and Craig define one form of knowledge as "justified true belief" (Moreland and Craig, *Philosophical Foundations*, 88).
18. Lewis, *Essay Collection*, 246.
19. Paul Brazier writes: "Bultmann's demythologizing agenda was typical of the dominant spirit of the age amongst intellectuals in the twentieth century. His attempt to identify how the Gospels had been constructed was through form criticism; the aim being to try to get back in time to how the Gospel had been written. This approach was controversial but popular in academic circles. Bultmann was at his most controversial when he applied this technique to John's Gospel claiming that it was simply theology in story form. Bultmann believed the Gospels had to be reduced so as to present and explain them to his intellectual contemporaries, which meant identifying that which did not fit in with a modern mind-set. Bultmann's technique is driven by skepticism, but with an unquestioning acceptance of a modern scientific worldview. He [Bultmann] asserted that it is not possible to use electric light and the radio and to avail ourselves of modern medical and surgical discoveries and at the same time believe in the New Testament world of demons and spirits. It has often been asserted that Bultmann carried form criticism to such an extreme that the veracity and historical value of the Gospels is done away with" (Brazier, *C. S. Lewis* 2:36).

have been popularized about other historical figures such as Plato, Aristotle, and Shakespeare and have been debunked by succeeding scholars. Lewis comments that he has been bemused by reading imaginary histories both of his own works and those of his friends, whose real history of their writings he knew:[20]

> This is done with immense eradition and great ingenuity. And at first sight it is very convincing. I think I should be convinced by it myself. . . . Until you come to be reviewed yourself you would never believe how little of an ordinary review is taken up by criticism in the strict sense, by evaluation, praise, or censure of the book actually written. Most of it is taken up with imaginary histories of the process by which you wrote it.

Lewis notes that critics who had postulated about what public events or which authors had directed or influenced his own writings had never been right in a single instance, that, in fact, "not one of these guesses has on any one point been right," and that they had a "record of 100 per cent failure."[21]

Lewis finds it to be particularly objectionable that theologians constantly apply the "principle that the miraculous does not occur." He objects to the practise whereby any statement made by Jesus that contains prophetic or predictive content is deemed to have been made after the event had occurred. Lewis points out that this practise is a logical consequence of adopting a belief that miraculous events never occur. "This is a purely philosophical question. . . . Scholars speak on it with no more authority than anyone else," he argues.[22] "If one is speaking of authority, the united authority of all the biblical critics in the world counts here for nothing. On this they speak simply as men; men obviously influenced by, and perhaps insufficiently critical of, the spirit of the age they grew up in" Lewis claims.[23]

Some of Lewis's harshest critique of liberal critics's anti-supernatural biases is contained in his fictional works. In his book *The Screwtape Letters*, he describes the liberal vicar of a local Anglican congregation as "a man who has been so long engaged in watering down the faith to make it easier for a supposed incredulous and hard-headed congregation,

---

20. Lewis, *Essay Collection*, 248.
21. Lewis, *Essay Collection*, 249.
22. Lewis, *Essay Collection*, 247.
23. Lewis, *Essay Collection*, 248.

that it is now he who shocks his parishioners with his unbelief, not *vice versa.*" He characterises the vicar as having undermined the Christianity of many of his parishioners and as having spared the laity of many of the less popular books of Scripture by confining his preaching to a "treadmill" of some fifteen favourites, feel-good psalms, in an effort to avoid preaching about subjects that contain truth-bearing, instructive, corrective, and life-changing elements.[24] Lewis satirizes various proponents of inauthentic Christianity in *The Screwtape Letters.* In one of the letters, various forms of the falsified historical Jesus are constructed, including one based "on Marxian, catastrophic and revolutionary lines"[25] and one modeled "on liberal and humanitarian lines."[26] Lewis points out in his fictional narrative that these falsified versions of the "historical Jesus" are intended to mask the reality of the truth about the historical Jesus[27] and are expected to be revised every few decades in order "to direct men's attention to something which does not exist."[28]

As Lewis said in his 1945 lecture in Wales, there can be no authentic version of Christianity that eliminates the supernatural, because Christianity is the one religion from which the miraculous cannot be excluded.[29] He believed miracles to be an essential component of authentic Christianity, including the supreme miracle, the resurrection. He found any theology that denies the historicity of nearly everything in the Gospels on which Christian life had been based for nearly two millennia to be untenable. Moreover, he found it difficult to reconcile any form of Christianity that denied the miraculous altogether or accepted the resurrection but

---

24. Lewis, *Screwtape Letters*, 231.
25. Lewis, *Screwtape Letters*, 251–52.
26. Lewis, *Screwtape Letters*, 251.
27. Paul Brazier notes that biblical scholar John Redford calls out Enlightenment methodology relating to historical situations for being scientifically deficient: "Redford, a Roman Catholic scholar, has critically demolished the post-eighteenth-century Enlightenment 'Quest for the Historical Jesus,' in part because of its innate prejudicial ground in believing that incarnation could not happen and that the miraculous never occurred," writes Brazier. Brazier opines that Redford has left the biblical criticism of the likes of Bultmann and Schweitzer shaken to its core, by exposing its "blinkered Enlightenment methodology." He finds certain biblical scholars' "sophisticated and widely-held conclusions deficient on scientific grounds" (Brazier, *C. S. Lewis*, 2:147).
28. Lewis, *Screwtape Letters*, 252.
29. Lewis, *God in the Dock*, 99.

denied the historicity of Jesus's miracles, such as the miraculous "feeding of the multitudes."[30]

Even though Lewis's critiques were written more than half a century ago, they offer readers a wealth of resources for responding to current challenges to an authentic, supernaturalistic Christian worldview.

6.3 CHALLENGES FROM DEISM

Although some of Lewis's criticisms of inauthentic Christianity may also apply to deism, Lewis seemingly devoted relatively little time to critiquing deism itself. However, some versions of deism contain certain features of Lewis's depiction of unorthodox, unauthentic Christianity and are therefore subject to the Lewisian critique. Charles Taylor has written that deism has drifted away from orthodox Christianity, whereby rather than being conceived as a Supreme Being, with relational qualities and properties analogous to what we call agency and personality, God is seen as relating to us only as the architect of the law-governed structure he had created. Taylor thinks that this results in the perception of humans having an existence within an indifferent universe, in which God is either indifferent or nonexistent. From Taylor's perspective, deism should be seen as a kind of "half-way house on the road to contemporary atheism."[31] Taylor writes: "The main attack against orthodoxy concerns the agency of God, as wielder of extra-systemic causal power, bringing about miracles, special providences, acts of favour and punishment, and the like . . . The grid that Deism and its successors operate with, blanks out communion almost totally."[32]

In a chapter titled "The Impersonal Order" in his massive 2007 work *A Secular Age*, Taylor offers valuable insights into the West's drift away from orthodox Christianity. Taylor's chapter offers significant parallels to Lewis's body of work. Taylor credits several strands of thought as being instrumental in the drift to deism. Just as Lewis did, he considers the perceived disenchantment of the cosmos as being one of the strands. A changing stance toward history, in which certain events came to be viewed as legendary, rather than historical, is cited as another factor. He notes that the revised stance toward history was instrumental in bringing

---

30. Lewis, *Essay Collection*, 243.
31. Taylor, *Secular Age*, 270–71.
32. Taylor, *Secular Age*, 280.

about a revised approach to biblical criticism whereby biblical accounts were judged for their historical accuracy in terms of which events were plausible, rather than whether or not they were historical. He cites the works of Spinoza and Hume as having influenced the various trends. As well, Taylor credits the growing confidence in the reliability of scientific endeavours as another factor in the drift away from orthodox Christianity and the slide toward deism. He cautions against explaining the rise of deism solely in the above terms, at the risk of falling into an implicit petition *principii*,[33] however.[34] Taylor notes that with the cultural and societal changes taking place, such as increasing economic prosperity, a move toward greater egalitarianism, and a growing, "commercial production-oriented elite," there may be a sense that religion, too, must change, and that orthodox, community-defined Christianity belongs to an earlier age.[35] Taylor summarises the processes that he thinks contributed to the slide toward deism:[36]

> So putting this all together, we see how a certain kind of framework understanding came to be constituted: fed by the powerful presence of impersonal orders, cosmic, social and moral; drawn by the power of the disengaged stance, and its ethical prestige, and ratified by a sense of what the alternative was, based on an elites's derogatory and somewhat fearful portrait of popular religion, an unshakeable sense could arise of our inhabiting an immanent, impersonal order, which screened out, for those inhabiting it, all phenomena which failed to fit this framework. We just need to add one thing which puts the lock on the door, as it were. Once one has adopted this take, one can be firmly entrenched in it by the enframing historical consciousness[37] which was developed in polite, commercial society.

In Taylor's opinion, cosmic forces, supported by social dynamics and fueled, in part, by an elitist, derogatory view of popular (Christian) religion, formulated an intellectual framework for bringing about a societal

---

33. Latin, "the fallacy of assuming in the premise of an argument what one wishes to prove in the conclusion; a begging of the question."

34. Taylor, *Secular Age*, 270–73.

35. Taylor, *Secular Age*, 289.

36. Taylor, *Secular Age*, 288–89.

37. Taylor's notion of an "enframing historical consciousness," which he elsewhere terms "social imaginary" (Taylor, *Secular Age*, 281), contains most, if not all, of the characteristics of a worldview.

worldview characterised as an immanent order, which was purposefully conceived as being impersonal.

Taylor notes that the drift toward deism and away from orthodox Christianity was commensurate with the rise of unitarianism. He opines that this drift was, in part, a consequence of modern Christian belief having been cut "loose from the soteriological doctrines of historical Christianity." Taylor claims that this revised form of Christianity deprived Jesus of his divinity and changed his role from one that "inaugurates a new relation among and with us, [thereby] restoring or transforming our relationship with God," to one in which Jesus's role is reduced to that of a moral teacher. Taylor claims that unitarianism wasn't confined solely to denominational Unitarianism but that elements of it have manifested themselves in various other denominations as well.[38] Much of Taylor's detailed analysis of the rise of deism notably parallels Lewis's critique of inauthentic Christianity.

6.4 CHALLENGES FROM PANTHEISM/PANENTHEISM

In the 1950s essay titled "Rejoinder to Dr. Pittenger," Lewis notes that he found pantheistic notions more of a hindrance to conversion than deism: "I see around me no danger of Deism, but much of an immoral, naive and sentimental pantheism. I have often found that it was in fact the chief obstacle to conversion," writes Lewis. In fact, in his response to Pittenger, Lewis notes that having observed this tendency to lace Christianity with pantheistic content, although believing God to be both immanent as well as transcendent, he emphasises God's transcendence more than his immanence.[39] In an essay titled "Difficulties in Presenting the Christian Faith to Modern Unbelievers" and later published as "God in the Dock," Lewis mentions that he had been mistaken in thinking that materialism was the only significant adversary in his public defense of the Christian faith. He notes that materialism was only one of many non-Christian creeds, which included theosophy and various forms of spiritualism. Lewis comments that he saw no sign that those alternative beliefs were diminishing. He observes that even where Christianity was being professed, it was frequently tainted with pantheistic notions.[40] In a chapter aptly titled,

38. Taylor, *Secular Age*, 291.
39. Lewis, *God in the Dock*, 181.
40. Lewis, *God in the Dock*, 240–41.

"Christianity and 'Religion'" in Lewis's *Miracles*, he writes that there is a natural human tendency toward pantheistic notions:[41]

> Pantheism is in fact the permanent natural bent of the human mind; the permanent ordinary level below which man sometimes sinks, under the influence of priestcraft and superstition, but above which his own unaided efforts can never raise him for very long. Platonism and Judaism, and Christianity (which has incorporated both), have proved the only things capable of resisting it. It is the attitude into which the human mind automatically falls when left to itself. No wonder we find it congenial. If "religion" means simply what man says about God, and not what God does about man, then Pantheism almost *is* religion. And "religion" in that sense has, in the long run, only one really formidable opponent—namely Christianity.

Lewis thinks that humanity, sometimes aided by superstition and accompanied by various rituals, naturally finds itself drawn to religion. He thinks that some form of pantheism is typically embraced to satisfy this natural impulse. In his opinion, although Platonism and Judaism have at times been successful in resisting it, Christianity is actually pantheism's only formidable opponent.

Lewis comments that while he is cognizant of the fact that many pantheistic notions are consistent with the current intellectual and cultural climate, he is also aware of some of its inconsistencies within the modern mind set. He notes that pantheism is immemorial in Eastern civilizations such as India; that the Greeks, at their peak, rose above it through the thought of Plato and Aristotle; and that Western Europe largely escaped it by embracing Christianity. He sees a return to elements of pantheism in Hegel, Spinoza, and Rudolf Steiner's theosophy and even finds popular versions of it in Wordsworth, Carlyle, and Emerson. Lewis finds it ironic that each reincarnation of this ancient, immemorial religion is hailed as the last word in novelty and emancipation.[42]

Lewis sees two major reasons for the preference of some form of pantheism over Christianity. He thinks that there is usually a fatally flawed sense of comparison between the two. One's understanding of the Christian faith is typically acquired, and therefore shaped, by childhood experiences; whereas pantheism is usually embraced during early adulthood and is perceived as encapsulating greater profundity, as a

---

41. Lewis, *Miracles*, 132.
42. Lewis, *Miracles*, 131–33.

consequence of having been discovered during a period of greater maturity. Christianity is therefore perceived as offering a simplistic account of God and hence unlikely to be true, while pantheism offers a sense of the mysterious and sublime and is perceived as being more sophisticated and therefore more attractive. Lewis thinks that this perceived profundity acts as a thinly veiled covering for the inconsistencies within Pantheism.[43] Moreover, Lewis thinks that the pantheistic God is found to be a more amicable God to believe in: "The Pantheist's God does nothing, demands nothing. He is there if you wish for Him, like a book on a shelf. He will not pursue you. There is no danger that at any time heaven and earth should flee away at His glance. If He were the truth, then we could really say that all the Christian images of kingship were a historical accident of which our religion should be cleansed," writes Lewis.[44] Lewis contrasts the pantheists's conception of God with the God of Christianity:[45]

> Pantheists and Christians agree that God is present everywhere. Pantheists conclude that He is "diffused" or "concealed" in all things and therefore a universal medium rather than a concrete entity,[46] because their minds are really dominated by the picture of a gas, or fluid, or space itself. The Christian, on the other hand, deliberately rules out such images by saying that God is totally present at every point of space and time, and *locally* present in none. Again, the Pantheist and Christian agree that we are all dependent on God and intimately related to Him. But the Christian defines this relation in terms of Maker and made, whereas the Pantheist (at least of the popular kind) says, we are "parts" of Him, or are contained in Him. Once more, the picture of a vast extended something which can be divided into areas has crept in. Because of this fatal picture Pantheism concludes that God must be equally present in what we call evil and what we call good and therefore indifferent to both (ether permeates the mud and the marble impartially). The Christian has to reply that this is far too simple; God is present in a great many different modes: not present in matter as He is present in man, not present in all men as in some, not present in any other man as in Jesus.

---

43. Lewis, *Miracles*, 134.

44. Lewis, *Miracles*, 149.

45. Lewis, *Miracles*, 134–35.

46. Lewis does not delineate between pantheistic and panentheistic elements; some characteristics may be described as elements of panentheism.

Lewis finds a lack of coherence in the pantheistic model and suggests some Christian responses to counter pantheistic notions. He finds a credible explanation for the existence of evil to be notably absent in pantheism and considers the lack of a coherent explanation for evil's existence to be a fatal flaw in the pantheistic worldview.[47] Harold Netland, in his book *Encountering Religious Pluralism: The Challenge to Christian Faith and Mission*, writes that the New Age movement in the West incorporates pantheistic notions in its intellectual framework: "The tendency to blur the distinction between God and humankind—either to bring God down to our level or to deify human beings—is a common feature of religion and can be found in the polytheistic religions of the ancient world as well as in many modern-day traditions. . . . It has become popular in the West in the New Age movement."[48] Lewis's body of work serves as a good background for current authors to counter pantheistic challenges to the Christian worldview.

6.5 CHALLENGES FROM NATURALISM/SECULARISM

In his foreword to one of Paul Brazier's four volumes on Lewis, professor of systematic theology Justyn Terry, at Ambridge's Trinity School for Ministry, writes: "Naturalism . . . has become one of the greatest challenges the church has faced since the Reformation."[49] In John West's opinion, the revised 1960 edition of *Miracles* is recognised as Lewis's most mature critique of naturalism.[50] If Terry's observation about the current religious climate is accurate, the Lewisian apologetic methodology may be just as relevant in the current era as it was in Lewis's day.

Terry observes that modern science's explanations of natural events without any reference to divine agency has made it difficult for Christians to speak about the supernatural realm. This development has made naturalism a powerful alternative to theistic religion, he claims. Terry notes that despite the inadequacy of naturalistic explanations, many would-be believers are reluctant to embrace Christianity for fear of being perceived

---

47. William James notes that "on the monistic or pantheistic view, evil, like everything else, must have its foundation in God; and the difficulty is to see how this can possibly be the case if God is absolutely good" (James, *Varieties of Religious Experience*, 131).

48. Netland, *Encountering Religious Pluralism*, 336.

49. Terry, "Foreword," 2:xiii.

50. West, "Darwin in the Dock," 130.

as superstitious or ignorant of scientific discoveries. He claims that naturalism's influence is instrumental in causing resistance to notions of the supernatural and "is most especially acute when the subject of our inquiry is Jesus Christ." He observes that the Christian faith is impoverished, leaving the Jesus of the New Testament unrecognisable if theologians have to shave away all references to divine revelations or miraculous powers. Terry writes: "To meet the stringent demands of naturalism, the traditional Chalcedonian claim that Jesus is fully God and fully man has to be set aside in favour of a much diminished view of a very limited and purely human Jesus."[51] He notes that while Jesus may perhaps remain as a great religious teacher who offers insight into the human experience, any claims to being the Son of God result in being withdrawn. As Ambridge's professor of theology, Terry is well positioned to observe the challenges that naturalism presents to authentic Christian faith.

As mentioned in the preceding chapter, the argument against naturalism is sometimes referred to as the argument from reason. Jay Richards writes that "Lewis's achievement was to make the argument from reason precise enough to be persuasive but accessible enough to be understood by millions."[52] John West views Lewis's *Miracles* as a valuable resource for countering the naturalist challenge. Other resources include *Mere Christianity* and some of Lewis's essays, such as "Rejoinder to Dr. Pittenger," "Is Theology Poetry," "Christian Apologetics," and "Reply to Professor Haldane." The content of these works has been covered extensively in previous chapters and need not be repeated here.

Terry notes that of all the Christian apologists who have sought to directly confront the challenge of naturalism, one of the most effective and enduring has been C. S. Lewis:[53]

> He was unusually well prepared for the task by his background and education. He could understand the thinking of a naturalist, having become an atheist in adolescence after losing the Protestant faith in which he had grown up in Belfast, Northern Ireland. He also knew of the world of imagination from his study of literature and poetry and could see how stifling to such thinking naturalism could become. In addition, he was well versed in philosophy, which gave him important tools to engage the ideas of naturalists.

51. Terry, "Foreword," 2:xiii.
52. Richards, "Mastering the Vernacular," 190.
53. Terry, "Foreword," 2:xiii–xiv.

As Terry notes, Lewis was well grounded to engage the naturalists on their own turf. As a defender of authentic Christianity, Lewis has few equals. His body of work yields a rich resource of information for countering the naturalist challenge.

6.6 CHALLENGES FROM PRAGMATISM/ UTILITARIANISM/NEW AGEISM

Contemporary Christianity is also challenged by a form of utilitarianism. This trend is sometimes manifested as a determination to embrace a certain belief system because of its practical utility. The decision to embrace a utilitarian notion or subscribe to a particular utilitarian philosophy is based on the belief system's perceived utility, rather than on its truth value. The decision is typically based on what works for the individual, rather than on whether or not the philosophical or religious corporeity is inherently true. This trend contains elements of consumerism and may also be described as a form of pragmaticism[54] or privatism. Typically, individuals who subscribe to a philosophy because of its utilitarian attraction do so because of the potential utilitarian value it holds for the practitioner. In their book *Philosophical Foundations for a Christian Worldview*, J. P. Moreland and William Lane Craig identify several forms of utilitarianism and note that advocates of a version of utilitarianism known as pluralistic utilitarianism are attracted to it because of its intrinsic system of values, including qualities such as "knowledge, love, beauty, health, freedom, courage, self-esteem, and so on."[55]

As mentioned in a previous chapter, although utilitarianism was originally conceived as an ethical model,[56] its influence has been extended well beyond its ethical origins. McGill University philosopher Charles Taylor claims that a form of utilitarianism, "materialist utilitarianism," is one of Western modernity's most suppressing movements. Even though it was formed as a movement that seeks to establish a form of life that is "unqualifiedly good," utilitarianism has become insensitive

54. "The term Pragmatism derives from the Greek *pragmata* . . . it has come to be associated with such slogans as 'Truth is what works.' . . . Truth is therefore relative. When applied to religion this means that a religion or any aspect of it is not to be valued for its own sake but for its psychological and moral effects" (Colin Brown, *Philosophy and Christian Faith*, 145–46).

55. Moreland and Craig, *Philosophical Foundations*, 434–35.

56. See sect. 4 in ch. 2.

and intolerant of alternate notions, including religious ones, he writes.[57] Taylor claims that the rejection of traditional religion and adoption of utilitarianism can have untoward consequences for a society. He notes that one such consequence may be a "doctrinaire utilitarianism where all value is homogenized in terms of utility consequences, and the difference between higher and lower motivations denied."[58]

Professor emeritus of English George Musacchio claims that emergent philosophical notions are indicative of the human need for meaning, a need that is sometimes manifested as a search for some metaphysical explanation for the universe. He opines that the decline of Christianity in the West, combined with the rise of modernity, which was followed by the resultant postmodernity, has produced a vacuum in the human soul. He notes that into this vacuum have rushed "things like irrational philosophy, superstition, occultism, the New Age movement."[59] James Anderson, professor of theology and philosophy at Reformed Theological Seminary, has noted the recent rise of New Ageism as well. In his 2014 book *What's Your Worldview*, he writes that Pantheism has "made significant inroads to the West in recent years through the New Age movement."[60] Some current New Age notions manifest utilitarian characteristics; the desired qualities associated with a particular utilitarian notion are often cited as reasons for having embraced it. It is important to note that Lewis converted to theism and, eventually, to Christianity because of his belief in theism's and, ultimately, Christianity's inherent truth, rather than in its utilitarian value.

Harold Netland observes a dramatic change having taken place in the religious landscape of the West during the past half century. He opines that although there is ample evidence of the historical ties of Christianity and the West, the culture in the West is gradually shedding its Christian heritage. He attributes this phenomenon, in part, to the active promotion of religious pluralism, whereby alternate notions of spirituality are advanced and encouraged. He notes, however, that the manner in which

---

57. Taylor, *Secular Age*, 613.

58. Taylor, *Secular Age*, 599.

59. Musacchio, "Exorcising the Zeitgeist," 229. In his 2017 book, British journalist Douglas Murray, who refers to himself as a nonbeliever, notes that in Europe this vacuum is seemingly fulfilled by a conversion to Islam. He opines that "it is because most branches of European Christianity have lost the confidence to proselytize or even believe in their own message" (Murray, *Strange Death of Europe*, 264).

60. Anderson, *What's Your Worldview*, 81.

pluralism is promoted goes beyond recognition of the entitlement to hold a given religious view. He views the present promotion of religious pluralism as the furtherance of the notion for the equality of all religions as disseminators of truths and equality in regard to soteriological (salvationist) effectiveness. Netland writes: "In this sense religious pluralism is a distinctive way of thinking about religious diversity that affirms such diversity as something inherently good, to be embraced enthusiastically. It is this latter ideological sense that poses special challenges to Christian faith." Netland thinks that the advance of Pantheistic notions in the West, which includes the "romantic Orientalists of nineteenth century Romanticism and Transcendentalism as well as more recent New Agers" is the result of a determination to find a "way of advancing the sense of superiority of Eastern spirituality over (Western) Christianity."[61]

Netland sees a marked difference in previous pantheistic notions and those of the current era. New Agers place a high value on freedom of choice on their spirituality, he claims. He also finds a sense of "consumerism" in their "marketplace of ideas" and notices their appreciation for the "immense array of alternatives." He notes that the "contours of one's worldview can no longer be taken for granted," that the first decision for New Agers is frequently the decision about whether or not to be religious at all, and that decisions about "how one expresses religious commitments are increasingly matters of choice."[62] Netland's analysis offers important insights into the pragmatic nature of some versions of New Age spirituality. Clearly, the expected benefit—the beliefs' perceived utility—is often a significant factor in a practitioner's choice.

Angus Menuge, professor of science and philosophy at Wisconsin's Concordia College, writes that postmodernist society, so-called, has experienced a surge in New Age religions because of the perceived failures of modernity. He notes that New Age religions are basically pagan but thinks that many individuals within these groups could be more accurately described by what Lewis had referred to as Post-Christians. Menuge writes: "Part of Lewis's greatness was that his corpus includes works addressed

---

61. Netland, *Encountering Religious Pluralism*, 122. Ironically, Douglas Murray cites the "Christian story" being the European continent's "foundational myth" as the key to the success and sustenance of European civilization. It is noteworthy that Murray considers the negation of the Biblical narrative and the ascendancy of naturalism, aided by Darwinism, as key to what he considers to be the decline of European civilization (Murray, *Strange Death of Europe*, 210–11).

62. Netland, *Encountering Religious Pluralism*, 154.

to the concerns of both groups."[63] Boston University's professor of education M. D. Aeschliman claims that the appeal of pantheistic notions was something that Lewis understood and withstood. In his opinion, the attractiveness of pantheistic notions "lies at the heart of occult 'New Age' spirituality and 'Deep Ecology,' and a good deal of 'Eco-feminism' today." Aeschliman notes that Romantic self-absorption and pantheistic Gnosticism are targets of Lewis's satire, and that although Lewis criticized radical empiricism and rationalism, he was too much of a classic rationalist "to countenance esoteric or occult mysticism and the depreciation of reason, . . . or defy science on romantic or gnostic grounds."[64]

Netland claims that "what had been countercultural and somewhat avantgarde became mainstream and chic in the form of the New Age movement" by the early 1990s. "The New Age movement is an eclectic and rather amorphous movement that combines elements of ancient paganism, the occult, Eastern religions and some Judeo-Christian themes with pop psychology and an obsession with what Paul Heelas has termed 'self-spirituality,'" he writes. Netland observes that New Ageism is not an organized religion as such but that it draws upon ancient Buddhist, Hindu, and Taoist teachings that have been legitimized through their acceptance by leading media and entertainment figures, as well as by some educational institutions.[65] He notes that in many of the polytheistic religions of the ancient world, as well as in many modern-day practises, there is a tendency "to blur the distinction between God and humankind—either to bring God down to our level or to deify human beings." Netland claims that this tendency is especially pronounced in the Hindu and Shinto traditions "and has become popular in the West in the New Age movement, which preaches the essential divinity of human beings."[66] Christian apologist James Beilby warns against attributing any form of divinity to oneself. He claims that John Calvin's notion of *sensus divinitatus*[67] gets warped into one's own desires and goals without the guidance of Scripture. He notes that Scripture was at the heart of Calvin's apologetics, because "Scripture alone distinguishes God, as Creator of

---

63. Menuge, *C. S. Lewis*, 17.
64. Aeschliman, "C. S. Lewis," 48.
65. Netland, *Encountering Religious Pluralism*, 208.
66. Netland, *Encountering Religious Pluralism*, 336.
67. Latin, "sense of divinity."

the world, from the whole herd of fictitious gods."[68] Beilby notes that Lewis supplemented Calvin's notion by pointing to the universal sense of longing that humans feel as being indicative of the presence of the Judeo-Christian Creator God and that he repeatedly advised his readers and listeners that he had embraced Christianity because he believed it to be true.[69]

Harold Netland advocates for what is known as a cumulative case approach[70] when countering present-day challenges to Christianity such as religious pluralism and New Ageism. He claims that while arguments defending the rationality of Christian belief are significant, they have limited value in dealing with the distinctive challenges of religious pluralism. He recommends that Christians should go beyond negative (defensive) apologetics and engage in positive apologetics:[71]

> On the theoretical level, positive apologetics is a difficult and complex endeavour, as it seeks to show, in appropriate ways, that Christian theism is true or is rationally preferable to alternative worldviews. Dissatisfaction with positive apologetics is often due to the manner in which it is sometimes carried out and the unrealistic expectations raised by some apologists.

Netland advocates for a cumulative case approach, because it is "based upon the idea that a reasonable case for the truth of Christian theism can be established through the careful accumulation and analysis of a wide variety of data from various dimensions of our experience and the world."[72]

Netland cautions against unrealistic optimism but notes that Lewis and others are prime examples of well-known apologists who have successfully employed a cumulative case approach for establishing the truth of the Christian worldview. As Michael Payne has written: "The story Christians need to tell is the one that makes all others intelligible. The Gospel is not one story among many. The Christian worldview is not one

---

68. Beilby, *Thinking about Christian Apologetics*, 57.

69. Beilby, *Thinking about Christian Apologetics*, 77, 143.

70. For an explanation of cumulative case apologetics, see Feinburg, "Cumulative Case Apologetics."

71. Netland, *Encountering Religious Pluralism*, 278.

72. Netland, *Encountering Religious Pluralism*, 279. Because of the multifaceted nature of the evidence for the Christian faith, Austin Farrer considers Christianity's truth claims to be facts: "Christian theism, to those who believe it, commends itself as fact, not theory, by the sheer multiplicity of its bearings" (Farrer, "Christian Apologist," 26).

option among a plethora of options, each of which will satisfy the human need for clarity and truth. The Christian worldview is true. As such, it makes the world intelligible and reveals the many half-truths in the aberrant worldviews in which it competes."[73] C. S. Lewis would agree.

---

73. Payne, "Philosophy among the Ruins," 356.

Chapter Seven

Conclusion

THE OBJECTIVE OF THIS thesis, as stated in the abstract, has been to investigate key challenges to contemporary Christianity from alternative worldviews, explore C. S. Lewis's circuitous spiritual journey to faith, and examine the philosophical and intellectual elements of his Christian worldview—this, for the purpose of analysing the manner in which Lewis's worldview affected his apologetics and ascertaining how key elements from Lewis's apologetics may be employed in dealing with present-day challenges to Christianity. This objective has been achieved via the process as described in chapter 1. The content of this dissertation is represented by the following key words: Worldview, Apologetics, Reason, Imagination, Metaphysics, Theology, Philosophy, Christianity, Theism, Deism, Pantheism, Naturalism, Darwinism.

Chapter 1 offered a brief introduction, gave the central theological argument, and provided an outline of the methodology to be employed. Chapter 2 introduced worldview as a concept, listed the worldviews that present major challenges to contemporary Christianity, and described their respective elements. Chapter 3 introduced C S. Lewis and provided a biography of the process by which Lewis came to adopt various worldviews prior to embracing Christianity. It included an exploration of the manner by which the various periods of Lewis's formative years affected the formation of his worldview and examined the role played by his various and diverse educational experiences. The chapter concluded by examining the early years of Lewis's academic career and his conversion to theism and, eventually, to Christianity. This chapter provided the background needed to put Lewis's circuitous spiritual journey in context, in which the role that imagination played in Lewis's progression from theism to Christianity was a critical component. It offered an important backdrop for the fourth chapter. Chapter 4 offered an extensive analysis of the Lewisian worldview's philosophical and intellectual elements. This in-depth analysis was essential to understanding the various and diverse intellectual and spiritual components of Lewis's Christian worldview.

Chapter 5 built on the content of the previous chapter. It argued that Lewis's best known nonfictional work, *Mere Christianity*, is an accurate representation of Lewis's worldview and examined the manner by which that worldview is manifestly evident in his fictional works, as well as in his nonfictional apologetics. Chapter 6 completed the thesis by exploring measures by which Lewisian apologetic methods might be applied to present-day challenges to the Christian faith.

To sum up, this study concludes that the young Lewis, after having been reared in a Christian home, because of the death of his much-loved Christian mother, despite the prayers for her healing, and, in part, because of the influence of alternate worldviews, abandoned the Christian faith of his childhood. It provides evidence that Lewis was periodically drawn to a range of worldviews, which included elements of materialism/naturalism, atheism, agnosticism, pantheism, and certain versions of idealism. It concludes that Lewis converted to theism and ultimately to Christianity, because he believed that the worldview as represented by the Christian faith best accounts for his perception of reality. Finally, this study examined how elements of Lewis's methodology may benefit present-day Christian apologetics.

As was outlined in chapter 1, this thesis holds that the core claims of the Christian faith are true and that it is important for Christian apologists to respond to the claims of alternative worldviews inasmuch as they contradict the truth claims of authentic Christianity. It holds that it is advantageous for individuals who are engaged in contemporary Christian apologetics to have an awareness of the core tenets of competing worldviews.

According to David Naugle, the concept of worldview stems from the German word *Weltanschauung*. The word originated in the late eighteenth and early nineteenth centuries and was popularized by Wilhelm Dilthey. James Sire characterises one's worldview as a set of presuppositions that we hold, consciously or subconsciously, about the basic makeup of the world and by which we perceive reality, and David Naugle,

Wilhelm Dilthey, and Steven Cowan outline the respective worldviews within the triad of naturalism, pantheism, and theism. As someone who had embraced various elements of this taxonomy of worldviews during his intellectual and spiritual journey, Lewis offers helpful insights in his writings for dealing with the challenges that other worldviews pose to an orthodox, authentic Christian worldview.

Lewis considered naturalism and liberal/non-supernatural Christianity to be the two of the greatest challenges to contemporary authentic Christian faith but considered pantheism as Christianity's most formidable competitor. Lewis used a bipartite method to challenge naturalism's viability as a credible worldview contender. When encountering subject matter with which he was intimately familiar, he unequivocally challenged naturalism's sufficiency as a viable worldview. In matters with which he was less familiar, however, his challenge was much more nuanced. For instance, in his book *Miracles*, Lewis refutes naturalism's candidacy as a valid worldview by posing a direct challenge to its explanatory power. He claims that naturalism repudiates itself when it postulates that the emergence and development of the human brain are a product of random processes. He argues that by ascribing mental processes to the motions of atoms in one's brain as naturalists do, naturalists are advocating for a worldview that refutes itself, because the process as postulated allows for no principled reason to believe one's beliefs to be reliable. Lewis argues that a strict naturalism is therefore self-contradictory. *Miracles* represents Lewis's most complete critique of naturalism's credentials as a worldview contender. Lewis argues that naturalism lacks the requisite explanatory power to be a credible explanation of reality; his challenge to naturalism in *Miracles* is unequivocal. Whereas his challenge in *Miracles* to naturalism's capability as a viable worldview with the requisite explanatory power is direct and unambiguous, Lewis's challenge to naturalism's adequacy for explaining the emergence and development of the biosystem is much more nuanced.

Lewis's correspondence with Bernard Acworth and his decision to publish the essays "Funeral of a Great Myth" and "Dogma and the Universe" serve as prime examples of Lewis's more inobtrusive methodology. Lewis's letters to Acworth reveal an acknowledgment of the limitations of unguided neo-Darwinian processes to account for the emergence of the biosystem, but they also disclose Lewis's reluctance to participate in Acworth's aggressive stance in challenging the accepted Darwinian worldview. Lewis wrote Acworth that he had neither the training nor the inclination to sufficiently research the subject and expressed concern that opponents of the Christian worldview might use his lack of expertise on the matter under debate to their advantage. In the two aforementioned essays, however, Lewis raises serious doubts about the capability of the neo-Darwinian theoretic structure's ability to achieve even a fraction of what it is asserted to have produced. While he lauds the grandeur of what is alleged to have been accomplished by what he refers to as evolutionary mythology, he argues that there is remarkably little evidence that random evolutionary processes are capable of anything close to what has been ascribed to them. Although he doesn't challenge the theoretic structure in a direct, combative manner, for perceptive readers, the result of this method is often as effective as a direct confrontation. The choices he made for determining the methodology to be employed are indicative of his unique ability to relate to the tenor of the times and to connect with his intended audience. In challenging the naturalist worldview both directly and indirectly as he does, Lewis serves as an exemplar for exercising versatility in apologetic methodology. Lewisian methodology for countering the challenges from naturalism is as applicable today as it was in Lewis's time.

Lewis found it difficult to deal with liberal Christianity and considered non-supernatural versions of the faith to be tantamount to a post-Christian condition. He considered anti-supernatural, liberal Christianity to be a serious challenge to authentic Christian faith. Pointedly, he thought it more likely that pagans would be converted to authentic Christianity than that adherents of anti-supernatural Christianity be restored to Christian orthodoxy. To counter this trend, he admonished believers to voice their supernatural Christian faith: "We must insist from the beginning that we believe . . . in a spirit-world that can, and does, invade the natural or phenomenal universe," he writes.[1] He saw certain forms of liberal Christianity as mere ethical systems and as impediments to authentic Christian belief. Medieval Christianity had more appeal for Lewis than the modern anti-supernatural version. This is consistent with his preference for what he referred to as the "discarded model"— the medieval worldview—over the modern post-Christian, mechanistic, contemporary worldview. Lewis's rational arguments in works such as *Miracles* and *Mere Christianity* are prime examples of his reason-based apologetics; his more imaginative fiction works, such as *That Hideous*

---

1. Lewis, *Essay Collection*, 128.

Strength and *The Chronicles of Narnia*, illustrate his skill in employing the power of imagination and his use of story for countering the twin challenges posed by naturalism and anti-supernatural Christianity. His skills in utilizing reason-based argumentation are manifestly evident in the former two, and his use of story and imagination are on full display in the latter.

Notably, Lewis viewed naturalism and anti-supernatural versions of Christianity not as competitors to authentic Christianity but as challenges to the faith. For Lewis, the only real competitor to authentic Christian faith was pantheism. Lewis provides some detail for his reasons for considering pantheism as authentic Christianity's primary competitor, and the account of his own spiritual journey offers additional insight. Having embraced and, eventually, rejected naturalism/materialism in his youth, Lewis was well aware of naturalism's shortcomings. It is noteworthy that once he had become aware of naturalism's inadequacy, he had embraced pantheism for a limited period of time. Even prior to his conversion to theism and, subsequently, to Christianity, he had decided that some form of idealism was the most likely candidate for his perception of reality. Although he eventually favoured theism as the worldview most likely to be true, Lewis likely never forgot the strong attraction that pantheism had held for him. In some of his writings, he comments on its appeal by depicting it as imposing few, if any, demands on its adherents and as relatively easy to embrace.

Lewis thought that there was a natural yearning in humans for filling an ever-present spiritual void. He considered pantheism to be a natural draw for the filling of that void, because it satisfied an inherent religious impulse, albeit only temporarily or partially. Lewis's perception of anti-supernatural Christianity, however, was that of a belief system devoid of spiritual power and influence. He considered it to be a watered-down replica of authentic Christianity. It may well be that, because of the inability of naturalism and anti-supernatural Christianity to fill the inherent spiritual void, he viewed them as challenges rather than as serious competitors. Conversely, pantheism appeared to help satisfy that ever-present vacuity and therefore presented itself as a major competitor to orthodox Christian faith. It is important to note that manifestations of pantheism, such as Hinduism and various forms of Buddhism, continue unabated in many countries in the Far East. Moreover, as the preponderance of New Age philosophies would indicate, pantheism's present-day influence in the West does not seem to have lessened since Lewis's time.

Accentuating the validity of the truth claims of authentic Christianity was key to Lewis's apologetics. Because of the growing popularity of pantheistic notions in the West, pointing out the lack of evidentiary claims supporting pantheism's seemingly unsubstantiated propositions would seem to be an important supplement to Lewisian methodology. Significantly, it was Lewis's belief in the truth claims of the Christian faith that had led to his conversion. The lack of evidentiary properties undergirding pantheistic notions almost certainly contributed to his abandonment of the pantheistic worldview. Employing the Lewisian method of asserting the truth claims of Christianity, while at the same time drawing attention to the lack of evidentiary claims supporting pantheistic notions and pointing out pantheism's inherent inconsistencies, would seem to be an effective methodology for responding to the competition that pantheism presents to authentic Christian faith.

Almost immediately after his conversion in 1931, Lewis began using his talents to commend what he had discovered to be true. His intellectual and literary skills enabled him to develop a methodology for his apologetics that have had a significant impact on Christendom. Lewis's influence, although appreciated by the public at large, was only grudgingly tolerated by many of his Oxford colleagues. Several of Lewis's friends recalled occasions on which Lewis commented about the disapproval, and even outright hatred, to which he had been subjected during his many years as an Oxford don. Most of Lewis's university colleagues thought that he should be dedicating himself to academic pursuits rather than defying university protocol by engaging in public addresses. Although Lewis's public outreach significantly impaired his academic career, Lewis remained undeterred, despite the opposition to his renowned public profile. His public appeal was held against him throughout his time at the University of Oxford's Magdalen College; it was not until he moved to the University of Cambridge that he was awarded a full professorship.

Lewis's body of work covers a variety of different themes and provides significant insight into the intellectual and spiritual makeup of its author. He had an uncanny ability to discern the temper of the times—the spirit of the age. His ability to understand the *Zeitgeist* or, to use Charles Taylor's terms, the "social imaginary" or "historical consciousness" of the day enabled him to communicate the Christian message in a manner that was readily understood by the public. Prior to his conversion, he had embraced many of the features of the worldviews shared by his diverse audiences, and this undoubtedly helped him to connect with them, speaking to them in a language they could understand, and enabled him to communicate truths that they could comprehend. Despite the disapproval and undisguised hostility that was directed toward Lewis by his Oxford colleagues, Lewis remained undaunted in his decision to continue with his public addresses.

Rather than addressing his audiences as a spokesperson for his own denomination, Lewis addressed them in a spirit of ecumenism, in a manner that appealed not only to members of the Church of England but also to members of other denominations. His audiences consisted of both believers and unbelievers, and Lewis structured his messages to give them an ecumenical, extramural quality. Although his diverse audiences were comprised of people who held widely divergent views, he did not hesitate to speak about what he understood to be the core elements of the Christian faith. Whereas even certain leaders of his own denomination tended to gloss over or even ignore some of Christianity's truth claims, Lewis refused to compromise with what he considered to be orthodox Christian beliefs. He believed Jesus to be the Son of God and spoke of it in a manner that caused his audiences to think that he believed in what he was expositing. He claimed that Jesus's statements about himself did not allow for the option of viewing him as merely an influential, moral teacher. Lewis likely never forgot that he had been a believing Christian for a limited period of time when he was first enrolled in the British school system. In *Surprised by Joy*, he credits his early, albeit intervallic, belief to being taught the Christian faith by people who believed what they were saying. Whatever his listeners thought about the content of his messages, he left no doubt about the sincerity of his own belief.

From what he has written about his early school experiences, Lewis had been a believer from age ten until about twelve or thirteen. It was the influence of the school matron, Miss Cowie, plus the burdensome characteristics of his conception of the Christian faith, that led to his unbelief. According to what Lewis has written, Miss Cowie's spirituality seems to have been a blend of pantheistic notions, likely akin to some version of what today would be known as New Ageism. In his biography, Lewis graphically depicts the attraction that these pantheistic notions had held for him. Undoubtedly, his involvement with this mélange of spiritual notions was instrumental in causing him to view pantheism as a formidable competitor to Christianity.

Lewis's body of work encompasses poetry, reason-based prose, and story. Once Lewis realized that he lacked the necessary skills to become a great poet, he concentrated on prose. His apologetics reflect the orthodoxy of his Christian worldview and might be characterised as the gospel message translated into the language of the day. He saw his role as asserting Christian orthodoxy, as it is reflected in *Mere Christianity*; statements in his body of work give insights into how he perceived his role as a speaker and writer. In addition to his public addresses, there are indications of his self-perception in his responses to readers's letters. In a letter written shortly after World War II, in response to John Beddow, a priest who had asked Lewis to write a book that would convey the Christian message to British "workers," Lewis tells Beddow that although he is sometimes referred to as a translator, he would prefer his function to become that of the "founder of a school of translation." And he advises Beddow to find individuals who could identify with the audience he had in mind and who had the necessary religious training required for the task. In Lewis's opinion, those were the people who should be encouraged to write the book Beddow had in mind. He concludes the letter with some general pointers about writing in the vernacular and offers to help edit the book once it has been written.[2] Lewis's letter to Beddow is reminiscent of his message to the conclave of junior Anglican clergy in Wales in 1945, in which he advised the attendees to address their respective congregations in words that were part of their parishioners's normal language. And he encouraged those who had the requisite writing skills to write books about non-Christian subjects in which the author's Christianity was latent.

Lewis's letter to John Beddow and his message to the assemblage of clergy are illustrative of Lewis's contribution to Christian apologetics. Lewis wrote in the everyday language of the public and avoided religious words and expressions that were not part of his readers's vocabularies. His Christian worldview had been carefully thought out over many years and was reflected in what he wrote and said. The immensity of his intellectual range is especially noticeable in his essays, many of which are filled with a profusion of analogies, similes, metaphors, and other literary devices. To paraphrase his close friends Tolkien and Barfield, Lewis had a capacious, although not infallible, memory; everything that he had heard and had read was in everything that he said and wrote.

Former University of Victoria professor Lionel Adey has written extensively on both C. S. Lewis and Owen Barfield, including their

---

2. Lewis, *Collected Letters*, 2:673–75.

renowned philosophical differences,[3] which Malcolm Guite has characterised as disagreements about the solution to humanity's crisis-laden existence. Barfield envisioned a solution coming from a Christian evolution of consciousness, whereas Lewis expected the solution to come through the rebirth of humanity patterned on the death and resurrection of Christ. Adey had predicted that the impact of Barfield's body of work would surpass the influence of Lewis's work. In reality, Lewis's influence has dramatically overshadowed that of Barfield, and Lewis's popularity is expanding with the passage of time. Notable examples include multiple chapters of the C. S. Lewis Society in various countries; millions of books in circulation; several full-length films, which include a biography and several Narnia-based films; lecture series on Christian apologetics by prominent professors based on Lewis's material; and multiple writer groups that feature Lewis's writings. Ironically, although Lewis frequently reminded readers that he was not a theologian, several professors are presently conducting seminary-level courses titled "The Theology of C. S. Lewis."

Lewis's argumentation in his reason-based works has stood the test of time, and Lewis has been widely acclaimed for this body of work. He had published a book of poems prior to his conversion, but his first book regarding Christian faith was an allegorical account of his intellectual and spiritual journey through various philosophies, titled *Pilgrim's Regress*, and concludes with his embrace of Christianity. It is his works of fiction for which he is best known, however. His Narnia series is comprised of seven children's fantasy novels, is considered to be a classic in children's literature, has been translated into approximately fifty languages, and is reported to have sold over a hundred million copies.

Lewis's understanding and usage of the power of imagination is a major component of his contribution to Christian apologetics. Lewis had a unique talent for utilizing imagery to communicate concepts or abstractions; he saw imagination as key to understanding elements beyond one's immediate environment. He had become a theist, largely by induction, but had found himself unable to progress beyond that. Aided by imagination's capacity to provide meaning to the incarnation, he had acquired greater insight and was eventually converted to Christianity. Imagination was a key element not only in his own conversion but also in his apologetics. He understood imagination's capacity to provide

---

3. Adey, *C. S. Lewis*.

meaning and employed it effectively in his use of story, especially in his fictional works.

Lewis was uniquely gifted in using imagery to stimulate readers's imagination. He writes that material for stories typically "bubbles up" in an author's mind. He notes that, in his case, ideas for stories generally began with mental images, such as a fawn coming to mind or the image of a lion coming into a mental scene. Understandably, Lewis's fictional works are replete with imagery. His use of imagery and imagination is evidenced in his application of a concept that he has characterised as *transposition*. This is a term for a notion that he also calls up-grading. Lewis uses the term to describe a method whereby God's revelation takes place in human minds. He perceives God as communicating and mediating his salvific truths to humans through various modes that include moving from a lower to a higher order, from the general to the particular, from the incomplete to the perfect, and so on. In Lewis's view, because the nature of the lower order remains in place after being "taken up" and loaded with higher-order knowledge, it will always be possible for individuals to ignore the up-grading and to perceive nothing but the lower order. Lewis's notion of transposition, moving from a lower medium to a higher reality, is exemplified when drawing pictures of the real world, in order to experience and express the greater reality. He cautions readers against concentrating on the pictures and ignoring the reality that the pictures represent. This is reminiscent of Plato's analogy about persons having been confined to a cave during their entire lives, the result of which is mistaking the shadows on the wall of the cave as the real thing, rather than understanding the images to be only shadows of what is actually present in the real world. Lewis is seen by some to be at his most philosophically theological when he invokes the concept of transposition to explain his perception about the processes whereby salvific truths are communicated via God's revelation.

Lewis's concept of transposition may add a new dimension to one's understanding of Scripture. This could apply to Jesus's references to the kingdom of God, his comparisons and contrasts with the natural world and the world to come, and so on. There is also a cautionary note in Lewis's portrayal of the revelatory process via transposition. Lewis encourages readers not to ignore their own interpretive shortcomings and reminds them to be on guard against reading meaning into the text that is not consistent with the totality of the scriptural message or with the orthodoxy of the creeds. Upon reflection, there is much in Lewis's notion of transposition that has the potential to enhance one's overall understanding and appreciation of the Scriptures. Lewis's body of work represents a significant contribution to Christianity; Lewis has had a major impact on Christendom. Although his contributions were made near the midpoint of the twentieth century, his influence is having a major impact on apologetics in the current one. It has been said of Lewis that he saw his role as a Christian apologist who breaks down the intellectual barriers to the Christian faith in order to make Christianity intellectually plausible.

He has not been exempt from criticism, however. Much of the criticism directed toward him has revolved around issues such as his seemingly dated notions about the role of women in the church, his personal habits such as smoking, and his involvement in what Austin Farrer characterises as "impossible difficulties" by articulating some of his speculative notions. This would include Lewis's public musings about the afterlife, including the possibility of there being a place for household pets, and so on. Despite the criticisms levelled against him, he has remained popular, especially among Evangelicals. He was a practising member of the Church of England, and his influence, although variously manifested, is interdenominational.

How Lewis's influence is variously manifested among diverse denominations is beyond the scope of this thesis and is perhaps best left as a possibility for a future project.

Bibliography

"About *Piers Plowman*." *Piers Plowman* Electronic Archive, n.d. http://piers.chass.ncsu.edu/about/piersPlowman.html.

"About Posthumanism Theory." Technical Communication Body of Knowledge, n.d. https://www.tcbok.org/wiki/posthumanism-theory/.

Acworth, Bernard. *This Progress: The Tragedy of Evolution*. London: Rich and Cowan, 1934.

Adey, Lionel. *C. S. Lewis: Writer, Dreamer, and Mentor*. Grand Rapids: Eerdmans, 1998.

Aeschliman, Michael D. "C. S. Lewis on Mere Science." In *The Magician's Twin: C. S. Lewis on Science, Scientism, and Society*, edited by John G. West, 47–58. Seattle: Discovery Institute, 2012.

The American Heritage Dictionary of the English Language. 4th ed. Boston: Houghton Mifflin, 2000.

Anacker, Gayne J. "Narnia and the Moral Imagination." In *The Chronicles of Narnia and Philosophy: The Lion, the Witch, and the Worldview*, edited by Gregory Bassham et al., 130–42. Chicago: Open Court, 2005.

Anderson, James N. *What's Your Worldview? An Interactive Approach to Life's Big Questions*. Wheaton, IL: Crossway, 2014.

Anscombe, G. E. M. *Metaphysics and the Philosophy of Mind*. Vol. 2 of *The Collected Philosophical Papers of G. E. M. Anscombe*. Minneapolis: University of Minnesota Press, 1981.

"Anthroposophy." Wikipedia, last edited Apr. 22, 2022. https://en.wikipedia.org/wiki/Anthroposophy.

Augustine. *The Confessions*. Hendrickson Christian Classics. Peabody, MA: Hendrickson, 2006.

Barefoot, Darek. "A Response to Richard Carrier's Review of C. S. Lewis's Dangerous Idea." The Secular Web, June 25, 2007. https://infidels.org/library/modern/darek_barefoot/dangerous.html.

Barfield, Owen. "Lewis and/or Barfield." In *C. S. Lewis & His Circle: Essays and Memoirs from the Oxford C. S. Lewis Society*, edited by M. Roger White et al., 214–22. New York: Oxford University Press, 2015.

———. *Owen Barfield on C. S. Lewis*. Oxford, UK: Barfield, 2011.

———. *Poetic Diction: A Study in Meaning*. Oxford, UK: Barfield, 2010.

———. *The Rediscovery of Meaning and Other Essays*. 2nd ed. Oxford, UK: Barfield, 2013.

———. *What Coleridge Thought*. Middletown, CT: Wesleyan University Press, 1971.

Behe, Michael J. *Darwin's Black Box: The Biochemical Challenge to Evolution*. New York: Free, 1996.

———. *The Edge of Evolution: The Search for the Limits of Darwinism*. New York: Free, 2007.

Beilby, James K. *Thinking about Christian Apologetics: What It Is and Why We Do It*. Downers Grove, IL: InterVarsity, 2011.

Bergson, Henri. *Creative Evolution*. Translated by Arthur Mitchell. Mineola, NY: Dover, 2016.

Beversluis, John. *C. S. Lewis and the Search for Rational Religion*. Rev. ed. Amherst, NY: Prometheus, 2007.

Bird, Alexander. "Thomas Kuhn." Stanford Encyclopedia of Philosophy, Aug. 13, 2004; revised Oct. 31, 2018. https://plato.stanford.edu/entries/thomas-kuhn/.

Boulay, Shirley du. *Beyond the Darkness: A Biography of Bede Griffiths*. New York: Doubleday, 1998.

Brazier, Paul H. "C. S. Lewis: A Doctrine of Transposition." *Heythrop Journal* 50 (2009) 669–88. https://www.researchgate.net/publication/229502269_C_S_LEWIS_A_doctrine_of_transposition.

———. *C. S. Lewis: Revelation and the Christ*. 4 vols. Eugene, OR: Pickwick, 2012.

Britannica, T. Editors of Encyclopaedia. "Entelechy." Encyclopedia Britannica, Mar. 1, 2022. http://www.britannica.com/topic/entelechy.

Brock, Dan W. "Utilitarianism." In *The Cambridge Dictionary of Philosophy*, edited by Robert Audi, 942–44. 2nd ed. New York: Cambridge University Press, 2006.

Brown, Callum G. *Religion and the Demographic Revolution: Women and Secularisation in Canada, Ireland, UK and USA since the 1960s*. Studies in Modern British Religious History. Rochester, NY: Boydell, 2012.

Brown, Colin. *Philosophy and the Christian Faith: A Historical Sketch from the Middle Ages to the Present Day*. Downers Grove, IL: InterVarsity, 1968.

Brown, Devin. "Planet Narnia Spin, Spun Out." C. S. Lewis, May 13, 2009. https://www.cslewis.com/planet-narnia-spin-spun-out/.

Bultmann, Rudolph K. *Theology of the New Testament*. Translated by Kendrick Grobel. New York: Scribner's, 1951.

Butts, Robert Earl. "Spencer, Herbert." In *The Cambridge Dictionary of Philosophy*, edited by Robert Audi, 869–70. 2nd ed. New York: Cambridge University Press, 2006.

Cannon, Lincoln. "Trust in Posthumanity and the New God Argument." Linoln Cannon, Oct. 3, 2010; updated June 25, 2021. http://lincoln.metacannon.net/2010/10/transcript-of-presentation-at.html#more.

Carnell, Corbin Scott. *Bright Shadow of Reality: Spiritual Longing in C. S. Lewis*. Grand Rapids: Eerdmans, 1999.

Carter, Craig A. "The Legacy of an Inadequate Christology: Yoder's Critique of Niebuhr's *Christ and Culture*." *Mennonite Quarterly Review* 77 (2003) 387–401. https://www.goshen.edu/mqr/2003/07/july-2003-carter/.

Chakrabarti, A. "Nirvana." In *The Oxford Companion to Philosophy*, edited by Ted Honderich, 659. 2nd ed. New York: Oxford University Press, 2005.

Christensen, Michael J. *C. S. Lewis on Scripture: His Thought on the Nature of Biblical Inspiration: The Role of Revelation and the Question of Inerrancy*. Nashville: Abingdon, 1989.

Clark, David G. *C. S. Lewis: A Guide to His Theology*. Malden, MA: Blackwell, 2007. https://books.google.co.za/books?id=oKOdKtrG4bUC&printsec=frontcover

&dq=clarke+CS+lewi s+a+guide+to+his+theology&hl=en&sa=X&ved=0ahUKE
wiQ_arg25PaAhVlAsAKHbUgCYUQ6A EIJjAA#v=onepage&q=clarke%20CS%
20lewis%20a%20guide%20to%20his%20theology&f=fse.
Clarke, Arthur C., and C. S. Lewis. *From Narnia to a Space Odyssey*. New York: iBooks, 2005.
Clarke, D. S. *Panpsychism and the Religious Attitude*. New York: State University of New York Press, 2003.
Coleridge, Samuel Taylor. *Coleridge: A Collection of Critical Essays*. Edited by Kathleen Coburn. New York: Prentice Hall, 1967.
———. *Samuel Taylor Coleridge: The Major Works*. Edited by H. J. Jackson. Oxford World's Classics. New York: Oxford University Press, 2009.
Como, James. "Lewis, C. S. (Clive Staples)." In *American Conservatism: An Encyclopedia*, edited by Bruce Frohnen et al., 495–96. Wilmington, DE: ISI, 2006.
Cootsona, Gregory S. *C. S. Lewis and the Crisis of a Christian*. Louisville, KY: Westminster John Knox, 2014.
Cousins, Lance Selwyn. "Nirvana." In *Concise Routledge Encyclopedia of Philosophy*, edited by Routledge Staff, 633–34. New York: Routledge, 2000.
Cowan, Steven B., ed. *Five Views on Apologetics*. Grand Rapids: Zondervan, 2000.
Davis, Bill. "Extreme Makeover: Moral Education and the Encounter with Aslan." In *The Chronicles of Narnia and Philosophy: The Lion, the Witch, and the Worldview*, edited by Gregory Bassham et al., 106–18. Chicago: Open Court, 2005.
Dorsett, Lyle W. *Seeking the Secret Place: The Spiritual Formation of C. S. Lewis*. Grand Rapids: Brazos, 2004.
Duriez, Colin. *The C. S. Lewis Handbook*. Grand Rapids: Baker, 1990.
Edwards, Bruce L. "Miracles: A Preliminary Study." In *The C. S. Lewis Readers' Encyclopedia*, edited by Jeffrey D. Schultz and John G. West Jr., 280–81. Grand Rapids: Zondervan, 1998.
Edwards, Mark. "Classicist." In *The Cambridge Companion to C. S. Lewis*, edited by Robert MacSwain and Michael Ward, 58–71. Cambridge Companions to Religion. Cambridge: Cambridge University Press, 2010.
Epstein, Greg M. *Good without God: What a Billion Nonreligious People Do Believe*. New York: HarperCollins, 2009.
Farrer, Austin. "The Christian Apologist." In *Light on C. S. Lewis*, edited by Jocelyn Gibb, 23–43. New York: Harcourt Brace Jovanovich, 1965.
Feinburg, Paul D. "Cumulative Case Apologetics." *Five Views on Apologetics*, edited by Steven B. Cowan, 148–206. Grand Rapids: Zondervan, 2000.
Fischer-Schreiber, Ingrid. "Nirvana." In *The Encyclopedia of Eastern Philosophy and Religion: Buddhism, Taoism, Zen, Hinduism*, edited by Ingrid Fischer-Schreiber et al., 248–49. Boston: Shambhala, 1989.
Ford, Paul F. *Companion to Narnia: A Complete Guide to the Magical World of C. S. Lewis's* The Chronicles of Narnia. Rev. ed. New York: HarperCollins, 2005.
Frame, John M. "Greeks Bearing Gifts." In *Revolutions in Worldview: Understanding the Flow of Western Thought*, edited by W. Andrew Hoffecker, 1–36. Phillipsburg, NJ: P & R, 2007.
Friedrichs, Kurt. "Moksha." In *The Encyclopedia of Eastern Philosophy and Religion: Buddhism, Taoism, Zen, Hinduism*, edited by Ingrid Fischer-Schreiber et al., 229–30. Boston: Shambhala, 1989.

Galloway, Ronald. *A Study in the Perception of Evil.* Salt Lake City: Sacred Tribes, 2013. Kindle.

Geisler, Norman L. *The Big Book of Christian Apologetics: An A to Z Guide.* Grand Rapids: Baker, 2012.

———. *Christian Apologetics.* Grand Rapids: Baker, 2013.

Giokaris, Glenn J. "The Philosophical Journey of C. S. Lewis." Stanford, June 3, 2017. https://web.stanford.edu/group/ww1/spring2000/Glenn/Lewis.htm. Site discontinued.

Gould, Stephen Jay. *Rocks of Ages: Science and Religion in the Fullness of Life.* New York: Random House, 1999.

Green, Roger Lancelyn, and Walter Hooper. *C. S. Lewis: The Authorised and Revised Biography.* London: HarperCollins, 2002.

Gresham, Douglas H. *Jack's Life: The Story of C. S. Lewis.* Nashville: Broadman & Holman, 2005.

———. *Lenten Lands: My Childhood with Joy Davidman and C. S. Lewis.* Glasgow: Collins Sons & Co., 1988.

Griffin, William. *C. S. Lewis: Spirituality for Mere Christians.* New York: Crossroad, 1998.

Griffiths, Bede. "The Adventure of Faith." In *C. S. Lewis at the Breakfast Table and Other Reminiscences,* edited by James T. Como, 11–24. Boston: Houghton Mifflin, 1992.

———. *The Golden String: An Autobiography.* London: Catholic Book Club, 1954.

———. *A Human Search: Bede Griffiths Reflects on His Life: An Oral History.* Edited by John Swindels. Liguori, MI: Triumph, 1993.

Guenther, Bruce L. "The 'Enduring Problem' of Christ and Culture." *Direction* 34 (2005) 215–17. https://directionjournal.org/34/2/enduring-problem-of-christ-and-culture.html.

Guite, Malcolm. *Faith, Hope and Poetry: Theology and the Poetic Imagination.* Farnham, UK: Ashgate, 2010.

Gunter, P. A. Y. "Bergson, Henri Louis." In *The Oxford Companion to Philosophy,* edited by Ted Honderich, 91. 2nd ed. New York: Oxford University Press, 2005.

Gustafson, James M. "Preface." In *Christ and Culture,* by H. Richard Niebuhr, xxi–xxxv. San Francisco: Harper, 2001.

Hacking, Ian. "Introductory Essay." In *The Structure of Scientific Revolutions,* by Thomas Kuhn, vii–xxxvii. Chicago: University of Chicago Press, 2012.

Harper, Katherine. "Anscombe G. E. M." In *The C. S. Lewis Readers' Encyclopedia,* edited by Jeffrey D. Schultz and John G. West Jr., 81. Grand Rapids: Zondervan, 1998.

Harwood, Alfred Cecil. "A Toast to His Memory." *Remembering C. S. Lewis: Recollections of Those Who Knew Him,* edited by James T. Como, 377–82. San Francisco: Ignatius, 1979.

Hasnain, Ahmed. "Coleridge on Imagination: Comparison with Wordsworth." Academia, n.d. http://www.academia.edu/8877771/Coleridge_on_Imagination_Comparison_with_Wordsworth_Introduction.

Herrick, James A. "C. S. Lewis and the Advent of the Posthuman." In *The Magician's Twin: C. S. Lewis on Science, Scientism, and Society,* edited by John G. West, 235–64. Seattle: Discovery Institute, 2012.

Hexham, Irving. *Understanding World Religions: An Interdisciplinary Approach.* 2nd ed. Grand Rapids: Zondervan, 2011.

Hinten, Marvin D. "Bluspels and Flalanferes." In *The C. S. Lewis Readers' Encyclopedia*, edited by Jeffrey D. Schultz and John G. West Jr., 101. Grand Rapids: Zondervan, 1998.

———. "Metaphor." In *The C. S. Lewis Readers' Encyclcpedia*, edited by Jeffrey D. Schultz and John G. West Jr., 273–74. Grand Rapids: Zondervan, 1998.

Hofstadter, Richard. "The Vogue of Spencer." In *Darwin*, edited by Philip Appleman, 389–99. 2nd ed. Norton Critical. New York: Norton, 1979.

Hooper, Walter. *C. S. Lewis: A Companion & Guide*. San Francisco: HarperSanFrancisco, 1996.

Hume, David. *An Enquiry Concerning Human Understanding*. Edited by Antony Flew. Peru, IL: Open Court, 1988.

Humphries, Chris, et al. *Oxford World Encyclopedia*. New York: Oxford University Press, 2001.

"Intelligent Design: What Is Intelligent Design?" Discovery Institute, n.d. http://www.intelligentdesign.org/whatisid.php.

Jacobs, Alan. "The Chronicles of Narnia." In *The Cambridge Companion to C. S. Lewis*, edited by Robert MacSwain and Michael Ward, 265–80. Cambridge Companions to Religion. Cambridge: Cambridge University Press, 2010.

James, William. *Pragmaticism: A New Name for Some Old Ways of Thinking*. New York: Longman, Greens, 1909.

———. *The Varieties of Religious Experience: A Study in Human Nature*. New York: Promotheus, 2002.

Keeble, N. H. "C. S. Lewis, Richard Baxter and 'Mere Christianity.'" *Christianity and Literature* 30 (1981) 27–44. https://doi.org/10.1177/014833318103000306.

Keller, James A. "Process Theology." In *The Cambridge Dictionary of Philosophy*, edited by Robert Audi, 748. 2nd ed. New York: Cambridge University Press, 2006.

Kilby, Clyde S. *The Christian World of C. S. Lewis*. Grand Rapids: Eerdmans, 1964.

King, Alec, and Martin Ketley. *The Control of Language: A Critical Approach to Reading and Writing*. London: Longmans, Green and Co., 1939.

Kinghorn, Kevin. "Virtue Epistemology: Why Uncle Andrew Couldn't Hear the Animals Speak." In *The Chronicles of Narnia and Philosophy: The Lion, the Witch, and the Worldview*, edited by Gregory Bassham et al., 15–26. Chicago: Open Court, 2005.

Kort, Wesley A. *C. S. Lewis: Then and Now*. New York: Oxford University Press, 2001.

Kreeft, Peter. *C. S. Lewis: A Critical Essay*. Grand Rapids: Eerdmanns, 1969.

Kuhn, Thomas. *The Structure of Scientific Revolutions*. Chicago: University of Chicago Press, 2012.

Leisola, Matti, and Jonathan Witt. *Heretic: One Scientist's Journey from Darwin to Design*. Seattle: Discovery Institute, 2018.

Lennox, John C. *God's Undertaker: Has Science Buried God?* Updated ed. Oxford: Lion, 2009.

Lewis, C. S. *The Abolition of Man*. In *The Complete C. S. Lewis Signature Classics*, by C. S. Lewis, 691–730. New York: HarperCollins, 2002.

———. *All My Road before Me: The Diary of C. S. Lewis, 1922–1927*. Orlando: Harcourt, 1991.

———. *Christian Reflections*. Edited by Walter Hooper. Grand Rapids: Eerdmans, 1967.

———. *Christian Reflections*. Edited by Walter Hooper. Grand Rapids: Eerdmans, 2014.

———. *The Collected Letters of C. S. Lewis*. Edited by Walter Hooper. 3 vols. San Francisco: HarperCollins, 2004–2006.

———. *The Discarded Image*. Cambridge: Cambridge University Press, 1964.

———. "'Early Prose Joy': C. S. Lewis's Early Draft of an Autobiographical Manuscript." *Seven: An Anglo-American Literary Review* 30 (2013) 13–50. https://www.jstor.org/stable/48599471.

———. *English Literature in the Sixteenth Century (Excluding Drama)*. London: Oxford University Press, 1954.

———. *Essay Collection: Faith, Christianity and the Church*. Edited by Lesley Walmsley. London: HarperCollins, 2002.

———. *An Experiment in Criticism*. Cambridge: Cambridge University Press, 1961.

———. *God in the Dock: Essays on Theology and Ethics*. Edited by Walter Hooper. Grand Rapids: Eerdmans, 1970.

———. *Image and Imagination*. Edited by Walter Hooper. New York: Cambridge University Press, 2013.

———. *The Last Battle*. London: Collins & Sons, 1956.

———. *Letters of C. S. Lewis*. Edited by Warren H. Lewis. Rev. ed. Orlando: Harcourt, 1966.

———. *Letters to Malcolm: Chiefly on Prayer*. New York: Harcourt, 1992.

———. *The Magician's Nephew*. New York: HarperCollins, 1955.

———. *Mere Christianity*. San Francisco: HarperCollins, 1952.

———. *Miracles*. San Francisco: HarperCollins, 1960.

———. *Of Other Worlds: Essays and Stories*. Edited by Walter Hooper. Orlando: Harcourt, 1994.

———. *Out of the Silent Planet*. New York: Scribner, 1938.

———. *Perelandra*. New York: Scribner, 1944.

———. *The Pilgrim's Regress*. Glasgow: Collins, 1984.

———. *The Problem of Pain*. New York: HarperCollins, 1996.

———. *Reflections on the Psalms*. London: HarperCollins, 1958.

———. "Rejoinder to Dr. Pittenger." *Christian Century* (Nov. 26, 1958) 1359–61. https://archive.org/details/sim_christian-century_1958-11-26_75_48/page/1359/mode/1up.

———. *The Screwtape Letters*. In *The Complete C. S. Lewis Signature Classics*, by C. S. Lewis, 179–296. New York: HarperCollins, 2002.

———. *Selected Literary Essays*. Edited by Walter Hooper. Cambridge: Cambridge University Press, 2013.

———. *The Silver Chair*. London: Geoffrey Bles, 1953.

———. *Spirits in Bondage: A Cycle of Lyrics*. New York: Casimo, 2005.

———. *Surprised by Joy*. New York: Houghton Mifflin Harcourt, 1955.

———. *That Hideous Strength*. New York: Simon & Schuster, 1945.

———. *They Stand Together: The Letters of C. S. Lewis to Arthur Greeves (1914–1963)*. Edited by Walter Hooper. London: Collins, 1979.

Lindskoog, Kathryn Ann. "Dom Bede Griffiths." In *The C. S. Lewis Readers' Encyclopedia*, edited by Jeffrey D. Schultz and John G. West Jr., 194–95. Grand Rapids: Zondervan, 1998.

Lipton, Peter. *Inference to the Best Explanation*. International Library of Philosophy. 2nd ed. New York: Routledge, 2004.

Logan, Stephen. "Literary Theorist." In *The Cambridge Companion to C. S. Lewis*, edited by Robert MacSwain and Michael Ward, 29–42. Cambridge Companions to Religion. Cambridge: Cambridge University Press, 2010.

MacIntyre, Alisdair. "Pantheism." In *Encyclopedia of Philosophy*, edited by Donald M. Borchert, 94. Detroit: Macmillan, 2006.

MacSwain, Robert. "Introduction." In *The Cambridge Companion to C. S. Lewis*, edited by Robert MacSwain and Michael Ward, 1–12. Cambridge Companions to Religion. Cambridge: Cambridge University Press, 2010.

Marsden, George M. *C. S. Lewis's Mere Christianity: A Biography*. Lives of Great Religious Books 24. Princeton, NJ: Princeton University Press, 2016.

Martindale, Wayne. "Myth." In *The C. S. Lewis Readers' Encyclopedia*, edited by Jeffrey D. Schultz and John G. West Jr., 287–88. Grand Rapids: Zondervan, 1998.

Martinich, Aloysius Patrick. "Theosophy." In *The Cambridge Dictionary of Philosophy*, edited by Robert Audi, 915. 2nd ed. New York: Cambridge University Press, 2006.

Marty, Martin E. "Foreword." In *Christ and Culture*, by H Richard Niebuhr, xiii–xix. San Francisco: HarperCollins, 2001.

Matthews, Gareth B. "Plato in Narnia." In *The Chronicles of Narnia and Philosophy: The Lion, the Witch, and the Worldview*, edited by Gregory Bassham et al., 169–79. Chicago: Open Court, 2005.

McGrath, Alister E. *C. S. Lewis—A Life: Eccentric Genius, Reluctant Prophet*. Colorado Springs, CO: Alive Communications, 2014.

———. *The Intellectual World of C. S. Lewis*. Chichester, UK: Wiley and Sons, 2014.

———. *Mere Apologetics: How to Help Seekers and Skeptics Find Faith*. Grand Rapids: Baker, 2012.

Meilaender, Gilbert. *The Taste for the Other: The Social and Ethical Thought of C. S. Lewis*. Grand Rapids: Eerdmans, 1978.

Menuge, Angus J. L. *Agents under Fire: Materialism and the Rationality of Science*. Lanham, MD: Rowman and Littlefield, 2004.

———, ed. *C. S. Lewis, Lightbearer in the Shadowlands: The Evangelistic Vision of C. S. Lewis*. Wheaton, IL: Crossway, 1997.

Mill, John Stuart. *Utilitarianism*. Amherst, NY: Prometheus 1987.

Miller, Michael Matheson. "C. S. Lewis, Scientism, and the Moral Imagination." In *The Magician's Twin: C. S. Lewis on Science, Scientism, and Society*, edited by John G. West, 309–38. Seattle: Discovery Institute, 2012.

More, Max. "H+: True Transhumanism." Metanexus, Feb. 5, 2009. https://metanexus.net/h-true-transhumanism/.

———. "A Letter to Mother Nature: Amendments to the Human Constitution." Max More's Strategic Philosophy, May 25, 2009. http://strategicphilosophy.blogspot.com/2009/05/its-about-ten-years-since-i-wrote.html.

Moreland, J. P., ed. *The Creation Hypothesis: Scientific Evidence for an Intelligent Designer*. Downers Grove, IL: InterVarsity, 1994.

———, and William Lane Craig. *Philosophical Foundations for a Christian Worldview*. Downers Grove, IL: InterVarsity, 2003.

Mosteller, Tim. "The Tao of Narnia." In *The Chronicles of Narnia and Philosophy: The Lion, the Witch, and the Worldview*, edited by Gregory Bassham et al., 94–105. Chicago: Open Court, 2005.

Murphy, Brian. *C. S. Lewis*. Mercer Island, WA: Starmont House, 1983.
Murray, Douglas. *The Strange Death of Europe: Immigration, Identity, Islam*. London: Bloomsbury, 2017.
Musacchio, George. "Exorcising the Zeitgeist: Lewis as Evangelist to the Modernists." In *C. S. Lewis, Lightbearer in the Shadowlands: The Evangelistic Vision of C. S. Lewis*, edited by Angus J. L. Menuge, 213–34. Wheaton, IL: Crossway, 1997.
Myers, Doris T. *C. S. Lewis in Context*. Kent, OH: Kent State University Press, 1994.
Nagel, Thomas. *Mind and Cosmos: Why the Materialist Neo-Darwinian Conception of Nature Is Almost Certainly False*. New York: Oxford University Press, 2012.
Nash, Ronald H. *Worldviews in Conflict*. Grand Rapids: InterVarsity, 1992.
Naugle, David K. *Worldview: History of a Concept*. Grand Rapids: Eerdmans, 2002.
Netland, Harold. *Encountering Religious Pluralism: The Challenge to Christian Faith and Mission*. Downers Grove, IL: InterVarsity, 2001.
The New Webster's Encyclopedic Dictionary. Canadian ed. New York: Lexicon Publications, 1988.
Niebuhr, H. Richard. *Christ and Culture*. San Francisco: HarperCollins, 2001.
Niebuhr, Reinhold. *Moral Man and Immoral Society: A Study in Ethics and Politics*. New York: Scribner's, 1953.
Nietzsche, Friedrich W. *Beyond Good and Evil: Prelude to a Philosophy of the Future*. Translated by Marion Faber. New York: Oxford University Press, 1998.
———. *Human, All Too Human: A Book for Free Spirits*. Translated by Marion Faber. Lincoln: University of Nebraska Press, 1984.
Olsen, Ted. "Apologetics: C. S. Lewis." *Christianity Today*, 2000. http://www.christianitytoday.com/history/issues/issue-65/apologetics-cs-lewis.html.
Ottaway, Kristine. "William Wordsworth (1770–1850)." In *The C. S. Lewis Readers' Encyclopedia*, edited by Jeffrey D. Schultz and John G. West Jr., 430. Grand Rapids: Zondervan, 1998.
Payne, Michael W. "Philosophy among the Ruins: The Twentieth Century and Beyond." In *Revolutions in Worldview: Understanding the Flow of Western Thought*, edited by W. Andrew Hoffecker, 318–58. Phillipsburg, NJ: P & R, 2007.
Perry, Mike W., and Jeffrey D. Schultz. "Mere Christianity." In *The C. S. Lewis Readers' Encyclopedia*, edited by Jeffrey D. Schultz and John G. West Jr., 270–73. Grand Rapids: Zondervan, 1998.
Persson, Ingmar, and Julian Savulescu. "Moral Transhumanism." *Journal of Medicine and Philosophy* 35 (2010) 565–669. https://doi.org/10.1093/jmp/jhq052.
Piehler, Paul. "Encounters with Lewis: An Interim Report." In *C. S. Lewis Remembered: Collected Reflections of Students, Friends and Colleagues*, edited by Harry Lee Poe and Rebecca Whitten Poe, 115–58. Grand Rapids: Zondervan, 2006.
Pietarinen, Juhani. "The Principal Attitudes of Humanity towards Nature." In *Philosophy, Humanity and Ecology: Philosophy of Nature and Environmental Ethics*, edited by H. Odera Oruka, 290–94. N.p.: Diane, 1996. https://books.google.je/books?id=AfN94sbTx2MC&printsec=frontcover#v=onepage&q&f=false.
Piper, John. "C. S. Lewis, Romantic Rationalist: How His Paths to Christ Shaped His Life and Ministry." Desiring God, Sept. 27, 2013. https://www.desiringgod.org/messages/c-s-lewis-romantic-rationalist-how-his-paths-to-christ-shaped-his-life-and-ministry.
———. "C. S. Lewis, Romantic Rationalist: How His Paths to Christ Shaped His Life and Ministry." In *The Romantic Rationalist: God, Life, and Imagination in the*

Work of C. S. Lewis, edited by John Piper and David Mathis, 21–38. Wheaton, IL: Crossway, 2014.

Pittenger, Norman. "Apologist versus Apologist: A Critique of C. S. Lewis as 'Defender of the Faith.'" *Christian Century* (Oct. 1, 1958) 1104–7. https://archive.org/details/sim_christian-century_1958-10-01_75_40/page/1106/mode/1up.

Plantinga, Alvin. "A Christian Life Partly Lived." In *Philosophers Who Believe: The Spiritual Journeys of 11 Leading Thinkers*, edited by Kelly James Clark, 45–82. Downers Grove, IL: InterVarsity, 1993.

———. *Warranted Christian Belief*. New York: Oxford University Press, 2000.

———. *Where the Conflict Really Lies: Science, Religion and Naturalism*. New York: Oxford University Press, 2011.

Pojman, Louis P. "Gnosticism." In *The Cambridge Dictionary of Philosophy*, edited by Robert Audi, 346. 2nd ed. New York: Cambridge University Press, 2006.

Purtill, Richard. "Apologetics." In *The C. S. Lewis Readers' Encyclopedia*, edited by Jeffrey D. Schultz and John G. West Jr., 83–85. Grand Rapids: Zondervan, 1998.

Ray, Christopher. *Time, Space and Philosophy*. Philosophical Issues in Science. New York: Routledge, Chapman & Hall, 1991.

Rea, Michael C. *World without Design: The Ontological Consequences of Naturalism*. Oxford, UK: Oxford University Press, 2002.

Reppert, Victor. *C. S. Lewis's Dangerous Idea: In Defence of the Argument from Reason*. Downers Grove, IL: InterVarsity, 2003.

———. "C. S. Lewis's Dangerous Idea Revisited." In *The Magician's Twin: C. S. Lewis on Science, Scientism, and Society*, edited by John G. West, 199–232. Seattle: Discovery Institute, 2012.

Rescher, Nicholas. "Idealism." In *The Cambridge Dictionary of Philosophy*, edited by Robert Audi, 412–13. 2nd ed. New York: Cambridge University Press, 2006.

Richards, Jay W. "Mastering the Vernacular: C. S. Lewis's Argument from Reason." In *The Magician's Twin: C. S. Lewis on Science, Scientism, and Society*, edited by John G. West, 179–98. Seattle: Discovery Institute, 2012.

Roberts, Austin. "Processing Theology with Cobb and Suchocki." Austin Roberts, June 2011. http://austinroberts13.blogspot.ca/2011/06/processing-theology-with-cobb-suchocki.html.

Ryken, Philip. "Inerrancy and the Patron Saint of Evangelicalism: C. S. Lewis on Holy Scripture." In *The Romantic Rationalist: God, Life, and Imagination in the Work of C. S. Lewis*, edited by John Piper and David Mathis, 39–64. Wheaton, IL: Crossway, 2014.

Savulesco, Julian. "Unfit for Life: Genetically Enhance Humanity or Face Extinction." YouTube, Oct., 2009. https://www.youtube.com/watch?v=PkW3rEQoab8.

Sayer, George. *Jack: A Life of C. S. Lewis*. 2nd ed. Wheaton, IL: Crossway, 1994.

Schaefer, Henry F., III. "C. S. Lewis: Science and Scientism." C. S. Lewis Society of California, n.d. https://www.lewissociety.org/scientism/.

Schakel, Peter J. *Imagination and the Arts in C. S. Lewis: Journeying to Narnia and Other Worlds*. Columbia: University of Missouri Press, 2002.

———. "Reason." In *The C. S. Lewis Readers' Encyclopedia*, edited by Jeffrey D. Schultz and John G. West Jr., 348–50. Grand Rapids: Zondervan, 1998.

Sellars, J. T. *Reasoning beyond Reason: Imagination as a Theological Source in the Work of C. S. Lewis*. Eugene, OR: Wipf and Stock, 2011.

Sherburne, Donald W. "Whitehead." In *The Cambridge Dictionary of Philosophy*, edited by Robert Audi, 971–74. 2nd ed. New York: Cambridge University Press, 2006.

Sire, James W. *Apologetics beyond Reason: Why Seeing Really Is Believing*. Downers Grove, IL: InterVarsity, 2014.

———. *Naming the Elephant: Worldview as a Concept*. Downers Grove, IL: InterVarsity, 2004.

———. *The Universe Next Door: A Basic Worldview Catalog*. 5th ed. Grand Rapids: InterVarsity, 2009.

———. *Why Good Arguments Often Fail: Making a More Persuasive Case for Christ*. Downers Grove, IL: InterVarsity, 2006.

Smart, Ninian. *The Long Search*. Boston: Little and Brown, 1977.

———. *Worldviews: Crosscultural Explorations of Human Beliefs*. Englewood Cliffs, NJ: Prentice Hall, 1983.

Smith, Andrew Philip. *The Secret History of the Gnostics: Their Scriptures, Beliefs and Traditions*. London: Watkins Media, 2015.

Sprigge, T. L. S. "Panpsychism." In *The Cambridge Dictionary of Philosophy*, edited by Robert Audi, 640. 2nd ed. New York: Cambridge University Press, 2006.

Stack, George J. "Rudolf Steiner." In *The Cambridge Dictionary of Philosophy*, edited by Robert Audi, 878. 2nd ed. New York: Cambridge University Press, 2006.

Stassen, Glen H. "It Is Time to Take Jesus Back: In Celebration of the Fiftieth Anniversary of H. Richard Niebuhr's *Christ and Culture*." *Journal of the Society of Christian Ethics* 23 (2003) 133–43. https://www.jstor.org/stable/23561532.

Suchocki, Marjorie Hewitt. "What Is Process Theology: A Conversation with Marjorie." Process and Faith, 2003. https://processandfaith.org/wp-content/uploads/2015/07/what-is-process-theology.pdf.

Taylor, Charles. *A Secular Age*. Cambridge, MA: Harvard University Press, 2007.

Teilhard de Chardin, Pierre. *The Phenomenon of Man*. New York: Harper & Row, 1955.

Terry, Justin. "Foreword." In *C. S. Lewis: Revelation and the Christ*, by Paul H. Brazier, 2:xiii–xv. Eugene, OR: Pickwick, 2012.

Tolkien, J. R. R. *The Letters of J. R. R. Tolkien*. Edited by Humphrey Carpenter. Boston: Houghton Mifflin, 1981.

Troyer, John, ed. *The Classical Utilitarians: Bentham and Mill*. Indianapolis: Hacket, 2003.

Unamuno, Miguel de. *The Tragic Sense of Life in Men and Nations*. Edited by Anthony Kerrigan and Martin Nozick. Translated by Anthony Kerrigan. Princeton, NJ: Princeton University Press, 1972.

Valantasis, Richard. *The Beliefnet Guide to Gnosticism and Other Vanished Christianities*. New York: Doubleday, 2006.

Van der Elst, Philip. *C. S. Lewis: A Short Introduction*. Continuum Icons. New York: Claridge, 2005.

Vanhoozer, Kevin J. "On Scripture." In *The Cambridge Companion to C. S. Lewis*, edited by Robert MacSwain and Michael Ward, 75–88. Cambridge Companions to Religion. Cambridge: Cambridge University Press, 2010.

Viney, Donald Wayne. "Charles Hartshorne." In *The Cambridge Dictionary of Philosophy*, edited by Robert Audi, 363–64. 2nd ed. New York: Cambridge University Press, 2006.

Walker, Andrew. "Scripture, Revelation and Platonism in C. S. Lewis." *Scottish Journal of Theology* 55 (2002) 19–35. doi:10.1017/S0036930602000121.

Walsh, Chad. *C. S. Lewis: Apostle to the Skeptics*. Reprint, Eugene, OR: Wipf and Stock, 2008.

———. *The Literary Legacy of C. S. Lewis*. London: Sheldon, 1979.

Ward, Michael. "The Good Serves the Better and Both the Best: C. S. Lewis on Imagination and Reason in Imagination." In *Imaginative Apologetics: Theology, Philosophy, and the Catholic Tradition*, edited by Andrew Davidson, 59–78. Grand Rapids: Baker, 2011.

———. *The Narnia Code: C. S. Lewis and the Secret of the Seven Heavens*. Carol Stream, IL: Tyndall House, 2010.

———. *Planet Narnia: The Seven Heavens in the Imagination of C. S. Lewis*. New York: Oxford University Press, 2008.

———. "The Seven Heavens." Planet Narnia, 2007–2008. http://www.planetnarnia.com/planet-narnia/the-seven-heavens.

Webb, Stephen H. "Aslan's Voice: C. S. Lewis and the Magic of Sound." In *The Chronicles of Narnia and Philosophy: The Lion, the Witch, and the Worldview*, edited by Gregory Bassham et al., 3–14. Chicago: Open Court, 2005.

West, John G. "The Abolition of Man." In *The C. S. Lewis Readers' Encyclopedia*, edited by Jeffrey D. Schultz and John G. West Jr., 67–69. Grand Rapids: Zondervan, 1998.

———. "Darwin in the Dock." In *The Magician's Twin: C. S. Lewis on Science, Scientism, and Society*, edited by John G. West, 109–52. Seattle: Discovery Institute, 2012.

———. "Evolution and C. S. Lewis: What Did He Really Believe?" YouTube, Apr. 5, 2012. https://www.youtube.com/watch?v=iZP9YlQhdfs.

———. "The Magician's Twin." In *The Magician's Twin: C. S. Lewis on Science, Scientism, and Society*, edited by John G. West, 19–46. Seattle: Discovery Institute, 2012.

———, ed. *The Magician's Twin: C. S. Lewis on Science, Scientism, and Society*. Seattle: Discovery Institute, 2012.

Wethmar, Conrad J. "Theology between Church, University and Society." In *Theology between Church, University and Society*, edited by Martin E. Brinkman et al., 217–38. Studies in Theology and Religion 6. Assen, Neth.: Royal Van Gorcum, 2003. https://doi.org/10.1163/9789004494459_018.

Wilson, Andrew Norman. *C. S. Lewis: A Biography*. New York: Norton, 1990.

Wilson, Fred. "John Stuart Mill." In *The Cambridge Dictionary of Philosophy*, edited by Robert Audi, 568–71. 2nd ed. New York: Cambridge University Press, 2006.

Wilson, John. "Short Reviews of *Planet Narnia*, *Beyond Left and Right*, and *Global Pentecostalism*." *Christianity Today*, Feb. 4, 2008. http://www.christianitytoday.com/ct/2008/february/18.80.html.

Wordsworth, William. *William Wordsworth: The Major Works*. Edited by Stephen Gill. Oxford World's Classics. New York: Oxford University Press, 2008.

Wright, D. H., ed. *Beowulf: A Prose Translation*. New York: Penguin, 1957.

Wright, N. T. "Welcome to the Real Narnia: The Hidden Medieval Message at the Heart of C. S. Lewis's Classic Chronicles." John Mark Ministries, Nov. 13, 2009. http://www.jmm.org.au/articles/23073.htm.

Wybrow, Cameron. "The Education of Mark Studdock: How a Sociologist Learns the Lessons of the Abolition of Man." In *The Magician's Twin: C. S. Lewis on Science, Scientism, and Society*, edited by John G. West, 265–92. Seattle: Discovery Institute, 2012.

Zaleski, Philip, and Carol Zaleski. *The Fellowship: The Literary Lives of the Inklings*. New York: Farrar, Straus and Giroux, 2015.

Index

Abbott, Edwin, 69
abduction, 154n315, 157n322
The Abolition of Man (Lewis)
   critique of societal values and morals, 143
   envisioning a future society, 193
   on progressive scientific social engineering, 146–147
   on radical intellectual secularism, 181–182
   referring to a "Green Book," 73
   as a series of three lectures, 189
the Absolute, 59, 65
absolute One, attaining oneness with, 9
absolute pantheists, 8
academia, concern about contemporary, 194
academic theologians, cannot afford to disregard Lewis, 117–118
Acworth, Bernard, 75, 219–220
Adams, Father Walter Frederick, 101
Adey, Lionel, 224–225
Aeschliman, M. D., 214
afterlife, 52, 227
aging and death, no longer tolerating, 146
agnosticism, 44n104
all-inclusive unity, as divine, 8
amendments, to the human constitution, 146
Anacker, Gayne, 172
analogia entis (the analogy of being), 179n39

analogia fidei (the analogy of faith), 179n39
Anderson, James, 212
Anglican Church, 117, 118, 141, 161
Anglican clergy, 39, 120, 123, 197
Anglicanism, forms of, 198
Anointed One, 137
anomaly, 117
Anscombe, G. E. M. (Elizabeth), 174, 174n27, 175, 176
Anscombe/Lewis debate, 175–176, 177
Anthroposophical Society, 47n119
anthroposophy, 41, 41n98, 47, 47n119, 153
anti-supernatural, liberal Christianity, 220
anti-supernatural biases, 202
anti-supernatural Christianity, 221
anti-supernatural drift, 94–95
anti-supernaturalism, present climate of, 12
anti-theistic naturalist movement, 7
apologetic gateways, deployed by Lewis, 152
apologetic issues, Lewis engaging at multiple levels, 160
apologetic methodology, of C. S. Lewis, 4, 16, 150, 155, 174
apologetics, 3, 140–162, 163–194, 215. *See also* Christian apologetics
apologists
   Christian, 3, 120, 121–122
   methods employed by, 150
apostate, Lewis became, 22, 23

applied technology, Lewis's concerns about, 145
"Araparg" secret charity fund, 161
architect of a universe, conception of God as, 13
argument from reason, 210
argumentation, Lewis using his fictional writings, 166
"Aristotelian analyses," 96
Aristotle, 67n46, 69, 88
Arnold, Matthew, 113
art, reverence ascribed to, 113
asceticism, mated with living of the cultural life, 107
Askins, Dr., 41, 48
Aslan the Lion, 142, 168–169, 170
atheism, 13, 26
atheists, 125, 191n75
athleticism, educational philosophy of, 31
atonement, as a word needing revision, 124
Augustine, 110, 112, 159, 178
authentic Christianity, 198, 200
autobiographical works, of Lewis, 155
"awakening," Lewis's discovery of Norse mythology as, 92
awe, myths inspiring, 96

Baker, Leo, 38–39
Barefoot, Derek, 175
Barfield, Mrs., 48
Barfield, Owen
  charity fund set up by, 161
  on Darwinian processes, 44, 45
  defined humanity as an entity in itself, 110–111
  on imagination facilitating discernment of meaning, 54n140
  influence on Lewis's epistemology, 183
  on Lewis's reluctance to discuss his conversion experience, 65, 94
  ongoing questioning by, 82
  on philosophy as a way, 190n75
  on reincarnation, 40
  Rudolf Steiner's notions and, 19n11, 42
  views on evolution, 81
Barth, Karl, 133n257
Basilidies, 36n78
Baxter, Richard, 184
beauty, 35, 38
Beilby, James, 214
Bentham, Jeremy, 13
Bergson, Henri Louis, 83n104, 87
Beveridge, William Henry, 123n235
Beveridge Plan, 123n235
Beversluis, John, 175
Bhagavad-Gita, 10n16
Bible, 131, 133n257, 139, 140
biblical criticism, revised approach to, 205
biblical inspiration, 135, 136
biblical miracles, 198
biography, Lewis's omissions from his, 94
biological evolutionary process, 71
bitter-sweet longing, Romanticism as, 63
blind faith, as unsuitable, 39
"blinkered Enlightenment methodology, exposing, 203n27
"Bluspels and Flalansferes" lecture, on reason and imagination, 68
body, human, 8, 9
bounding lines, fixing clearly, 197
Bradley, sense of the Absolute, 49
Brazier, Paul
  on Bultmann's demythologizing agenda, 201n19
  on Christianity as the worldview, a *Weltanschauung* for Lewis, 187
  on John Redford calling out Enlightenment methodology, 203n27
  on the Lewis/Anscombe debate and the period after, 178n36, 179n39
  on Platonism as fundamental to Lewis's work, 179
British Social Security system, plan for, 123n235
Brown, Colin, 11n23
Brown, Devin, 89, 89n127
Brunner, Emil, 133n257

brutes, possibility for the immortality of, 158
Buddhism, 9n15, 10n16, 221
Bultmann, Rudolf K., 201–202

C. S. Lewis: A Guide to His Theology (Clark), 73n68
C. S. Lewis and the Crisis of a Christian (Cootsona), 86
C. S. Lewis and the Search for Rational Religion (Beversluis), 175
C. S. Lewis: Apostle to the Skeptics (Walsh), 182
C. S. Lewis at the Breakfast Table and other Reminiscences, 104n173
C. S. Lewis: Eccentric Genius, Reluctant Prophet (McGrath), 90
C. S. Lewis Handbook (Duriez), 61
C. S. Lewis on Scripture (Christensen), 139
C. S. Lewis Society, in various countries, 225
C. S. Lewis's Dangerous Idea: In Defence of the Argument from Reason (Reppert), 175
cabdriver, overwhelmed by Aslan's voicing, 172
Calvin, John
  affirmed the full authority of Scripture, 128
  on the historicity of Job, 131, 132
  notion of *sensus divinitatus*, 214
  as transformationalist or "conversionist," 110
Campbell College, 18
Cannon, Lincoln, 145
Carlyle, 207
Carnell, Corbin, 62n31, 87, 96
Carter, Craig, 108
Cartesians, on animal life as a mechanism, 136
categories, single ideal-typical set of, 100
catholic, as a word needing revision, 124
"causal tools," lack of in the naturalist toolkit, 189
cave allegory, in Plato's *Republic*, 180

Center for Science and Culture, at the Discovery Institute, 80n87
centrists, 106
Chakrabarti, Arindam, on nirvana, 9n16
characters, as distant to us in myths, 96
charity, as a word needing revision, 124
Cherbourg School, Lewis attended, 18
chess game, Lewis making reference to, 51
Chesterton, G. K., 87
The Chicago Statement on Biblical Inerrancy, 130
Christ. *See* Jesus Christ
Christ above Culture category, 101, 106–108
Christ against Culture category, 101–102
Christ and Culture in Paradox category, 101, 111–117
Christ and Culture (Niebuhr), 98
Christ of Culture category, 101, 102–105
Christ the Transformer of Culture category, 99, 101, 108–111
Christensen, Michael
  on biblical inerrancy, 139
  on biblical inspiration, 134
  on Lewis "giving fresh and fluid expression to old ideas," 127–128
  on Lewis's worldview, 140
  on neoorthodox theologians, 133n257
  on Platonism in Lewis's body of work, 179
Christian, as a word needing revision, 124
Christian apologetics, Lewis's contribution to, 16, 224
Christian apologist, 3, 120, 121–122
Christian beliefs, 215, 223
Christian faith. *See also* faith
  alterations to, 196
  as best explanation for Lewis's perception of reality, 141

(Christian faith continued)
  conflict between science and elements of, 71
  embracing meaning individual selfsurrender, 110
  exploration of, 150, 151
  influence on Lewis's perception of the world, 57
  intellectual world represented by, 159
  Lewis abandoning, 23
  Lewis expressing the reasonableness of, 153
  Lewis valuing logic and reason in matters of, 177
  philosophical basis for, 178
  shaped by childhood experiences, 207–208
  supernaturalistic content of, 198
Christian message, preserving as distinct from one's own ideas, 122–123
Christian mythology, idea that it might after all be true, 93
Christian orthodoxy, as reflected in *Mere Christianity*, 224
Christian Platonism, in Lewis's *The Last Battle*, 181
Christian story, as full of meaning for Lewis, 66
Christian theism, 7, 177
Christian vision of reality, 160, 160n335
Christian worldview
  categorizing alternatives to, 4
  of Lewis, 16, 224
  Lewis defending his, 83
  Lewis not wavering in his commitment to, 177
  as true, 216
Christianity
  as the actualization of the entelechy, 67–68
  apologists defending, 122
  challenges from inauthentic, non-supernatural, 196–204
  as the "church of the center," 106
  conflict with scientism, 70–71
  contemporary challenges to, 5–15
  defining relation to God, 208
  embraced as the ultimate worldview, 195
  as God expressing Himself through "real things," 54
  grasping the reality of through imagination, 54
  hazardous to offer a watered-down form of, 199
  impoverished without its supernatural quality, 7
  lacing with pantheistic content, 206
  Lewis hampered in embracing, 53
  of Lewis understood by discerning readers, 163
  Lewis's concept of the common doctrines of, 184
  as a main genre of Lewis, 142
  methodological naturalism coexisting with, 7
  as not even the best religion, 26
  notional, transdenominational form of, 186
  offering a simplistic account of God, 208
  as the one religion from which the miraculous cannot be excluded, 203
  resisting pantheism, 207
  on salvation obtained through a common faith, 10
  same kind of thing as all the rest, 22
  as the story of a loving God revealing himself to mankind, 67
  supra-naturalistic notions of, 28
  utilitarian-like notion manifested in, 14
  validity of the truth claims of authentic, 222
"Christianity and Culture" (Lewis), 112
The Chronicles of Narnia and Philosophy (Webb), 168
Chronicles of Narnia series, 88, 89, 152
Church of England, 118
Church of Ireland, 30
Clark, David

INDEX 245

on forming a culture, 107
on "The Green Book," 73n68
on Lewis leading people to faith, 142, 161
on *That Hideous Strength*, 149
Clarke, Arthur C., 74
clergy. *See* Anglican clergy
Coburn, Kathleen, 164
Coleridge, Samuel Taylor
   on imagination, 45, 46
   influence on Lewis, 30n54, 165, 183
   Lewis well acquainted with the writings of, 47
   understanding imagination's role, 164
Coleridge: A Collection of Critical Essays (Coburn), 164
Coleridgean view of the world, 166
collectivism, Lewis distrusted, 196n4
common descent, evolution as a theory of, 80
The Commonitory (Lerins), 184n57
Communion, Lewis's first, 26
community worship and prayer, Lewis devoted to, 161
Como, James, 196n4
Companion to Narnia (Ford), 172
conditioner-induced global tyranny, 193–194
conditioners, creating an artificial *Tao*, 147
Confucius, 104
"congealed Darwinism," implications of, 82
conservative thought, touchstones of Lewis's, 196n4
consumerism, 211, 213
contemporary society, human's biology and psychology as unfit for, 144
conversion, 65, 94
cooperative society, achieved by training, 103
Cootsona, Gregory, 86, 188–189
core elements
   of the Christian faith, 4, 197, 223
   essential for Christian apologetics, 125

within myths, 95
core tenets of the faith, 198
cosmic philosophy, evolution as, 80
cosmic theory, making evolution into, 77
cosmogony, 38
Cousins, Lance Selwyn, 10
Cowan, Steven, 2, 219
Miss Cowie (C.), 20, 22n22, 41, 223
creative, as a word needing revision, 124
Creative Evolution (Bergson), 83n104
creativeness, New Testament leaving no room for, 107
creativity, of C. S. Lewis, 168
criticism, Lewis not exempt from, 227
Croce, Benedetto, 113
cross, as a word needing revision, 124
crucifixion, as a word needing revision, 124
crystallisation, process of, 183n53
cultural critique, of Lewis, 5
cultural setting, in early New Testament times, 97
culture, 98–117
   as the "artificial, secondary environment," 109
   aspiring for symmetry with Christianity, 106
   Christian faith and, 112–113
   encouraging people to think they were already good, 143
   Lewis's use of the word, 113n197
   in the Niebuhrian context, 109
   not held up as something important in the Scriptures, 107
   relationship between Lewis and as complex, 116
cumulative case approach, Netland advocating for, 215
current worldview, Lewis's reservations about, 61

Darwin, Charles, 43
Darwinian controversies, Lewis's caution about participating in, 75–76

Darwinian natural selection, as the object of Lewis's attack in *Miracles*, 86
Darwinian notions, Lewis's characterisations of, 44
Darwinian processes, scrutiny of Lewis's views regarding, 74–75
Darwinian theory, Lewis's reservations about, 76
Darwinism, 45, 82
Davis, William, 178
death, of Lewis's mother, 18
debunkers, proclivity for destabilizing society, 193
deductive reasoning, 154n315
degenerative changes, outweighing improvements, 79
deism, 12–13, 185, 204–206
demythologised version, of Christianity, 200
demythologized theology, of Rudolf Bultmann, 185, 201n19
denominations, 118, 186
Descartes, 178
Desire, 63
"devil-led organization," N.I.C.E. as, 150
dialectic approach, to Lewis's relationship with his cultural environs, 116
"The Dialectic of Enjoyment and Renunciation," Lewis exhibiting, 115
diary, kept by Lewis between 1922 and 1927, 39
Dilthey, Wilhelm, 2, 218, 219
dipolarity, God conceived as, 11
The Discarded Image (Lewis), 59, 79, 89
Discovery Institute, 79n87
"Divine pressure," God exercising, 136
"Divine protection," withdrawal of Lewis from, 23
divine punishments, as also mercies, 24
divinity, Christ's, 52
doctrinaire utilitarianism, homogenizing all value, 212
doctrine, plain expositions or imaginative realizations of, 155
dogma, as a word needing revision, 124
"Dogma and the Universe" (Lewis), 83–84
Donne, John, 90
Dorsett, Lyle, 101–102, 111, 161
downward trend, in the universe as a whole, 84
dualism, 112n192
Duriez, Colin, 61
dying god, notion of among ancient cultures, 97
Dyson, Henry Victor (Hugo), 53n136, 67, 174n27

early church fathers, emphasising canonicity, 139
"Early Prose Joy" (Lewis), 50
earth, as stationery in the pre-Copernican worldview, 90
Eastern cultural framework, 104–105
Eastern spirituality, 108, 213
ecclesiastical distinctiveness, 186
ecumenism, Lewis's spirit of, 223
educators, teaching there are no objective truths, 172
Edwards, Bruce, 188
Edwards, Mark, 179n41
Emerson, 207
empirical reality, as the only reality, 71n58
empirical theist
    arriving at God by induction, 50
    Lewis as, 66, 66n43, 91, 183
empiricists, such as Locke and Hume, 50n127
"enduring problem," of culture, 113
English countryside, Lewis's reaction to, 31
English literature, 95, 140
English Literature in the Sixteenth Century (Excluding Drama) (Lewis), 88, 140
English public school system, Lewis's dissatisfaction with, 31, 190

the Enlightenment, adapted to local contexts, 118
Enlightenment figures, marginalizing imagination's role, 165
Enquiry Concerning Human Understanding (Hume), 30n54
entelechy, 67, 67n46
entropy, as the real cosmic wave, 84
epistemological issues, Lewis wrestling with, 45
Epstein, Greg, 12
ethical model, utilitarianism developed as, 14
ethics, pantheists striving to lead moral lives, 9
Ethiopian Eunuch, reading Isaiah 53, 137
Evangelicals
 on biblical inspiration, 130
 converting people, 109
 deploying the idea of worldview extensively, 2n5
 discomfort about Lewis's scriptural views, 131
 Lewis popular among, 227
 Lewis siding with on worldview and revelation, 139
 on revelation and Scripture, 134
 uniting with Anglo-Catholics, 184
The Everlasting Man (Chesterton), 49
"everywhere and by all" (*ubique et ab omnibus*), from Vincentius of Lérins, 184n57
evidence-based solutions, desire to find, 51
evil, explanation for the existence of absent in pantheism, 209
evil *archon*, rebelled against the heavenly *pleroma*, 36n78
evil demiurge, Gnostics belief in, 36n78
evil spirits, things animated by, 26
evolution, 77–78, 80
 having many different meanings, 80
evolutionary myth, 83
evolutionary processes, little evidence about, 220
evolutionary theory, defenders of, 76

evolutionism
 described, 80
 as different from Evolution, 71
 as myth, 71n61, 77
ex Deo (out of God), universe created by, 8
ex nihilo (out of nothing), as a belief of theism, 8
existence
 of God, arguments for, 125
 moving from "almost zero" to "almost infinity," 78
experience, supernatural elements of, 59
An Experiment in Criticism (Lewis), 95–96
experimentation, indiscriminate, 74
experts, opinions taking precedence over beliefs of the early church, 200

Faerie Queen (Spencer), 90
"fagging," custom of, 24
fairy-tales, Narnian novels as, 173–174
faith, 27, 122, 169n12. See also Christian faith
Faith, Hope and Poetry: Theology and the Poetic Imagination (Guite), 164
faith and science, relationship of in Lewis's worlview, 70–87
false gods, 24
falsified versions, of the "historical Jesus," 203
fancy, 46
Farrer, Austin, 154, 157, 215n72
The Fellowship: The Literary Lives of the Inklings (Zaleskis), 176
fiction, Lewis's usage of, 173
fictional works
 of Lewis, 220–221, 226
 worldview elements in Lewis's, 164–181
fire, becoming invisible, 10n16
first Communion, of Lewis, 26
Fischer-Schreiber, Ingrid, 9n16, 10n16

flalansfere, contracted Flatlander's sphere to, 69
flame of self, blowing out, 9n16
flat-Earthers, Barfield's reference to, 82
Flatland (Abbott), 69
Ford, Paul, 172–173
form criticism, identifying how the Gospels are constructed, 201n19
forms, finding, 181n46
Frame, John, 180n46
Freud, Sigmund, 27
fundamentalists, 133, 139
"The Funeral of a Great Myth" (Lewis), 77, 79
futurists, 143

Galloway, Ronald, 193n86
Gardener, Helen, 79
Geisler, Norman, 8, 9, 10, 12
generosity, of Lewis, 161
Genesis, versus the scientific view, 75
Giokaris, Glenn, 94
"giving an account of the world," Lewisian ways of, 5
Gnosticism, 36, 36n78
God
   as the architect of a law-governed structure, 13
   as the architect of the law-governed structure, 204
   blurring the distinction with humankind, 214
   contrasting the pantheists's conception of with the God of Christianity, 208
   deism's concept of, 12
   depending on the world, 11
   guidepost to lead humanity to its, 64
   pervading all things, 7
   postulating some sort of, 44, 50
   in process theology, 11n23
   reasons for revealing himself as he has, 133–134
   simplicity of in pantheism, 8
God and world, interrelated as mind and body, 11

God-Man, Jesus as, 119
Golden Age, of Lewis as a public apologist, 150
"a good deal further," as authentic faith in the risen Lord Jesus Christ, 200
Good without God (Epstein), 12
goodness, 52, 179
Gospels, 49, 97, 125, 199
Gould, Stephen Jay, 44n104
Great Bookham, 17, 30
"greatest teachers," Lewis's list of his, 29
Green, Roger Lancelyn, 29
Greeves, Arthur, 25, 26, 29, 34
Gresham, Douglas, 142n283, 161
Gresham, Joy Davidman, 161
Griffiths, Dom Bede
   account of Lewis's conversion, 92
   became a Catholic monk, 102
   differences with Lewis, 103, 104n173
   establishes a monastery in India, 105
   on philosophy as a way, 190n75
Guenther, Bruce, 99n157
Guite, Malcolm, 164, 166, 225
Gustafson, James, 99

Haldane, John Burdon Sanderson (J. B. S.), 71, 72, 188, 188n67
Hardman, Donald, 31–32
Harper, Katherine, 174n27
Hartshorne, Charles, 11n23
Harwood, Cecil, 40, 41, 162
Hasnain, Ahmed, 46
head, ruling the bely through the chest, 190
"health and wealth gospel," form of Christianity, 14
heavenly *pleroma*, evil *archon* rebelled against, 36n78
Heelas, Paul, 214
Hegel, 49, 207
Herrick, James, 73, 143, 144, 148
Hexham, Irving, 9n14, 10
Higher Thought, spirituality of, 20
Hindu and Shinto traditions, 214

Hinduism, 9n15, 104, 221
Hinten, Marvin, 67, 69
historical accuracy, biblical accounts judged for, 205
historical Jesus, 30, 203
historical truth, not every statement in Scripture as, 127
historicity, of the Gospel account, 199
history, pantheists seldom talking about, 9
Holy Scripture. *See* Scripture
Holy Spirit, 127
Hooper, Walter, 29, 37, 47n119
"Hound of Heaven," Lewis's reference to, 95
human constitution, Mother Nature's poor job with, 146
human history, birth of Christ as a turning point in the course of, 93
human life, 113, 136
human soul
 emphasis on by Lewis, 111
 enjoying some object never fully given, 64, 115
 moving from body to body in the cycle of transmigration, 9n14
 rise of modernity producing, 212
humanism, 7, 144n290
humanity
 as an amalgam of individual lives for Lewis, 110
 God using fallible, 135
 restoring a sense of into contemporary culture, 6
 wishing for a tidier vehicle for God's word, 133
Hume, David, 27, 30n54, 46, 47
Huxley, Aldous, 64
hypotheses, 6n8

"The Idea of the Holy" (Otto), 156n321
idealism
 acceptance of some form of, 42
 cannot be lived, 191n75
 Lewis and, 221
 priority to the mental over the material, 42n100
 Romantics having more in common with, 57n7
idealist philosophy, Lewis raised in the tradition of, 158
ideal-typical options, 100
ideas, 46, 54n140
Iliad (Homer), Lewis learning Greek from, 29
illusion, universe as, 8
imagery, of Lewis, 159, 225, 226
imaginary histories, Lewis bemused by reading, 202
imagination
 aroused by the beauty of a natural event, 172
 breaking apart and combining ideas, 46
 elements of, 46
 giving meaning to events, 94
 Lewis's appreciation for the power of, 166
 Lewis's beliefs about, 30n54
 Lewis's enabled him to comprehend the meaning of Christian faith, 66
 Lewis's frustration about, 48
 Lewis's skill in employing the power of, 221
 Lewis's understanding and usage of the power of, 225–226
 Lewis's views regarding the capacity of to convey meaning, 164
 providing insight that is unattainable by reason alone, 49
 role in accuiring knowledge, 45
 Wordsworth's notion of, 47
Imagination and the Arts in C. S. Lewis (Schakel), 98n151
imaginative breakthrough, brought Lewis to Christian faith, 55
imaginative capacity, of Lewis, 183
imaginative man, in Lewis versus the religious writer or the critic, 173
imaginative qualities, within literature, 92
"imaginative reasoning," as a special form of reasoning, 166

imaginative skills, of Lewis in his works of fiction, 141
imaginative writing, argument appearing in, 166
immortality, Steiner's notion of, 40
impersonal order, primacy of, 13
improvement, as somehow a cosmic law, 72
inauthentic Christianity, Lewis satirizing proponents of, 203
incarnation
    Lewis comparing to Scripture, 135
    not believed or understood, 138
    talk with Dyson and Tolkien helped Lewis realized the meaning of, 92
    as a turning point in the history of religion, 93
    uniqueness of, 125
inconsistencies, in the New Testament, 127
individual man, "theological Lewis" writing of, 110
induction, process of, 91
inerrancy, 139, 140n275
inner life, of Lewis, 31
innovators, proponents of the search for a new morality as, 192
inspiration, 127, 139
intellectual endeavours, Lewis's preference for, 31
intellectual framework, 82, 205–206
intellectual luminaries and theorists, on remaking society, 143
The Intellectual World of C. S. Lewis (McGrath), 95
intelligent design, theory of, 80n87
intense longing, 62, 63. *See also* longings
interconnectedness, flash of insight discovering, 50
interdenominational Christian spokesperson, Lewis's role as, 126
International Council of Biblical Inerrancy (ICBI), 130
Isaiah, on Jesus, 137
Isherwood, Christopher, 64

Jacobs, Alan, 182
Jainism, 9n15
James, William, 209n47
Jefferson, Thomas, 102
St. Jerome, on Moses describing Creation, 131
Jesus Christ
    benefitting believers in a practical manner, 14
    body of doctrine/belief held in faith by all, 184n57
    divinity of as a seminal belief, 39
    faulting disciples for not believing what the prophets had said, 137
    as a great religious teacher, 102, 210
    as merely a man, 103
    not entrusting the Great Commission to professional theologians, 130
    personal information about, 201
    as the second meaning of Scripture, 137
    as the Son of God, 52–53, 119
    un-historicity of some narratives of, 127
Jews, importance of, 104
Job, historicity of the book of, 131–132
John's Gospel, as simply theology in story form, 201n19
Joy, 33, 55
Judaism, resisting pantheism, 207
Judas, difference in the accounts of the death of, 127
Judeo Christian values, in matters of understanding, 171
"justified true belief," 201n17

Kant, 178
karma, 9, 9n14, 9n15
Keeble, Neil, 185
Kierkegaard, Søren, 133n257
Kilby, Clyde S., 71n61, 126
Kinghorn, Kevin, 169, 171
Kirkpatrick, William
    of C. S. Lewis, 32
    at Great Bookham in Surrey, 17–18

as a kindred spirit for Lewis's naturalism, 28
Lewis's reason honed to be sharp as a razor under, 188
never disparaged someone else's religious views, 29
rational form of atheism, 26
tutelage of Warren Lewis, 24
knowledge, 36n78, 42n98
Kort, Wesley, 5, 6
Kreeft, Peter, 141, 142
Kuhn, Thomas, 50n130, 60n23

Lamarckian evolution, elements of, 43n104
landscapes, in Romantic poetry, 45n110
Langland, William, 92–93, 92n134
languages, taught to Lewis by Kirkpatrick, 29
laws of thought, as the laws of things for Lewis, 66
"lay student of theology," Lewis as, 130
lectures, of Lewis, 68
Leisola, Matti, 6–7n8
Lennox, John, 140n276
letters, written by hand by Lewis, 161
Letters to Malcolm (Lewis), 199–200
Lewis, Albert (father of C. S. Lewis), 17, 21, 37
Lewis, C. S.
close to a neoorthodox position, 133n257
drawn to the Christians at Magdalen, 49
methodology for critiquing contemporary secular culture, 6
as the most influential Christian apologist of the twentieth century, 3, 195
moved in with Mrs. Moore and her daughter, 40
moved to Great Bookham to continue his education, 25
philosophical and spiritual journey of, 16–55

preference for metaphors of light, 169n12
Romanticism and, 57–66
scepticism regarding his friends attempting to organize a commune, 101
on Scripture as carrying the word of God, 132–133
Lewis, Florence (mother of C. S. Lewis), 17
Lewis, Warren (brother of C. S. Lewis), 17, 21, 24, 25, 37, 161
Lewis/Greeves letters, 25n35
liberal Christianity, 196–197, 220
liberal/non-supernatural Christianity, 219
liberals, 109, 134
library, of Lewis's parents in *Surprised by Joy*, 98n151
Lion. See Aslan the Lion
The Literacy of C. S. Lewis (Walsh), 36
literary background
of Jesus's audiences, 97
of Lewis, 130
literary knowledge, breadth of Lewis's, 97
"literary Lewis," versus "theological Lewis," 111
literary persona, as "the imaginative man in me," 173
literary themes, constituting a rational testimony to the myth of truth, 94
literary works, ability of myth to convey meaning, 93
literature
God's word expressed through, 136
Lewis and, 87–98
Logan, Stephen, 57, 58, 59
logic, Kirkpatrick's rigorous, 28
logician, Lewis as a skilled, 66
Loke, creating discord among other gods, 26n38
longings, 155, 215. See also intense longing
Lord Digory, on "all in Plato, all in Plato," 179

The Lord of the Rings (Tolkien), 53n137
Luke, how he obtained/assembled his material, 127
Luther, Martin, 128
Lyrical Ballads, of Wordsworth and Coleridge, 45n110

Macdonald, George, 87
machines, "Evolution" happening in the history of, 78
MacIntyre, Alisdair, 7–8
MacSwain, Robert, 57, 117–118, 163
Magdalen College, Lewis's fellowship at, 43
magicians, power seemingly exhibited by, 21
The Magician's Nephew, 166–167, 169
Malvern College, Lewis attended, 18
man, achieving total control over himself, 193
manliness, English parents wanting their young boys to exhibit, 31
Mark Studdock, key figure in *That Hideous Strength*, 148
Marsden, George, 118–119n224, 143, 186
Marty, Martin, 99, 112
materialism
    coming back from to a belief in God, 50
    examining the general problem of, 175
    lacking explanatory power for encompassing reality, 42
    Lewis's disenchantment with, 43
    Lewis's doubts about the sufficiency of, 87
    Lewis's strong belief in, 32
    as only one of many non-Christian creeds, 206
    refuting itself, 85–86
    science parted company with the classical form of, 84
    since the publication of Charles Darwin's *Origin of the Species*, 178
Materialist, holding different beliefs from a Christian, 68
materialist philosophy, deadening effect of, 164–165
materialist utilitarianism, 14
materialistic post-Christian England, Lewis dealing with, 185
materialistic worldview, identifying central characteristics of, 175
materiality, problem of as the foundation of all Gnostic systems, 36n78
Mathews, Gareth, on Lord Digory, 179–180
matter, 36, 39, 40n93
"Matter=Nature=Satan," with Beauty on the other side of the equation, 35
McGrath, Alister
    on the Anscombe debate as uncomfortable for Lewis, 176
    apologetics described, 150
    on atheist caricature of faith as wish-fulfillment, 27
    on Baxter believing religious controversies, 186
    chapter on "Lewis's Apologetic Method," 160
    crediting J.R.R. Tolkien, 54
    extensive commentary on Ward's thesis, 90
    on inference, 154
    on Lewis as "perhaps the greatest apologist of the twentieth century," 195
    on Lewis seeing God as an intellectual sun, 159
    on Lewis's account as a process of crystallisation of connectedness, 50
    on Lewis's approach to apologetics, 151–152
    on Lewis's argumentation as abduction, 157n322
    on Lewis's conversion to theism, 52n134
    on Lewis's notion of Joy, 33

on Lewis's notion of unfulfilled
desires, 159–160
on Lewis's writings as they relate to
Anglicanism, 118
on a myth weaving together truth
and meaning, 95
seeing a change in focus in Lewis's
apologetics, 182
support of Ward's thesis, 91
meaning, comprehended through
imagination, 54
medieval cosmological model, based
on Ptolemaic astronomy, 89
medieval cosmology, featuring in the
Narnia chronicles, 88
medieval model, attraction for Lewis,
61, 88, 91
medieval period, 59, 87–88
medieval planets, listing of, 90
medieval romance, Lewis's world of,
58–59
medieval worldview, 60, 220
memory, on Lewis's capacious,
93n138, 224
"Men without Chests" essay (Lewis),
190
mental faculties, 46
mental images, 226
mental processes, 219
Menuge, Angus, 175, 213–214
mere Christianity, 185, 187
Mere Christianity (Lewis)
on explaining and defending belief,
118
expressing Lewis's conception of
Christianity, 198
as fairly succinct, 181
largely reason-based, 183
as Lewis's finest work of Christian
apologetics, 186
presenting the Christian faith as
reasonable account of life, 159
providing readers with the basics of
authentic Christianity, 187
representing the Lewisian worldview, 182

as the theological core on which
different Christians can agree,
184
trilemma stated in, 103
metaphorical language, power of, 69
metaphysical framework, Lewis's
search for, 38
metaphysical views, of Lewis undergoing changes, 34
methodological naturalism, 6, 6n8
methodology, examples of Lewis's,
219
microevolution, Lewis accepted the
concept of, 78
military experience, of Lewis, 34
Mill, popularized utilitarianism, 13
Miller, Michael M., 72–73
ministry, 140–162, 197
miracles, 8, 131, 203, 204
Miracles (Lewis)
challenge to Naturalism, 182
as a critique of metaphysical naturalism, 181
as a defence of reason, 188
largely reason-based, 183
making the strongest case for the
Christian worldview, 85
representing Lewis's most comprehensive critique of naturalism,
187, 219
misdirectedness, drawing attention
to, 158
"Modern Theology and Biblical Criticism" (Lewis), 199
modernists, embarrassed by both
Christian fathers and pagan
philosophers, 60
modernity, 5, 61, 213
moksha, defining, 10
monasticism, Niebuhr crediting, 102
Moore, Janie, the family matron, 39
Moore, Maureen, 39, 43, 75
Moore, Mrs., 40n91, 43, 48
Moore, Paddy, 39–40
moral absolutes, abandonment of, 194
moral imagination, engaging, 172
moral law, 9, 143, 152

Moral Man and Immoral Society: A Study in Ethics and Politics (Niebuhr), 112
moral relativism, critique of, 190
moral standard, rejecting the notion of any absolute, 7
moral subjectivism, predicted by Lewis, 194
moral teacher, Jesus's role reduced to, 206
"Moral Transhumanism" (Persson and Savulescu), 144
morality, 27
More, Max, 145–146
Mormon Transhumanist Association, 145n293
Mosteller, Tim, 171
Murphy, Brian, 140–141
Murray, Douglas, 212n59, 213n61
Musacchio, George, 212
Myers, Doris, 145n292, 148, 173n25
mystical imagination, loss of, 88
mystical intuition, of Lewis, 104n173
myth, 92, 94, 95
mythical imagination, 79
mythologies, religions as, 26

Narnia, 178, 179
The Narnia Code (Ward), 89
Narnia series
  arranged within the medieval perception of the world, 89
  characters of, 171–172
  comprised of seven fantasy novels, 225
  as fairy-tales, 173
  illustrating scenarios, 169
  significance of seven, 90
Nash, Ronald, 2
National Institute of Coordinated Experiments (N.I.C.E.), 148–150
natural causes, hypothesizing, 6n8
natural events, modern science's explanations of, 209
natural law, 145n292, 193
natural moral laws, 171
natural order, 7, 85
natural selection, 80, 81
natural world, 86, 168
naturalism
  causing resistance to notions of the supernatural, 210
  challenges from, 86n116, 209–211, 219, 221
  form of, 16
  found wanting by Lewis, 60
  as incompatible with reason, 189
  inconsistencies within, 85, 174
  lacking explanatory power to be an explanation of reality, 219
  Lewis rejecting while embracing a form of pantheism, 35
  Lewis well aware of shortcomings of, 221
  Lewis's gave way to a form of pantheism, 33
  Lewis's rejection of, 176
  not accounting for Lewis's perception of reality, 86
  repudiating itself, 219
  sufficiency/adequacy of, 114
  summarised, 16n1
naturalist worldview, Lewis challenging, 220
naturalistic causes, liberal theologians searching for, 134
naturalistic worldview, Lewis adopted, 27
naturalists, 86, 188, 219
nature
  admiring while being oblivious to the creative genius of its Creator, 115
  aesthetic enjoyment of advanced by Jesus, 114
  as not everlasting, 84
  perceived as an evil creation of Satan, 38
  so-called power over, 147
Nature of God, pantheism on, 8
nature of the universe, pantheism on, 8
nature-spirits, 26
Naugle, David, 2, 218
neo-Darwinian processes, 219

neo-Darwinian theoretic structure, 220
Neo-Darwinism, as the modern form of Darwinism, 43n104
neoorthodoxy, Lewis distancing himself from, 133n257
Netland, Harold
  advocating for a cumulative case approach, 215
  on the culture in the West shedding its Christian heritage, 212–213
  on the New Age movement, 209, 214
  on Theosophy, 19n11
New Age movement, 209, 214
New Age pantheistic notions, 15
New Age philosophies, 221
New Age spirituality, 213
New Ageism, 212, 214
New Agers, 213
New Testament
  cultural setting in, 97
  demanding the abandonment of anything "conflicting with the service of God," 114
  inconsistencies in, 127
  leaving no room for creativeness, 107
  old orthodoxy undermining, 200
Newman, John Henry, 114
Newton, 165
N.I.C.E. (National Institute of Coordinated Experiments), 148–150
Niebuhr, Reinhold, 100, 102, 112, 113n197
Niebuhr, Richard, 98–99
Niebuhr's five-model framework, 100–101
nirvana, 9–10, 10n16
Noll, Mark, 186–187
nonfiction writings, of Lewis, 141
nonfictional works, worldview elements in Lewis's, 181–194
non-supernatural versions of Christianity, challenging authentic, salvific Christian faith, 196
Norse mythology, Lewis reading, 23
"Northernness," 25, 96

numinous, concept of, 156n321

object of contemplation, myth introducing us to a permanent, 96
objective moral code, named the *Tao*, 190
objective moral judgments, denying the validity of, 191
objective truth, apologetic material representing for Lewis, 187
objective values, 73, 145n292, 192
occultism, 19n14, 21
Odin, deified after his death, 30
old orthodoxy, undermining of, 200
Old Testament, same sort of material as any other literature, 132
Old Western Man, Lewis called himself, 197n4
"on our own steam," acknowledging, 152
opposition, bitterest from semi-believers of all complexions, 151
"Oracles of God," understanding the Bible to be, 131, 132
organic life, evolution not explaining the origin of, 77
originality, as the prerogative of God alone, 107
Otto, Rudolf, 156n321
Out of the Silent Planet (Lewis), 74
outer life, of Lewis, 31
Oxford don, Lewis as, 43–55, 222
Oxford faculty, Lewis as an enemy of the progressive element of, 183
Oxford student and military officer, Lewis as, 33–43
Oxfordian idealism, of Lewis, 190n75

pagan philosophers, having much in common with the medieval Christian fathers, 60
Paganism, 104
pain, existence of, 155
panentheism, 7, 10–11, 208n46
panpsychism, 40n93
pantheism
  competitor to orthodox Christian faith, 221

(pantheism continued)
  definition of, 17n2
  found in other religions, 7
  on God as equally present in evil and good, 208
  as immemorial in Eastern civilizations, 207
  inroads to the West in recent years, 212
  Lewis drawn to, 17, 221
  as the natural bent of the human mind, 207
  sense of the mysterious and sublime, 208
  union with the divine, 105
pantheism/panentheism, challenges from, 7–12, 206–209
pantheistic beliefs, key characteristics of, 8–9
pantheistic notions, 207, 213, 222
paradox, 116, 158
Paul, 122, 127, 135
Payne, Michael, 215
Sister Penelope CSMV, 101, 198, 198n7
Pentecostals, receptive to the power of the Spirit, 109
perceived reality, terms referring to, 160n333
perceptual range, expanding, 146
Perelandra (Lewis), 74, 115
perpetuation of our own species, as the supreme moral end, 72
personal, as a word needing revision, 124
Personal God, relation to the absolute Godhead, 105n173
personality, Bultmann notion of, 201
perspective, understanding impacted by, 171
pessimism, Lewis harboured in his adolescence, 21
Phantastes (MacDonald), 33
phenomenon
  Lewis as, 117
  troublesome leading to new knowledge, 123

The Phenomenon of Man (Teilhard), 76, 76n79
philosophers, not understanding metaphysical things, 69
Philosophical Foundations for a Christian Worldview (Moreland and Craig), 211
philosophical influences, Lewis challenging the prevailing, 154–155
philosophical "muddle," in which Lewis found himself, 41–42
philosophical training, Lewis's worldview influenced by, 96
philosophy, utilitarian attraction of, 211
physical sciences, relying on experimental observations, 71
physical world, as psychical, sentient or conscious, 40n93
Piehler, Paul, 24n31
The Pilgrim's Regress (Lewis)
  accepting the Christian faith, 93
  concluding with his embrace of Christianity, 225
  critiquing Wordsworth, 45n110
  describing "intense longing," 55
  preface to, 63
  related to Lewis's journey to Christianity, 94
Piper, John, 59
Pittenger, Norman, 118–119, 119n224
Planer Narnia (Ward), 89
Plantinga, Alvin, 86n117, 175
Plato
  analogy about persons confined to a cave, 226
  on argument from reason, 178
  foretelling the translation of souls after death, 179n41
  idealism in the West dating from the teachings of, 42n100
  imagery traced back to, 159
  intent to avoid illusion through philosophy, 181
  on a king governing through his executive, 190
  on the physical world consisting of forms, 180

Platonic Idealism, Lewis presupposing the validity of, 179
Platonic imagery, Lewis's novels endowed with, 181
Platonism, resisting pantheism, 207
pluralistic utilitarianism, 211
poems, 35, 45n110
poets, 69, 141
"The Poison of Subjectivism" (Lewis), synopsis of *The Abolition of Man* in, 190
positive apologetics, 215
posthumanism, 144, 144n290
posthumans, becoming, 145
post-modernism, utilitarian elements of, 15
post-positivist era, Lewis never quite at home in, 154
potentiality and actuality, God consisting of, 11
Pragmatism, 211n54
pragmatism/utilitarianism/new ageism, challenges from, 211–216
preferential treatment, putting forward a claim for, 116
pre-life notion, of reality, 76n79
The Prelude (Wordsworth), 45n110
"preoccupation," of Lewis with the supra-rational and the "transrational," 58
prescience, in Lewis's fictional works, 74
preternatural, Lewis's fixation on, 21
priests, as honest men, 197
primary imagination, as universal, 46
primitive, as a word needing revision, 124
principles, within the *Tao*, 192
The Problem of Pain (Lewis), 81, 156
process theology, 11, 11n23
progression, of Lewis from reason and argumentation to imaginative and devotional literature, 187
prophetic content, in Lewis's writings, 142, 143–150
prose, Lewis concentrated on, 224
Protestantism, needing to find an authority, 128

providential deism, 13
Ptolemaic cosmological model, graphic of, 88
public addresses, Lewis continuing with, 223
public at large, Lewis addressed his writings to, 163
public outreach, of Lewis, 222
public school system, as a "tragicomedy," 31, 190
public school years, of Lewis, 17–25
Purtill, Richard, 121

quantum mechanics, 85
quantum theory, metaphysical implications of, 82

"race of conditioners," configuring society, 147
rational argument, 154
rationalism, 71n58, 142
rationalist
    Kirkpatrick as, 29
    Lewis describing himself as a, 57
rationality, Lewis straining beyond the bounds of, 58
Rea, Michael, 175
real objects, 42n100
reality
    Christian worldview as the best explanation for, 57
    Christianity representing the totality of, 68
    consisting of spirit as matter, 36
    credible explanation of, 219
    divided into knowable and unknowable, 44n104
    Lewis's nuanced perception of, 3
    mutually exclusive ways to perceive, 2
    as somehow mind-correlative or mind-coordinated, 42n100
    ultimate understanding of as unattainable, 61
"realization," as a standard for Lewis, 20
reason
    combining with imagination, 54

(reason continued)
  complemented by wisdom, 179n39
  impacting how one interprets imaginative events, 94
  inadequacy, of relying on alone, 153
  led Lewis to theism, 66, 91
  limitations of, 42, 153
  not based solely on natural cause and effect, 189
  predating creation, 179n39
  taking us only so far in matters of religious faith, 49
reason-based apologetics, of Lewis, 220
Reasoning beyond Reason: Imagination as a Theological Source in the Work of C. S. Lewis (Sellars), 70
redemption, Lewis puzzled by the doctrine of, 53
Redford, John, 203n27
The Rediscovery of Meaning and Other Essays (Barfield), 82
Reflections on the Psalms (Lewis)
  commentary on biblical inspiration, 130
  on incarnation being analogous to Scripture, 136
  Lewis's overview of scriptural formation in, 133
  miracles, acceptance of, 131
  never setting forth a "doctrine" of scripture, 134
  not intended as an apologetic work, 150–151
  on the supernatural elements of Scripture, 198–199
Reformation, England's protracted, 185
reincarnation, 9, 40
"Rejoinder to Dr. Pittenger" (Lewis), 119, 206
relativism, 73
relevance, of Lewis for present-day Christian apologetics, 195–216
religion, 22, 44n104, 156, 207
religious convictions, conveying via symbolic and mythopoetic imagery, 173
religious diversity, 213
religious faith, Lewis shaping, 118
religious orders, affection and appreciation of Lewis for members of established, 101
religious pluralism, promotion of, 212–213
religious values, discovering in literature, 92
religious writings, of Lewis, 155
renaissance, of Lewis, 23
"Reply to Professor Haldane," not published until after Lewis's death, 72
Reppert, Victor, 174–175, 178
resurrection
  of Jesus, prophecy of, 138
  as the supreme miracle, 203
revelation, 179n39, 226
revivalist preachers, emotionalism of, 120
Richards, I. A., 113
Richards, Jay, 189, 210
right conduct, 152
Roman Catholics, 133
Romantic affinities, of Lewis have been obscured, 58
Romantic Movement, in poetry, 45n110
Romanticism, 57–66
  described, 57n7
  as an example of words losing their meaning, 62n31
  key figures in literature, 57n7
  Lewis's commitment to, 58
  Lewis's theory of, 61–62
  as a main genre of Lewis, 142
  representing Joy for Lewis, 63
romantic-rational blend, of Lewis, 142
Rosicrucianism, 19n12
Ryken, Philip, 129, 131, 133, 139

salvation, Langland celebrating, 93n134
salvific Christianity, doctrines of, 197
samsara, 9, 10
Savulescu, Julian, 143–144
Sayer, George, 94, 174n27

Sayer, Jack, 31, 33
scepticism, about values as disingenuous, 191
Schaefer, Henry, III, 149
Schakel, Peter, 97–98n151, 187–188
school life, of Lewis, 24
schooling, summary of Lewis's, 17n4
science, 44n104, 84–85, 149
scientific decision-making, 73
scientific endeavours, 205
scientific knowledge, 70
scientific materialism, 148
scientific method, 71n58
scientism, 71n58, 72, 73
The Screwtape Letters (Lewis), 202–203
scriptural authority, as oft-disputed, 128
Scripture
    at the heart of Calvin's apologetics, 214–215
    interpretations of, 184n57
    Lewis's concept of transposition and, 226
    Lewis's rules on divine authority of, 127
    Lewis's understanding of, 125–126
    as the supreme authority for Lewis, 129
    as the vehicle of God's word, 135
    viewed as the "paper-Pope of Protestantism," 128
    as the word of God, 198
secondary imagination, as the purview of artists and poets, 46
A Secular Age (Taylor), 5, 12, 160n333
secular humanism, as another manifestation of secularism, 7
secular modernity, countering the trend toward, 5
secularism, 6, 11
secularism/naturalism, challenges from, 5–7
Sehnsucht (wistful yearning), 64, 129
self, regarding in two ways, 116
self-contradiction, relativists escaping, 191
self-perception, of Lewis, 224

self-renunciation, near the core of Christian ethics, 116
Sellars, Jeff, 70, 166
seminary-level courses, titled "The Theology of C. S. Lewis," 225
sensory experience, transcending, 59
sensory perceptions, 35, 46
"sentimental" value system, advocating for, 192
sentiments, Lewis objecting to, 35
separation of church and state, 6
seven kingdoms, of the seven planets, 90
seven planets, 90, 91
sexual appetite, Lewis relaxing the restraints on, 23
shadows on the wall of the cave, mistaking as the real thing, 226
shadowy figures, as the true reality, 180
Shermer, Michael, 47–48n119
Shinto traditions, 214
Siege Perilous, in the Arthurian legend, 64
Siegfried and the Twilight of the Gods, 23
signposts, not mistaking for the real objective, 129
The Silver Chair (Lewis), 180
Sire, James, 2, 163, 218
skepticism, Bultmann's technique driven by, 201n19
Smart, Ninian, 10, 160n333
Smewgy, 29
Smith, Andrew, 36n78
social experimentation and social engineering, Lewis concerned about, 74
"social imaginary," as an "enframing historical consciousness," 205n37
social life, Lewis never enjoyed in college, 24
society
    deism's impact on contemporary, 12
    role of government in bettering, 111n191
Socrates, 180, 201

Socratic Club, 57n4, 67, 174
solutions, to humanity's crisis-laden existence, 225
soul. *See* human soul
sound, mystery of, 168–169
sound of singing, encompassing the entire world, 167–168
speculative notions, of Lewis, 158
Spencer, Edmund, 90
Spencer, Herbert, 43, 43n104, 44n104
Spencerian notions, Lewis's characterisations of, 44
Spinoza, 207
spirit, as a force for good, 36
Spirits in Bondage (Lewis), 37, 38, 87
Spirits in Prison (Staples), 35–36
spiritual, as a word needing revision, 124
spiritual essence, 44
"spiritual forces," which Steiner found everywhere, 40–41
spiritual God, created spiritual bodies and humans, 36n78
spiritual immaturity, of Miss C., 19
spiritual journey, analysing Lewis's, 195
spiritual life, of Lewis, 3, 18
spiritual problems, preventing people from seeing the truth about God, 169
spiritual void, 221
spiritual world, contacting, 47n119
spiritualism
   akin to dabbling in the occult, 48
   described, 19n13
   as eccentric, 41
   embraced by Steiner, 42n98
   as non-Christian, 206
spiritualists, feeling the presence of the divine, 109
spirituality, of Miss Cowie (C), 20, 223
Stassen, Glen, 108–109
Steiner, Rudolf, 19n11, 40, 41n98, 47n119, 207
story of Christ, as simply a true myth, 54
subjectivism, philosophy of, 73

supernatural elements, demonstrated in the voice's creative power, 168
supernaturalism, 125, 166
supernaturalistic Christianity, 185
supernaturalists, 184, 185
Surprised by Joy (Lewis)
   on the abandonment of Lewis's Christian faith, 19
   on Askins's mental deterioration, 48
   depiction of his Romantic/rational dilemma, 142
   difficult period for Lewis described, 17
   earlier version of, 50
   experiencing a sensation of imaginative longing, 33
   on Joy as a pointer to something other and outer, 128–129
   on Lewis's behaviour at Malvern College, 24
   on philosophy as a way, 190n75
   title from a Wordsworth sonnet, 45n110
   on wishing to remain a sound atheist, 87
Swedenborg, Emanuel, philosophy of, 19n11

Tacitus, mentioning Jesus' execution in the Annals, 30
tactical advantage, of the apologist, 122
the Tao, 145n292, 171, 190, 192–193
The Taste of the Other: The Social and Ethical Thought of C. S. Lewis (Meilaender), 115
taxonomies, creating a framework for analysis worldviews, 2
Taylor, Charles
   insights into the West's drift away from orthodox Christianity, 204
   on Lewis communicating the Christian message, 222
   on materialist utilitarianism, 14, 211
   on present-day influence of deism, 12–13

on social imaginary, 160n333
on Western society becoming more secular, 5
teaching methods, Lewis quickly took to Kirkpatrick's, 29
Teilhard de Chardin, Pierre, 76
temper of the times, Lewis's ability to discern, 222
tenure, artificial intellectual environment protected by, 194
Terry, Justyn, 209, 210
That Hideous Strength (Lewis)
  on Christian faith and science, 70
  confronting the modern reverence for science, 148
  on culture gone berserk, 111
  fictional treatment of the ideas in *The Abolition of Man*, 193
  on the inherent dangers of scientism, 73–74
  on Nietzschean science allied with government bureaucrats, 189
theism
  embraced by Lewis, 51, 52, 61
  Lewis attracted to, 17, 55
  Lewis came to by rational means, 141
  passage to Christianity for Griffiths and Lewis, 93
theistic religion, naturalism as a powerful alternative to, 209
theistic worldview, viewing reality as, 51
theists, 8, 93
theologian, Lewis as an inept, 119
theologians, applying the "principle that the miraculous does not occur," 202
theological approach, seeking a setting for the incidents of pains, 157
theological belief, as not a philosophical position, 155
theological language, Lewis advising the clergy to revise, 123–124
theological training, Lewis never received any, 117

"theologised science-fiction," as a genre, 173
theology, Lewis and, 117–140
Theology of the New Testament (Bultmann), 200
Theology through the Arts course, 165
theosophy, 19n11, 206
things, forming concepts of, 181n46
threats, posed by fixating on gifts, 116
Tolkien, Christopher, 81
Tolkien, John Ronald Reuel (J. R. R.), 53n137, 54, 67, 81
traditional values, authors debunking, 192
transcendence, 11–12, 206
transhumanism, 144, 144n289
transposition, 136n268, 226, 227
trench warfare, Lewis engaged in, 34
Trinity, Coleridge found haven and firm footing in, 165
"a true myth," Lewis's understanding of, 66
truth, 125, 184n57, 211n54
truth claims, 4, 151, 187, 222
tutelage
  of C. S. Lewis, 25–33
  of Warren Lewis, 24
typologies, as heuristic devices, 99

unbelievers, failing to see the Bible as anything more than literature, 138
Uncle Andrew, effect on of the Lion's singing, 170–171
Underland, beneath the Narnian world, 180
"Unfit for Life: Genetically Enhance Humanity or Face Extinction" (Savulescu), 143
unintelligible language, of highly cultured clergymen, 120
unitarianism, rise of, 206
universal sense of right and wrong, Lewis appealing to, 143
universe, 11, 27, 40n93
University of Cambridge, Lewis awarded a full professorship, 222

unsatisfied desire, as more desirable, 58
Upanishads, on *turya*, 10n16
utilitarian religious philosophy, 14
utilitarianism, 13, 211–212
utility, 14

Valantasis, Richard, 36n78
values, that the innovator uses, 192
Van der Elst, Philip, 68
Vanhoozer, Kevin, 134, 138, 138n269
Vedanta, 10n16
Vendantism, 64
the vernacular, 124, 151–152, 224
view of the world, Guite writing about, 166
Vincentius of Lérins, key work *The Commonitory*, 184n57
The Vision Concerning Piers Plowman, 92–93, 92n134
voice, bringing a whole new world into existence, 168

Wagnerian music, Lewis listening to, 23
Walker, Andrew, 181n47
Walsh, Chad
  assessing Lewis's writings, 87
  on content in *That Hideous Strength*, 149
  on Lewis being born six hundred years late, 60
  on Lewis combining reason and imagination, 69
  on Lewis completing a children's book, 182
  on Lewis having a "fluctuating philosophy," 36
  on Lewis's ability to use Aristotle's tools of logic, 69
  on Lewis's conversion, 56–57, 141–142
  on Lewis's embrace of Christianity, 38
  on Lewis's "fluctuating philosophy," 37
  on Lewis's theory of Romanticism, 61–62
  on the medieval model as appealing to Lewis, 60
Ward, Keith, 139n275
Ward, Michael, 90, 91, 195
"watchmaker" model, of deism, 12
Webb, Stephen, 168
Weldon, Thomas Dewar, 50
Weltanschauung (world perspective), 2, 187, 218
Weltbild (world picture), 2
West, John G.
  on *The Abolition of Man* (Lewis), 189, 194
  on Lewis distancing himself from evolution's uncritical boosters, 80
  on Lewis's critique of naturalism/materialism, 86, 189
  on Lewis's interest in the topic of evolution, 79–80
  on Lewis's mature critique of naturalism, 209
  on Lewis's *Miracles* countering the naturalist challenge, 210
  on "The Way," 190–191
Wethmar, Conrad, 194
What Coleridge Thought (Barfield), 45
"what has been held always, everywhere, by everybody" (*quod ubique, quod semper, quod ab omnibus*), 184n57
what is true for them, practitioners choosing, 15
"what sort of person" we are, perception dependent on, 171
"what works," choice based on, 14
Whitehead, Alfred North, 11n23
William Heinemann Company, 35
Wilson, Andrew Norman, 79, 174, 177
Wilson, John, 89
Wilson, Kristine Ottaway, 45n110
Witt, Jonathan, 6–7n8
Word of God, carrying, 133
words, Lewis's list of, needing revision, 124
Wordsworth, William
  influence on Lewis, 30n54

influence on Lewis's epistemology, 183
Lewis well acquainted with the writings of, 47
mystical experiences of the presence of God, 33
passages in fraught with meaning, 62
references to the power of imagination, 45
return to elements of pantheism in, 207
work of men's minds and hands, as culture, 109–110
"the world," of Lewis, 97–98, 109
world picture, Lewis's, 56, 160n333
World War II, Lewis's letters written during, 111n191
worldview(s)
    challenges to Christianity from alternative, 1
    Christian apologists responding to alternative, 218
    Christian faith and science in Lewis's, 70–87
    as a concept for perceiving reality, 1
    described, 160n333
    dimensions of in Lewis's apologetics, 163–194
    dimensions of Lewis's, 56–162
    influences of alternative, 3
    of Lewis, 3, 163, 181
    Lewis periodically drawn to a range of, 218
    Lewis searching for a comprehensive, 51
    as the mind's formation of a cosmic or world picture, 2
    of paramount importance in any scientific endeavor, 86
    reason and imagination in Lewis's, 66–70
    understanding of contemporary, 2
    Western society embracing a variety of mutually exclusive, 2
Wybrow, Cameron, 193
Wynyard School, 18, 20

yearning
    Lewis's described by Logan, 58
    Lewis's objective to "simulate" in his readers, 59
    simulating to transcend the limits of sensory experience, 58
    for something beyond the natural world, 64
Yeats, poetry of, 32
Yeshua, regarded as a god, 26–27
yoga, on *niribja-samadhi*, 10n16

Zaleski, Philip and Carol, 176

www.ingramcontent.com/pod-product-compliance
Lightning Source LLC
Chambersburg PA
CBHW050342230426
43663CB00010B/1962